Amy,
As fellow travelers, your mom and I
connected. No doubt our story offered a little
vicarious travel to her wandering spirit.

Tightwads on the Loose

A SEVEN YEAR PACIFIC ODYSSEY

I hope this light hearted tale
brightens what has probably been
a challenging year.
♡
Wendy Hinman

Wendy Hinman

SALSA PRESS, SEATTLE, WA

ISBN-13: 978-0-9848350-0-3

Library of Congress Control Number: 2012905240

Cartoon by Jennifer M. Smith

Velella profile under sail by Carl Cox

Author photo by Mike Wann

All other photographs are from the author's collection.

Drawings by Garth Wilcox.

Salsa Press, Seattle, WA

First edition trade paperback
Printed in the United States of America

Tightwads on the Loose

LOOSE

A SEVEN YEAR PACIFIC ODYSSEY

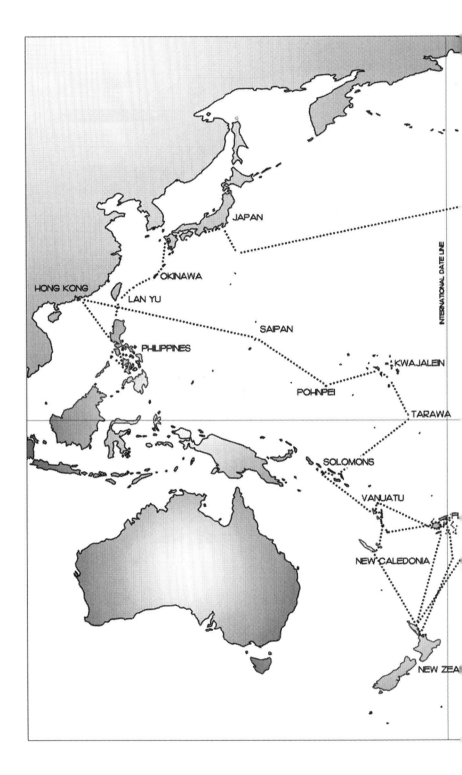

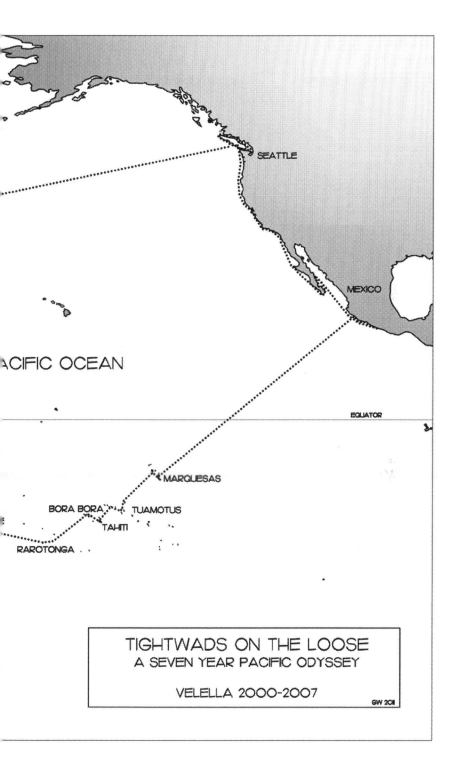

SEATTLE

MEXICO

PACIFIC OCEAN

EQUATOR

MARQUESAS

BORA BORA
TUAMOTUS
TAHITI

RAROTONGA

TIGHTWADS ON THE LOOSE
A SEVEN YEAR PACIFIC ODYSSEY

VELELLA 2000-2007

GW 2011

AUTHOR'S NOTE

This is a true story, dredged from my own imperfect recollections. Where my memory was fuzzy, I called upon the encyclopedic memory of my faithful companion, Garth. I am thankful I kept as detailed notes as I did of our daily doings, despite endless razzing from my comedian husband.

Distilling seven years of adventure into a book you wouldn't need a crane to lift required I skip notable events and compress others. Some names have been changed and many people who enriched our journey are missing—from those who shared our vagabond lifestyle to countless locals who generously welcomed us into their country, culture, and homes.

I hope you will enjoy this adventure as much as I enjoyed living it.

Wendy Hinman

CONTENTS

PART I
BREAKING AWAY

PLOTTING ESCAPE

You might say it was inevitable.

I was named after Wendy from *Peter Pan,* though I had more in common with Peter.

I suppose you could blame my restless childhood. We moved every two or three years to culturally diverse places like Guam, Hawaii, and Washington, D.C., which sparked my intense curiosity about new places and people.

You could note my natural affinity for the water—diving and swimming independently at the age of two.

You could say it started with my father's decision to buy a sailboat (when I was six) and sign the family up for sailing lessons, after which we spent weekends and vacations sailing the Hawaiian Islands and the Chesapeake Bay.

Or you could mention my parent's well-traveled friends, who told stories over cocktails about wandering the world under sail when they thought I wasn't listening.

Most likely you'd point to my father's dream of extended blue water cruising that filled our bookshelves with such enticing titles as *Survive the Savage Sea* and *Adrift* (which may explain why my mother was *not* interested). These disaster tales infused me with my first hit of adrenaline, the start of an addiction that has afflicted me since.

Then you might say that my condition was compounded by a family charter in the Virgin Islands when I was twenty-two, when I tasted this simple but rich lifestyle.

Yes, I suppose you'd be justified in saying it was no surprise I developed an incurable case of wanderlust and that it might find its expression in a saltwater adventure. Especially after I married a man who had already sailed around the world.

It wasn't a matter of *if* we'd take off sailing—more a matter of *when*.

🌴

"It's perfect, Wendy," said my husband, Garth, looking around the interior.

"Perfect?" I said. "But you can't even stand up straight!"

"I can stand up here," he said with a devilish grin. His thick brown hair poked up through extra space provided by an open hatch just above his head—a total of four square inches in which he could align his head with his spine. Unless he was on the centerline of this boat, he had to stoop to move around. I cracked a smile and shrugged. Usually *he* provided the voice of reason.

"It's certainly capable. It's already sailed around the Pacific, and it's within our budget," he added. My impulsiveness must have rubbed off on him. For months we'd been shopping for a boat in which we could go voyaging, but every boat we'd seen that fell within our microscopic budget was a disaster. Garth had finally found this one on the Internet only an hour's drive from Seattle, once he'd relaxed his requirements *yet again*.

In the ten years we'd been married, I'd changed jobs frequently to quell my wanderlust and infuse the regular dose of change which was normal to me. Every few years, I'd decide that I had learned everything interesting about an industry and set my sights on something new. I'd convince some unsuspecting soul that I could create a new export department that would sell millions of dollars' worth of fresh produce worldwide. Or I'd tout my modest computer skills to persuade a company to hire me to build websites or edit technical papers. Though I was never quite sure how I'd tackle the challenge, the risk of failure would propel me into learning at an accelerated pace and infuse the task with an excitement that I might otherwise find lacking.

Meanwhile Garth, Mr. Steady-Eddie, had been designing tug boats and fish processors for March Shipyard in Seattle since before we'd gotten married. The shipbuilding business is highly cyclical, and the industry was heading into another downturn, which Garth could hardly stomach again. He was ready for a change.

Of course, I was always ready for change. When I was born all of my great-grandparents were alive except one. Most of my ancestors lived long lives, often into their mid nineties. So my chances of living a long life looked promising. Yet I had always possessed a sense of urgency. I was someone who would jam pack more into a day or a week than anyone I knew—as though, if I didn't, I might miss something. I barely left time to reflect on one encounter before the next began. Friends might describe me as an "experience junky" accumulating them like girl scouts collect merit badges. I was nearly always game to try anything once. I wouldn't say that I was a dare-devil—though I've never been particularly fearful. When I went skydiving in college with a boyfriend who'd already been skydiving once, I couldn't fathom his agitation before our jump. I mean, *what was the big deal?* I relished a few moments escape from the pull of gravity and the wide open vista that lay before me. Mostly my curiosity drove me to find out what *something—whatever-it-was—* was like. A serious car accident the second year Garth and I were married reinforced this sense that life was short and we needed to make the most of it.

For a couple of experienced sailors, taking off for an extended cruise seemed natural. The "cruising" lifestyle would combine transportation to a tropical paradise with a place to stay. Now, we just had to find a boat we could afford to get there, wherever we decided "there" would be. But this boat was only thirty-one feet, the size of a modest weekender.

"Are you sure?" I said, remembering how long we'd struggled to find a small car that could reasonably fit his large frame. Usually I forget the size difference between us until seeing our reflection gives me a chuckle. He's powerfully built and moves deliberately. Next to him, I look and flit about like Tinker Bell.

"Well, it sure beats everything else we've looked at," Garth said, his voice taking on an earnest tone. "And it's well built to handle ocean passages."

Compared to the sparse, cramped interior of our little red racing boat, *Atomic Salsa*, this boat felt enormous and plush. I was impressed that we could afford a boat with upholstered seats and fine varnish that sparkled like honey. "It's so pretty," I said, lust beginning to overtake all rational thought.

We'd given little thought to where we would go or how long we'd be gone. Our first priority was to simplify our lives so we'd have the freedom to make choices. We made an offer, and soon it was ours. I never imagined I'd spend the next nine years living in this tiny space.

🌴

Garth and I met twelve years earlier in Washington, D.C., the day he moved in.

When I graduated from the University of Michigan in 1986 with a degree in Economics, I dreamt of an international career full of travel and glamour, but when a well-paying job didn't materialize upon graduation, I moved into the basement of my sister's group house, near the washer and dryer. In an expensive city like Washington, D.C., young professionals often split expenses to live in a nice suburban house, which they otherwise couldn't afford. With limited savings and no job, I had few options.

The morning Garth moved into the group house, I was nursing a hangover and reading the comics, thinking guiltily that I should help him. By the time I lazily hauled myself off the couch to help, this Spartan guy had finished carting all his belongings in from the front seat of his Fiat Spyder, which he'd named "Boris" after the Who song. I later learned that he'd only learned to drive in the last year at the age of twenty-six, *after* he'd bought the car.

As he reassembled the twin bed he'd designed from wood scraps, I peppered him with questions. Once I pushed past his shyness and finally got him talking, I discovered he was a great storyteller with a wry sense of humor and plenty of fascinating tales to tell. I learned that before he was eighteen, he'd sailed around the world with his family and gotten a taste of the life of Robinson Crusoe after an unfortunate encounter with a Fijian reef left a hole in their boat large enough to drive a car through.

This man is an original, I thought. Not like anyone I'd ever met before. He was full of contradictions that intrigued me. He was so sure of himself, yet humble and gentle. He possessed a maturity and depth that defied his years. I found him easy to be around. He introduced me to bluegrass music, public radio, and windsurfing. Together we sampled a broad spectrum of music, made pies, and shared a frugal approach to life that featured occasional dumpster diving. Then one night, after months of "hanging out," everything suddenly felt *different* and our relationship turned romantic. As though it were inevitable.

Garth had amassed a stunning breadth of knowledge from books he'd read to stem the boredom of days at sea where he saw few kids his age (or any age). His clear understanding of history appealed to my insatiable curiosity. Who knew an encyclopedia could come in such handsome packaging? He was killer at the game of Trivial

Pursuit, though I could beat him whenever it came to questions about sitcoms he'd missed while out voyaging.

While we were dating that family charter sparked my imagination. Relaxing in the cockpit after an easy sail in tropical water, I concluded that I'd found the ultimate way to live. Upon my return, I passionately lobbied Garth to seek jobs as captain and first mate on a charter boat—to which Garth patiently replied, "I have no intention of being anybody's lackey. When I go cruising, I'll go where I want on my own schedule."

I pointed out this wasn't likely to happen anytime soon, since he still owed his parents money for four years at MIT. He retorted by urging me to find a job worthy of my college degree. Eventually I found a job with an international consulting firm, where I worked with people who traveled the world. Working there didn't mean *I* actually got to go anywhere, but I did learn about countries I never knew existed and got to meet people with exotic accents while I developed my prowess in that most essential office skill—photocopying.

After two years of dating, Garth and I married. By then Garth had gotten a job in Seattle, and our six-month cross-country romance was getting inconvenient and expensive. And I was restless. Garth employed the time-tested technique for urging me to join him in Seattle. I found a ruby ring that I coveted, and Garth mailed me a $300 check annotated, "for services rendered." I knew we'd sealed the deal when he agreed to let someone poke him with a needle for the requisite marriage license blood-test. I figured life with this man would prove ever interesting.

For our honeymoon, we chartered an inexpensive boat in Greece using gift money from Garth's folks, and we sailed as captain and first mate at last—or captain and admiral, as Garth tells it. Garth swears he was never a Boy Scout, though you wouldn't know it, as his credo is "Always Be Prepared." He brought his sail-repair bag along on our honeymoon, explaining that "you just never know." Sure enough, on day two of our rock-bottom charter, Garth was busy sewing the ripped mainsail and splinting broken oars.

Despite a record heat wave, no wind, and a broken refrigerator, I relished bobbing around naked, drinking gallons of warm sun tea and dousing each other with buckets of salt water to cool off, and finishing the day in a new foreign port. On a day when previously nonexistent wind appeared all at once, I got a thrill from single-handedly crashing from wave to wave in high winds while Garth endured a migraine. Little could I have imagined how much our honeymoon foreshadowed our future life.

At the close of our 1988 Grecian honeymoon, I didn't return to Washington, D.C. Instead, I flew with Garth to Seattle, where I discovered it rained *a lot*. For a wedding present, Mr. Worst-Case-Scenario gave me a full set of foul weather gear, possibly the most expensive outfit I have ever owned, though hardly the sexiest. I had to admit it was infinitely useful in the ever-present Seattle drizzle, especially since we started sailboat racing nearly every night of summer and almost every weekend the rest of the year.

For ten years, Garth and I tucked the idea of going voyaging into the back of our minds and went about pursuing careers, a bigger bank account, and first place on the water. We were financially conservative; in fact, many people might describe us as cheap. We devoted our income to saving money and paying down a mortgage, though we did succumb to buying our own racing boat. We spent vacations motoring our little red sailboat past alluring anchorages on the way to regattas and dreaming of a time we could linger instead of rushing back to work.

A vacation with friends for Antigua Race Week 1998 featured an encounter with people living the "cruising life" we coveted. The experience sparked conversations about making a change, which quickly evolved into boat shopping.

Garth dismissed a number of larger boats in our budget, declaring, "I spent five years struggling to sail around the world in a tub that could barely move and was impossible to fix. I'm not going to do that again." And he'd launch into a story about how his family's boat, the *Vela,* became unwieldy in even moderate winds, forcing them to reduce sail area or risk being catapulted over the side by the force of the tiller. With carefully timed pauses and a twitch of his lip, he'd describe how difficult the *Vela* was to repair because it was outfitted with aircraft components, which are not widely available to the general public and are even less so in Fiji, Sudan, or Cocos Keeling.

Though we had dreams of a fast, sleek boat, our tiny budget injected a harsh dose of reality. We wanted to go *now*...so we bought that thirty-one-foot boat in which Garth couldn't stand or sit comfortably.

Once we took ownership, we named the boat *Velella* after tiny jelly fish-like sea creatures that sail by the wind, as we planned to do. The name also paid tribute, in a way, to the boat that Garth's family had sailed around the world, almost like it was a miniature— albeit much sleeker—version of the *Vela.*

In our excitement to put a name on our new boat, we carefully studied fonts and colors at the graphics store, but missed an important detail. A week later, on a sunny August day, we were sipping beers in the cockpit of our newly named boat with veteran sailors Steve and Elsie. Steve casually remarked, "Our old boat was also named *Velella.*"

No!

"But we spelled it differently."

"How did you spell it?" Garth asked, cautiously.

"V-E-L-E-L-L-A," Steve said.

Garth and I looked at each other a moment, then stuck our heads over either side to check what was printed there: "Valella."

Hmmm. I fished out our boat documentation to see what it said. "*Velella.*" Crap.

Like a couple of contestants on the Wheel of Fortune, we sheepishly returned to the graphics shop to buy a couple of E's— one for each side of the boat.

Once we'd gotten the *right* name on the boat, we prepared it to go offshore. Ms. Pollyanna (me) thought that meant buying groceries and untying the lines, while Mr. Worst-Case-Scenario (Garth) thought that meant rebuilding the boat. We negotiated something in between. After getting intimidated by boat magazines touting safety equipment we "couldn't live without" (most of which hadn't yet been invented when Garth had sailed around the world in the 1970s), we settled on items we could afford.

While Garth's parents and my dad could hardly complain about our plan to sail around the world, my mother and many friends acted as though we'd lost our minds. They hinted that we were heading off on a dangerous voyage. Yet we would be moving at five miles an hour, where there's little to hit, while they regularly drove seventy-miles-an-hour protected by a few millimeters of metal or plastic. I had friends who slaved in jobs they hated, only to spend everything they earned to pamper themselves for their sacrifice. I guess you could say insanity is in the eye of the beholder. Maybe it was the size of the boat people thought was crazy. To us, the logic was simple: Our budget was tiny, so our boat was tiny, because we were too impatient to wait.

The next step was to move aboard. Whittling down a house full of stuff into 300 not-very-square feet presented numerous opportunities for negotiation. We sorted everything into major piles: stuff that got to go sailing, stuff that got to stay in storage (a room we built in our basement or placed in the care of friends/ family so we wouldn't have to pay for storage), and stuff that went to Goodwill or the garbage. Of course, we had differences of opinion about which items qualified for keeping. Each of us insulted the other by casually referring to the other's treasures as "junk," then secretly hid the other person's "junk" at the bottom of the garbage can while the other wasn't looking. Two hotly disputed items were a tent—complete with news imprints from Garth's attempt at waterproofing before biking 5,000 miles across the country—and a set of wind chimes that needed restringing. Did I mention that we were frugal?

Down at the boat, the pile of items that needed a home aboard far exceeded the remaining space. We packed lockers as though we were completing a jigsaw puzzle. We tried to restrict ourselves to essentials that had multiple uses, but even the tiniest things came into question.

Garth called into question every item I packed, saying something like, "The nail polish has to go.... A Frisbee? What are we going to do with a Frisbee?"

I'd reply, "The Frisbee can be used for trading, playing, and also as a serving plate," trying to keep a straight face, "and you can use the nail polish to mark engine parts or slow the corrosion on the zincs." Then I'd flash a smile at my cleverness while Garth formulated his counter argument.

Or, with a hand on my hip, I'd point out, "I think five chart plotters seem excessive."

And on it went. For a couple of "paper-magnets" like us, leaving a single book behind was a struggle. A crisis for us would be vacationing in a mansion with nothing to read. Nearly every book made the cut—our 8,000-pound boat carried hundreds of pounds of books alone—but I finally convinced Garth to leave behind the fourth and fifth books about emergency navigation.

Once we were living aboard, many bills we had dutifully paid each month simply vanished. Electric, sewer, water, and garbage were included in our monthly moorage bill, which, once we were at anchor, would also disappear. Before everyone was a budding environmentalist, we prepared to live off the grid, using power and water that we collected ourselves. There was nothing like having to produce it in the first place to get us to use less of it. We rented our house and the income helped reduce the steady drain on our bank account that had begun with our quest to find and prepare a boat for voyaging.

As those last nine months in Seattle passed, we made more budget cuts, eliminating all restaurant meals, concerts, movies on the big screen, and ice cream. The public library provided free entertainment as well as heat and electricity during a cold, wet Seattle winter. Most evenings we settled in at the library with others seeking refuge, most of whom were showered and sober.

When we finally made our last mortgage payment, one bill still lingered: the monthly moorage for our old racing boat that we still hadn't sold. After owning two boats for over a year and a half, we ultimately convinced a dreamer that he needed a fast race boat for the occasional Sunday sail. The deal put cash into our hands and ended the monthly moorage fees that were hemorrhaging our finances. Our bank account was still anemic, but we were finally free.

Our first priority was to untie the lines that made demands on our finances and our time. We gave little thought to the idea of returning except to refrain from selling anything we could store for free. As long as we spent less than the $1,000 rent that the house brought in each month, our lifestyle was sustainable—provided we had no big surprises and counted every penny. That meant we had about $33 per day to cover groceries, boat maintenance, clearance fees, communications costs, and anything else that might come up.

We had no idea how long we'd be gone and had no firm route in mind, though our limited budget favored developing countries. Weather dictated our options more than anything else. We were drawn to the tropics, as anyone who's endured a Seattle winter could understand. Fall storms along the Pacific Northwest coast gave us incentive to head south by late summer. But first we decided to spend the summer months testing our skills and equipment locally in an extended "trial run."

In early June 2000, two days after quitting our jobs, we left Seattle to sail around Vancouver Island. Circumnavigating Vancouver Island gave us 1,000 miles of rugged sailing to make sure we knew what we were doing before we left the Pacific Northwest, its selection of well-stocked marine stores, and the convenience of our car.

After a long first day of sailing, we pulled into our first foreign port: Victoria, British Columbia. From the customs dock, we called to clear into the country. The official on the phone asked for a full inventory of the alcohol we had on board. We had no idea. In the week before we set off, friends kept arriving with congratulatory bottles in hand, some of which we consumed with them before we set sail. I'd stuffed bottles into illogical places, wherever they would fit in our rush to push off the dock. After Garth revised his guesstimate twice, the official on the phone told us to "sit tight." Someone would be down shortly for a full inspection.

The senior customs officer, who appeared as if she'd just graduated from high school, asked us to sit outside while she and an even-younger-looking colleague searched the boat. I wondered what would happen if our guess was wrong.

They poked methodically under seat cushions, asking, "What's in here?"

"Water tank," Garth replied.

"And here?"

"Another water tank."

They worked their way forward while I worried about stowaways I'd forgotten. When their eyes settled on the heaping mound of sails, clothes, bags, and boxes of yet-unsorted items in the V-berth, they looked at each other and shrugged.

Garth and I fought to suppress a snicker—we hadn't wanted to tackle that daunting pile either.

They let us go.

Over the next two months, we lost track of time with the awe of small children immersed in the wondrous world of nature, spotting sea otters at play, whales breeching, and dolphins frolicking. On days when we weren't sailing, we spent days climbing rocks, walking beaches, and hiking through rain forests dripping with moss. I watched bemused as graceful eagles turned into street brawlers over fishermen's discards in Port Hardy. Acting like a flock of oversized pigeons, their dignity vanished as they clamored around fish-cleaning stations, revealing white pantaloons beneath awkwardly lifted dark skirts.

Our route through narrow channels tested our navigation skills, and had us estimating speeds and distances, timing rapids so as to pass through when currents were minimal.

On the ocean side of Vancouver Island, I encountered ocean swell for my first time in years. I felt queasy after we rounded Cape Scott and wondered aloud if something I'd eaten didn't agree with me—to which Garth flatly replied, "Maybe you're just seasick."

I vehemently denied the possibility, my pride injured, but damn if he wasn't right. One Bonine and my stomach immediately felt better.

With short distances between anchorages, we studied our guidebooks and charts to find a protected bay to stop each night. One afternoon about halfway through our trial cruise, we entered Smith Cove on the west side of Vancouver Island, unsure about the location of a submerged rock. Garth steered the boat forward slowly, while I watched the depth-sounder readings. The numbers instantly changed from twenty feet to eight feet, and *bang!*

Garth smashed into the frame supports for the dodger, and I fell on top of him. After I climbed off Garth, I reached down and put the engine into reverse.

"I guess we found the rock," Garth said.

Another crash echoed from below. I checked for leaks and noticed that the oven had come off its gimbals. After anchoring, Garth noticed the dodger frame was askew and carefully winched it back into position with a line. Since it was Garth's birthday, we tried to pretend that our little accident hadn't happened, though we did have to reposition the oven before I could cook dinner. We knew we'd have to fix the damage to the keel eventually, but there was little we could do on the unpopulated west coast of Vancouver Island.

I urged Garth to linger in Hot Springs Cove for several days longer than we originally planned because I relished soaking beneath a natural steaming waterfall in a rocky basin that looked out over a bay sprinkled with islets. Twice a day, I passed reverently beneath towering evergreens along a mossy boardwalk for an impromptu hot-tubbing social hour with other boaters in a stunning natural setting while Garth cherished moments alone with a book. I'd never been so clean.

I indulged my obsession with waterfalls, caves, seashells, and rocks, barely able to contain my excitement whenever some crevice revealed a potential cave or a trickle of water a potential waterfall. Later, Garth would roll his eyes at my fixation, but at first, he seemed as content as I was to explore each one.

I was completely enchanted with this lifestyle, with each day different from the one before, and I wanted more. At Marble Cove I collected marble rocks, inflating their value based on the cost of remodeling our bathroom years earlier. Garth quietly returned my collection to the wild when I wasn't looking—our own version of catch and release which I barely noticed.

We learned some valuable lessons during our two-month trip: that I needed to stow things more carefully (after a box of oatmeal disgorged its contents all over the floor, got wet, and turned into a new form of cement); that store-bought cookies and crackers came with an unsustainable amount of packaging (which we then had been forced to carry for weeks until we found a "proper garbage receptacle"); and that our lack of fishing prowess not only had made buying a $100 Canadian fishing license a bad investment, but called into question our plans to subsidize our budget with freshly caught sea life.

Mostly, we were profoundly struck by how much pleasure we got from just appreciating what nature had to offer. In an area where few, if any, people lived, we had no cell phones and no Internet access. With the complexities of our lives gone, we were able to enjoy where we were at that moment. Nature provided vast entertainment, all for free—fortunately, given our budget.

We had one last obligation before we left the Pacific Northwest, which we'd almost forgotten about: I'd scheduled an official bon voyage party back in Seattle, yet here we were, still over 150 miles away.

Three mornings before the party, dawn arrived with fog so thick we could barely see the bow of our own boat. With no time left to wait for better conditions, we had to go anyway or stand up the friends gathering to wish us well. Garth pulled up the anchor, and I slowly retraced our GPS track out to clear water. In the Straits of Juan de Fuca, we couldn't see more than a hundred feet in front of us.

For the next eleven hours, Garth and I peered into blank whiteness on high alert, struggling to decipher outlines of obstacles before we hit them. I felt as though I were driving through a cloud, the sun so obscured that I had no cues which direction I was pointing without studying the compass. Periodically, a drifting runabout would suddenly appear ten feet from us, giving me heart palpitations.

So much for the calm that came from two months spent communing with nature. Garth's insistence on meeting Coast Guard requirements to the letter—indicating our position in dense fog by sounding a horn every two minutes—nearly lost me the rest of my sanity until I begged him to stop the migraine-producing noise. He finally relented, partly because blowing his family's bronze lung-powered horn made him light-headed.

By the time we arrived in Seattle, less than twenty-four hours before our party, I felt the euphoria of overcoming obstacles that had once seemed daunting.

Our trial cruise had also taught us that our new lifestyle suited both our personalities. We worked together towards a common goal for very different reasons. Garth thrived working steadily to test our systems and skills, prepare the boat, and reach interim milestones, while I relished the daily diet of change and the exciting opportunities each new place offered.

After a blowout bon voyage party, we spent the next couple of weeks back in Seattle madly handling last-minute details before we left to sail down the coast. There wasn't space enough for both of us to work on any project simultaneously aboard. Feeling a twinge of homelessness, I vacated the boat while Garth ripped apart the entire living space to improve on some boat system or another. Meanwhile, I foraged for groceries and arranged several last, *last* goodbyes with friends, unsure whether I'd find adequate social opportunities once we ventured offshore.

We identified a trustworthy, efficient, and inexpensive manager (my mother) to handle our business matters. She would prove to manage things far more effectively than we might have, though in the process, I learned the guilt involved gave new meaning to such terms from my college Economics classes as "cost-benefit analysis" and "no free lunch."

Finally, I identified a friend willing to buy our car but let us continue using it until we left. (Ultimately, we left him a trunk filled with an electric space heater, a life ring, and other items that we couldn't fit aboard. Whether he thought that was a perk or a liability, I am still not sure.)

A quick swim—very quick—in Puget Sound's fifty-five-degree water—to check the keel using the Braille method had confirmed that we needed to haul out before leaving the region to fix damage from hitting that rock. We chose a boat yard on our way out of Puget Sound and sailed to Port Townsend near where my mother had moved five years earlier. Garth sanded, epoxied, and painted the keel in the boat yard while, in my mom's kitchen, Mom and I prepared fried chicken, smoked salmon, pasta, and potato salads so I wouldn't have to cook offshore on my first ocean passage.

Once Garth finished fixing the keel and there was nothing more we could think of to prepare, Garth suggested we leave with the 5:00 a.m. tide. I cajoled him to wait until 9:00 a.m., so my mom could see us off after breakfast.

"Okay, but you're probably not going to like it," he said.

Leaving against the tide was a decision I would come to regret.

AND THEY'RE OFF

When the tiny figures waving on the beach at Port Hudson disappeared from view, I realized the folly of my scheduling. The boat crashed into each wave, sending spray flying, and stopping us in our tracks.

"Did you latch the forward hatch?" Garth asked. I couldn't remember. The answer became immediately clear as I watched the hatch open wide, swallow a big gulp of saltwater, and slam shut. Thoughts of the carpet flashed through my mind, and I hurried below to save it before it was too late. The water gurgled towards me at twice my speed, and I was losing the race. I slammed down on my knees and reached for the soggy edges just as a gush of saltwater flooded the carpet. The carpet squished between my fingers as I wrestled to roll it up and move it out of the way.

To close the tiny hatch, I had to crawl over the pile in the V-berth—which we still hadn't addressed—to the cramped point inside the bow. As I reached the hatch, it bounced open again, inviting a fresh jet of icy cold saltwater onto my face and hair and down the neck of my jacket and shirt.

This is closing the barn door after the horses are out, I thought grumpily. When I scrambled to my feet, a pile of cloth clung to my ankles. When I looked down, I realized that clothes once so neatly folded on the horizontal surface above now sloshed in the muddy water as it flowed across the floor below. *Arrgghh!* Clearly, I still hadn't learned my lesson about stowing things. Underway for only a few hours, and I already had a stack of saltwater-soaked laundry that started the clock on the first of many experiments in mildewing.

As we continued our wet, miserable sail, an hour of violent motion knocked free the wedges that held the mast in place. With each wave, the mast shifted radically inside the hole where it went through the deck, its wild motion making a terrible racket—as though the boat was tearing itself to pieces.

We had a serious problem. The rig could come crashing down, or rip a huge hole in the deck—or both. And we hadn't even reached the ocean yet.

Garth pushed the tiller into my hands and rushed below. He grabbed some line and quickly wrapped it four times around the mast. Then he shimmied it up into the hole and wedged it in as tightly as he could, using a mallet and a piece of wood to pound it in.

The alarming sway of the mast abruptly stopped.

I exhaled.

He watched for a moment, and then joined me in the cockpit.

"Phew! That was close," he said as he absently reached for the tiller. "I think it'll hold, but I'll double check it when we get to Port Angeles." His quick action and confidence soothed my shattered nerves.

The first thirty mile of fighting the tide took twelve stressful hours, soaked our gear, and jeopardized the rig. Not an auspicious start.

The next day—*with* the tide this time—we made it another forty miles to Neah Bay, perched on the western edge of Washington.

A benign weather forecast for the next few days encouraged us to head for San Francisco. With light winds, low clouds, and full of nervous anticipation, I steered for the ocean with a push from the early morning tide.

Hours later, we sat at the entrance to the strait with our sails hanging loosely like laundry on a line. Then the tide began to come back in, carrying us with it. To avoid getting swept past our starting point, Garth turned on the engine, and we motored southwest several hours further into the ocean. We had two months to get to San Diego, where we planned to join a sailing rally to Mexico, but at this rate, we might have walked there faster.

Daylight slowly faded, and lights appeared on shore five miles away. I imagined people going about their business. The thought of friends and families crawling into bed for a full night's sleep while we alternated sleeping in three-hour shifts made me wonder about the sanity of our plans, especially when Garth went down to get some sleep, leaving me in charge in the darkness. I had only the stars and a distant AM music station for company. I needed to make sure we didn't hit anything and ensure that we sailed in the right direction.

For the first hour, I worried about all the lights on the horizon. I hadn't known any boats were there before it got dark and didn't know how far away they were. I had confidence in my million-candlepower spotlight. While it blinded me, I could at least point it at anything that seemed close and then at my sails to pantomime, "Hey you, over there. I'm here, and I'm a sailboat."

As darkness descended, so did the temperature. Despite it being late August, it didn't take long to get chilly. Every few minutes, I wanted another hot drink. Never a big coffee drinker (despite living in Seattle, the coffee capital of the world), I started to worry whether we had sufficient hot chocolate mix at the rate of four cups per hour to reach San Francisco, some 800 miles away. Then I became acutely aware of the downside to consuming all that liquid. Every twenty minutes or so, I peeled off waterproofs and three layers of fleece to reduce the pressure on my bladder. Each visit below to the bathroom took an extra several minutes for disrobing…which did help pass the time.

Rarely had I studied a clock more closely. So much time just to think was a bit unsettling. I realized how much of my life I'd spent rushing around doing things that had seemed vital, most of which I couldn't even remember at the moment. The waters slapped lightly at the hull, and the lines groaned in their blocks, but we were ghosting along almost silently in the darkness, in our own little universe.

Still not used to sailing at night, I feared that a reading light would wreck my night vision. (Fortunately, that fear was short-lived; later I blew through stacks of books, relishing the luxury of so much time.) I huddled under the dodger, struggling to stay alert while a mechanical wind vane steered a better course than I might have. The wind vane left us free to move around (or visit the bathroom). We had nicknamed our wind vane "Jacques" because it came from Montreal, and because occasionally he became finicky when the winds changed. Fortunately, he didn't demand coffee or cigarettes, which earned him my respect as a valuable crew member.

When Garth took over at the end of my watch, I had the luxury of snuggling under the covers for some long-anticipated sleep. Once allowed, of course, sleep eluded me. I must have drifted off at some point because I awoke in a panic, sure that I was sleeping when I wasn't supposed to be. My off-watch was all too short, and as soon as I was again in charge, and Garth slept, I had no trouble relaxing into a comatose state.

"Having a nice nap?" Garth quipped when he relieved me at the end of my shift.

For the rest of this passage we were both awake together for only a few hours in the middle of the day, so we hardly saw one another. We struggled to get enough sleep, feeling like parents of a newborn, snatching rest every chance we could. Our change of watch in the middle of the night went something like this:

"Get some sleep?"

"I guess."

'"Awake yet?"

"Maybe."

"Good. There's a ship over there heading away from us, and that one over there is bearing three-hundred-and-forty degrees and getting closer. G'night."

Coming up late for a watch was an inexcusable offense. At ten minutes before a watch change, the sound of a stopwatch alarm would be greeted with glee by the soon-to-be-asleep person and a groan by the other—for whom rest had been all too brief. If the *on-watch* person saw no sign of movement, he'd knock on the deck to awaken his slumbering relief. (I say *he* meaning *he or she*, but I was fashionably late more often than Garth. I quickly learned that the extra minute or two of sleep wasn't worth the pout and the silent treatment.)

I was glad that we'd spent so much time sailing and taking navigation classes before we'd left that I could do this in my sleep, because that's what it felt like. Each of us checked our progress at the end of our watch, studying the GPS, and then marking our position on the chart. I was disappointed when the three miles we sailed in the last three hours did not magically become fifty, and the new dot identifying our current location on the chart was hardly distinguishable from the last. Fixated on our original estimate, I forgot about the relationship between time, speed, and distance, and blithely assumed that we'd cover the 800 miles to San Francisco in eight days, no matter how slowly we sailed.

While I could pretend that we were purists intent on proving our sailing skills at all costs, mostly an acute aversion to noise kept us from turning on our engine. We would do almost anything to avoid listening to that drone, including drift at barely perceptible speeds for days on end. Carrying only eighteen gallons of fuel contributed to our decision.

Though we knew how to eke every knot of speed out of a boat while racing, we were surprisingly lazy now. Garth had suggested we switch to a larger headsail on the first day, but sure that the wind would come up any second and dreading the prospect of having to change sails in the middle of the night, I nixed the idea. But the wind hadn't come up, and in our drowsy state, we lacked the energy to change to a larger headsail that might have helped us make better use of the light wind that we had. With fairly flat water, the motion was gentle, even pleasant, for a while . . .

On the sixth day, we started to feel a bit of swell as a distant weather system began to affect us. Without enough wind to fill the sails and propel us forward, we rolled in the swells like a harpooned whale. The sails slammed back and forth, rattling our nerves and our dental work. Somehow through all this—possibly due to severe sleep deprivation—I got better at catching sleep in snippets and ignoring the perpetual motion that jostled me awake every time I nodded off.

Just as I was about to suggest putting up more sail area so we could get there before Christmas, the wind came up. It arose abruptly, as though attempting within a few short hours to make up for all our loitering. Suddenly we were rocketing down huge waves at twice our typical speed. Each wave seemed to pick us up and hurl us towards San Francisco, and we rapidly closed the intervening miles. With wind, life aboard got more exciting. Like campers, we found challenge in the simplest tasks of meeting our basic needs, but now with the added predicament of doing so while on a waterlogged amusement park ride that failed to end after four minutes.

We ate our way through all the fancy food I'd prepared before we left, served in Ziploc bags—not exactly Martha Stewart-style. We didn't much care. We did our best to ignore the assault on our noses from our ripening carpet. And bodies. The idea of bathing lacked appeal under the present conditions, and we decided that as long as we were equally smelly, we could maintain an uneasy truce.

Reaching San Francisco marked the first major milestone in our journey, the conclusion of our first offshore passage. While normally we might wait offshore until we could safely navigate into port in daylight, these were Garth's home waters. His family had celebrated the completion of their five-year circumnavigation when they'd sailed the *Vela* under the Golden Gate Bridge twenty-five years earlier. Garth relished sailing under the Golden Gate Bridge in his own boat with his own "family" (me), at the start of his own voyage, yet when we reached this monumental landmark, the wind shut off as completely as if someone had turned off a switch, and we sat becalmed and frustrated, the city lights taunting us in the near distance. Anxious to get there, we overcame our aversion to the engine and motored the last mile into the bay. It was 3:40 a.m. when we pulled into San Francisco Municipal Marina after eight days of continuous sailing.

I was a blue water cruiser at last.

LEARNING THE ROPES

In early October, we began working our way south to San Diego. We spent our days either sailing south or exploring coastal refuges along the way. Interacting with no one besides Garth never struck me as monotonous because each day offered new scenery and brimmed with possibilities highlighted in my Pacific Coast guidebook. I felt the constraints of society fall away like shackles from the newly-freed. Instead of employing the chameleon-like survival skills I'd developed after years of frequent relocations and navigating the conflicting expectations of others, I followed my own compass, indulging my desire for adventure. Smitten as a honeymooner, I relished working seamlessly with Garth to forge a new life that let me breathe. When our plans to stop in San Simeon to explore Hearst Castle were aborted by thick fog, my disappointment quickly gave way to plans for hiking in the Channel Islands.

As we worked our way south to progressively balmier weather, we shed layers of clothes, and bathing became less of an ordeal. In northern waters, before bathing, we'd first heat a kettle of water since water from our tanks sat only a thin layer away from fifty-five-degree water. Of course we didn't have a hot water heater. But even with kettle-heated water, soaping up in the brisk air had seemed brutal. I couldn't wait to reach the tropics where bathing would be synonymous with swimming and snorkeling.

Off Point Conception, the waves turned sloppy. As we bounced around in the waves, the wind caught the wrong side of the mainsail. A line preventing the boom from swinging across the boat wasn't well rigged, and it caught on an open hatch when the boom suddenly crashed across the boat, with a loud bang. I noticed the center hatch didn't look quite right.

Hearing the clatter, Garth, clambered out of bed in a daze. I was busy cursing while Garth squinted at me sleepily, unable to focus without his contact lenses in the moonless darkness.

"What's going on?" he asked with a hint of whine in his voice.

I started to explain, but when I paused for a moment, something in his demeanor indicated that he didn't grasp the complexity of the situation, so I stopped talking and just said, "Here, just hold the tiller," and went forward to straighten things out.

Wondering why I'd left the hatch open in the first place, I removed the line from the inside of our now-mangled hatch, set the sails, and reset the wind vane to steer again, then released Garth to sleep once again.

In daylight, Garth seemed surprised to see the wrecked hatch, confirming just how oblivious he'd been in the night. With his usual wry humor, he pointed out, "You know, large holes on boats are not good; boats are kind of wet, especially when the wind and waves get big." He gave me a big grin, then went about taping it shut until he could fix it when we reached San Diego. He seemed almost pleased to have a new project to tackle.

🌴

We spent a long, stressful night off Point Loma, just outside San Diego Bay, barely moving in imperceptible winds. We were within sight of a drifting ship displaying a lighting combination for a "vessel not under command." What that means exactly, I haven't a clue, but that night it meant we couldn't relax for a moment.

When dawn arrived, the city was shrouded in a hazy marine layer typical of the area. San Diego felt familiar because my parents had been stationed there while I was in college, but it had never felt like home. It was in San Diego where they'd spent the last few years of their marriage. My infrequent holiday visits left me oblivious to the growing strain in their relationship until, shortly after Garth and I married, I discovered that my mother had purchased and decorated her own Coronado Island condominium to mirror the one she'd once shared with my father. Visiting one holiday, Garth and I found ourselves hopelessly confused, wondering which condo housed our clothes.

We motored through an oily calm the last ten miles into San Diego Bay and discovered that all the anchorages were filled with boats waiting to head for Mexico at the end of hurricane season. We finally found a spot to anchor beneath the flight path for San Diego International Airport. Whenever a plane took off or landed—which happened every few minutes given that it was an international airport—jet engines roared at full throttle, and all conversation ceased until we could hear one another without yelling. Since airports tend to cover vast tracts of real estate, that also meant our location was miles from anywhere. From our boat, getting to the closest marine store involved an hour-and-a-half row to Shelter Island or a shorter row directly to shore followed by a long walk beside the freeway. One day's row to the marine store against short choppy waves gave me blisters that lasted a week. Most cruisers secured a slip and rented a car or at least used a motor-powered inflatable. Not us. That cost money we didn't have. Obtaining that money would have meant forfeiting our freedom, so we lived without.

We had scores of last-minute errands to run. Each errand became vastly more complicated without a car, taking two or three times as long as we expected. Picking up mail my mother had sent to a friend and voting by absentee ballot in the 2000 presidential election that pitted George W. Bush against Al Gore took the better part of a day. So did finding an Internet café to check email and buying charts and guidebooks that would take us to Mexico and across the South Pacific to New Zealand, once we'd decided to follow our friends on this popular sailing route. But it was all part of the adventure.

One day at dawn, in an attempt to handle laundry and groceries in a single trip, we sailed across the bay to Coronado Island, where we could tie up for free at a dinghy pier for six hours. As we walked the mile and a half to the laundromat, each of us holding a full bag of smelly laundry, it began to pour. Our water-permeable laundry bags got heavier and heavier, absorbing water, until, by the time we reached the laundromat, I could barely lift my bag.

We threw our laundry into washing machines, and after the rain stopped, we headed for the grocery store, a half mile further inland. By the time we returned to the boat, laden like a couple of pack mules with groceries and clean laundry (now encased in *non*-water-permeable garbage bags), we were exhausted.

After hearing stories about how isolated Garth's family often was during their voyage, I was surprised to realize just how many other sailors were also embarking on this vagabond lifestyle. Some things had changed in the twenty-five years since Garth had been voyaging. I convinced Garth to join the Baja Ha-Ha, a sailing rally into Mexico, because I worried about feeling isolated. The Baja Ha-Ha organized a large group of sailboats to sail to Mexico in a flotilla with stops and social events along the way. I'd been reading about the event for years in sailing magazines. At a kick-off party a week before the rally began, we met other cruisers like us, who we encountered whenever we went about our errands. Instead of the lonely life of a sailor that

I'd anticipated, cruising was starting to look like one big roving social marathon.

"Who was that again?" Garth would ask as we walked away from a lively conversation on a street corner near the marine store.

"That was Cathy from the boat *Felicity*," I'd explain. "Don't you remember? We met her and Ken at the kick-off party."

"God, you know everybody!" he'd say, surprised at how many fellow cruisers stopped to chat with us.

We had the smallest boat in any anchorage, usually by more than ten feet. Whenever we went aboard other boats, we realized just how simple our boat was in comparison. Friends' boats had hot-water showers, movies, ice-cold beers, and ice cream. In comparison to their floating palaces, we lived in a floating pup-tent. Occasionally I was envious, of course, especially when my attempts to host a dinner morphed into a party aboard our friends' boat, as though I'd just invited myself over.

Gradually, though, I realized just how much all that luxury cost when cocktail-party discussions turned to problem-solving sessions about complicated on-board systems we didn't own—water makers, water heaters, generators, and radars. And that our lack of amenities ultimately enhanced the adventure we were undertaking.

After a couple weeks around the nervous energy of the sailing fleet trying to plan for every possible contingency, I was beginning to second-guess every decision we'd made. Every time I ran into a fellow sailor, I learned of something else I had forgotten to worry about, such as buying a cable and a lock for the dinghy. I wondered whether anyone would want to steal our flat-bottomed inflatable, considering how badly it rowed—particularly when everyone else had motorized high-speed rigid inflatables—but with little else to occupy my mind, I worried about it anyway. Garth's vast cruising experience eased some of the anxiety, though I was beginning to wonder how much else had changed in the twenty-five years since he'd last been voyaging.

Two days before we set sail for Mexico on Halloween, Baja Ha-ha organizers hosted a costume party. Garth donned a fright mask to wear with his t-shirt and swim trunks, while I dressed as the Statue of Liberty. Over a white bathing suit, I wrapped a white bed sheet, toga-style, and accessorized it with a hand-crafted crown and torch cut from cardboard.

We didn't win the costume contest.

As the official party came to a close, Anders, a crazy Swede, said, "Let's go back to my boat for drinks."

Ten of us wandered back to his slip in the marina and proceeded to empty his liquor cabinet. At one point in the evening—probably the moment the liquor ran out—we headed for a nearby hot tub. When a sudden squall brought a heavy downpour, the party scattered instantly. Garth and I grabbed our costumes and took off.

Suffice it to say that we were not quite at a hundred percent when the San Diego Police took a keen interest in a soggy couple walking in the pouring rain along the barrier next to the freeway. A patrol car slowed, a window rolled down, and an officer said, "We had a report of a naked woman walking down the street."

My white bathing suit looked rather like underwear now that I had slung the drenched bed sheet around my neck. The cardboard crown had long since melted in the rain.

"I'm not naked," I said. "I'm the Statue of Liberty."

He looked over at his partner.

"We just came from a Halloween party. We were in the hot tub, and it started to rain," I added a little too enthusiastically.

"Where are you headed?" he asked, cutting me off.

"Home."

"Where's that?"

"We're anchored under the flight path, next to the helicopter pad," Garth explained.

He paused, then asked, "How much have you had to drink?"

"I have no idea," Garth replied, enunciating as carefully as he could.

They studied us for a moment, then rolled up the window and pulled away.

They must have concluded that rowing under the influence was hardly a threat.

PART 2
SAILING IN COMPANY

CHAPTER
4

MEXICO: MARGARITAVILLE IN MANANA LAND

En masse with a hundred newfound friends, we arrived in Cabo San Lucas, Mexico, after ten days of sailing. We were surprised to learn that the election we'd missed had not yet been decided—a problem I thought was limited to thinly disguised dictatorships in the developing world. While news reporters and election officials analyzed hanging chads and debated the finer points of constitutional law—which the Supreme Court ultimately ignored—we wandered among brightly painted stucco buildings drenched in shimmering sunshine in step with the tuba-punctuated wail of Mexican love songs that blared over cheap, portable radios.

Checking into Mexico felt like a roving cocktail party, minus the refreshments, as we stopped to chat and share directions with fellow sailors about the locations of Customs, Immigration, or the Port Captain's Office. Between making photocopies of our entry forms (because in Mexico you could never have too many) and securing official stamps for our vast array of paperwork, we found a cheap taqueria where we lingered over 50¢ fish tacos bathed in fresh cilantro, tomatoes, and lime. We spent several days in Cabo, basking in beach chairs and dipping in the pools of the posh hotels along the beach while spending nothing, simply because we were pale enough to pass as hotel guests. I wondered why we hadn't ditched work and set sail sooner.

In mid-November, from Cabo, we sailed north into the Sea of Cortes to catch a glimpse of this barren coast before the weather turned cool. We set off early one morning, planning to reach the nearest anchorage, Los Frailes by dark. The wind was against us, creating a short chop that prevented us from making fast headway. Friends on other boats motored, but we stubbornly refused while we had adequate wind to sail. We were used to warm summer days in the Pacific Northwest during which we had daylight until 9:00 p.m., followed by a leisurely sunset in which the sun lingered on the horizon for an hour or two, giving us plenty of warning about its intentions. We were surprised when the strong Mexican sun simply vanished at 6:00 p.m. Garth suggested we sail on through the night to the next bay 45 miles to the north: Los Muertos.

Had we had our radio on, we might have realized that our newfound friends were calling to offer assistance. It simply never occurred to us that, while we sailed on in silence, our new floating community was working together in an impressive show of solidarity, using the radio, lights, and dinghies, to guide anyone caught out after dark into the bay. (Had we had our radio on, we might also have discovered sooner why our radio calls to ships when unanswered: our radio could only broadcast about twenty-five yards.)

I figured we'd catch up with our friends the following day, but a strong northerly wind discouraged anyone from continuing north for several days. Once we reached Los Muertos, Garth and I read books and played cards for a while, and then I struggled with what to do to fill my suddenly endless time while Garth mentally designed our next cruising boat. Meanwhile, in Los Frailles, twenty boats organized potluck dinners and games on the beach. *And I missed it!*

When the wind abated, we made a dash for La Paz. When we pulled into Puerto de La Paz, we noticed a current river, so we parked on the side closest to shore, sure that our flat-bottomed rubber dinghy would be difficult to row across such a strong current. After we rowed ashore, we learned that we'd anchored in a (virtual) marina, which faced one minor challenge—it still had yet to be built. The "marina" fee of $2 per day included free use of the showers and pool that served the associated hotel, so we decided to splurge, as we were desperately in need of showers.

To our delight, when we settled our bill two weeks later, it incorporated the mandatory port fee, which meant that we ultimately paid less than those who'd anchored in the "free" spots. I wasn't quite sure how the math added up, but I wasn't about to argue.

As our first Thanksgiving approached, we heard about a fancy traditional "Thanksgiving feast" arranged by permanent U.S. expatriates who sailors passing through derisively called "park-aboards," but the price seemed prohibitively expensive. Instead, we decided in favor of steaks in a waterfront restaurant. For days, I looked forward to celebrating with a special meal off the boat.

On the big day, Garth and I sat down with fellow sailors at a long table covered with vividly colored blankets, chatting idly with one another about family traditions we were missing and imagining our friends and family wrapped in sweaters and fleece sitting down to huge, stuffed turkeys back home. Shortly after ordering but before our steaks could arrive, the wind piped up. Our boats began leaping and swaying violently. One by one, couples hastily settled their bills and disappeared. This would be the first of countless weather-aborted events.

Lesson one in sailing: *The weather trumps all plans.* Lesson two: *The weather trumps all plans.* Lesson three: *The weather trumps all plans.*

A few days later, I caught up to Garth, who was standing at the head of the docks of Marina de La Paz. As I reached him, I noticed he was bouncing on the balls of his feet. He wore a crooked smile and his eyes danced.

"The *Vela* is here!" Garth said, looking at me as though he expected a reaction. He was as excited as I'd ever seen him.

"What?" I said, shielding my eyes from the bright sunshine.

"The *Vela* is right here in this marina." It took a moment for the news to sink in.

"You're kidding! Where?"

"See that wooden mast about halfway down on the right?" He pointed down the dock and then looked back at me expectantly.

I trained my eyes in that direction, but all I saw was a forest of masts shifting restlessly in the breeze.

"Not really," I said, "What makes you think it's the *Vela*?" How could he recognize the masthead of a boat he hadn't seen in twenty-five years from 200 yards?

"I know every inch of that mast," Garth said with certainty.

I looked at him for a second. He held my gaze.

"Let's go find out."

I couldn't believe he hadn't rushed down there the moment he saw it. I'd heard countless stories about this notorious member of the Wilcox family and seen the grainy pictures of the boat in the Seychelles or Sudan. In nearly every photo, what caught my eye was the rust streaking down the sides, visible even from a great distance. What I remembered most clearly was the *San Francisco Chronicle's* photo of the family squinting skeptically at the camera. In the days of celestial navigation, families sailing around the world for pleasure were extremely unusual, and many local papers had featured the Wilcox's story upon their return.

We hurried down the dock, ignoring the rising chorus of halyards slapping against metal. There it was. The *Vela* was an unusual looking boat, though no beauty. It was a narrow-sterned double-ender, wide in the middle, like a snake that had swallowed a rat. It barely resembled the elegant drawings and paintings Garth had made as a teenager. His depictions still decorated his mother's living-room wall. Green and yellow stripes had replaced the original red and grey ones. I chuckled at the telltale hints of the rust that had haunted his family throughout their voyage.

"Wow, it still has splices I made as a teenager. Yikes, those are two and a half decades old!" Garth paused and licked his lips. "Guess they haven't sailed much."

I remembered Garth's jokes about how badly the boat sailed, and I could see why. I smiled.

"The guy bought it to live aboard. He tried to trade his TR3 for it, but my folks couldn't imagine even owning a car at that point, much less a British sports car."

I tried to picture his parents in a British sports car, but the incongruity of it stopped me. My frugal in-laws made even Garth look like a spendthrift, but, besides that, Garth's mother began losing her vision soon after their return. She never did drive a car again. The first few months after their return, Garth and his mother had bicycled from their house in Palo Alto to Redwood City to repaint the boat so they could sell it.

"I made those splices in Sudan and redid the backstay in Israel. That must have been 1976." He shook his head. "I can't believe it hasn't changed in all this time." He walked farther down the dock alongside the boat, his eyes taking full inventory.

"That's new," he said, pointing to an ugly generator mounted on the back deck. He shook his head, and then shuddered. "Not an improvement."

I laughed then caught myself. "Shssshh," I whispered. "Someone might be aboard."

Just then, a small, fit older man appeared.

"Hi," he said, as he hopped from the boat onto the dock.

"You probably won't believe this, but I sailed around the world on this boat twenty-five years ago," Garth said to him.

A smile spread across the man's face. "Then you must be Garth Wilcox."

Garth's mouth opened and then clicked shut. The man laughed and added, "I'm Scott, the guy who bought the boat from your family." They shook hands and Garth introduced me.

Garth said, "Sorry, I didn't recognize you."

"Well, it has been twenty-five years." Scott smiled and cocked his head. "Would you like to come aboard for a look?"

Garth nodded. I couldn't believe I was getting to see the boat, which cast such a long shadow over our own journey. I felt as though I were finally meeting an old friend from Garth's most formative years.

Scott led us aboard. "I finally got the engine going after it seized on you in Panama. I'll never forget the stories about your eighty-seven-day passage, when you nearly ran out of food." Without an engine, they'd struggled to make headway in light winds while the boat fell apart around them. "I loved the part about getting swept past the Galapagos and hearing goats in the darkness."

"Boy, I'm amazed you remember the stories," Garth said, barely able to restrain a smile.

"They were fascinating."

Scott took us inside. As our eyes adjusted to the dim light, I tried to imagine four people sharing this small space for five years. I pictured Garth completing schoolwork at the table while his mother tried to cook breadfruit or taro, not quite knowing what it was, or what to do with it.

At the age of fourteen, Garth worked side by side with his father to patch the Volkswagen-sized hole in the boat and reconstruct the interior so the family could resume voyaging. When I asked about the exact location of the hole, Garth described how they'd scarfed in new wood to patch it, and then replaced the gutted interior. My eyes traced the white-painted surfaces trimmed with oak, and I imagined a young Garth with a furrowed brow, carefully measuring and sawing pieces of wood.

Garth hungrily took in each detail, with an expression on his face as though he were a million miles away. A faint smile revealed his affection for this old boat he'd cursed so many times. On board, he'd traveled the world and learned how to be self-sufficient on the high seas and in remote foreign lands. We were drawing upon those very skills for our own voyage.

As we walked away later, Garth turned around several times to look at the boat again, as though to prove that he hadn't imagined the encounter. He shook his head again. "You know what really blows me away?"

"What?"

"I spent months re-rigging *Velella* before we left Seattle. When the mast wedges came out in the Straits, I thought we'd lose the rig before we'd even gotten into the ocean. I was more spooked than I let on. Yet somehow, this tub made it all the way from San Francisco to Mexico with forty-year-old rigging that was beat!"

🌴

We spent several weeks in early December in the Sea of Cortes. Instead of the steady drizzle of a Seattle December, when we'd be rushing from house-to-car-to-office ensconced in fleece, we were in shorts under a blazing sun, surrounded by layers of red rock that evoked memories of family road trips to the Grand Canyon. Dry scrub and cactus dotted the shorter hills. Our days were filled with snorkels, hikes, and books instead of meetings, deadlines, and email. Yet we still had a schedule, now dictated by the seasons.

After a few tranquil weeks, we rode a screaming northerly wind south from the Sea of Cortes to reach Zihuatanejo in southern Mexico. As we neared Lazaro Cardenas, a large commercial port, *Velella* was ghosting along with a spinnaker under a silvery moon in light-to-moderate winds, the kind of conditions every sailor dreams of. Balmy air danced across my skin; it was the perfect temperature for a t-shirt and shorts, a long-sleeved shirt and pants, or no clothes at all.

I noted the position of Orion the Hunter, the constellation that kept me company through my night watches. His belt and sword stood proudly against an inky black sky. He'd only traveled a short distance across the sky, indicating that I wasn't more than an hour into my shift. Why did time seem to crawl on night watch, yet felt like only a blink when I was nestled in my bunk?

In the distance, I saw the green-and-white running lights of a ship, which indicated that I was looking at its starboard side. *Probably on its way to the Panama Canal, a memory within minutes.*

A few minutes later, I noticed that this ship wasn't moving quite as swiftly as the others had. In fact, it seemed closer.

I altered course, sailing a little higher, figuring I'd pass behind the ship, though that took me towards the shore. I didn't think it would take long for it to pass.

The ship's lights gleamed more vividly, menacingly. I grew nervous. My evasion hadn't worked. Now I was trapped between land and a ship that seemed drawn to me like a magnet. I regretted our decision not to take down the spinnaker before nightfall. Now that Garth was in bed, and I was in a tight situation, quick maneuvering could result in a tangled mess, with the spinnaker wrapped around the head stay.

When the moon disappeared, I realized that the ship was smaller and far nearer than I'd realized. A man's silhouette sauntered down the deck and paused to light a cigarette. He was close enough that I could see the ember flash. *Oh shit.*

"Oh God, oh God," I said aloud, pressing my hands flat against my cheeks, my mouth open in a silent scream.

"What's going on?" Garth said, giving me a jolt as he suddenly emerged from the bunk below. "What are you doing up here, praying?"

I flushed with embarrassment, wishing I'd had a few more seconds to react so that Garth wouldn't have awoken to discover my stupidity like this.

"I've gotten scary-close to a ship," I said. "I thought it was headed away from me, but instead it must have been drifting slowly towards me. I didn't pay close attention, and now it's right there, hovering over us." I had been daydreaming when I should have been tracking the ship's movements more closely, and then I'd been too lazy to take down the spinnaker to grant me better maneuverability when I realized I had an issue. My miscalculation had put us in grave danger.

Garth rushed up the steps and forward to release the spinnaker pole. In the cockpit, I released the sheets as he gently lowered the sail. Once he got it down, I turned on the engine, and put some distance between us and the ship, which I now realized must have been loitering off the port of Lazaro Cardenas until morning and moving on a far less-predictable course than I had assumed.

We quickly recovered from the incident, though my self-flagellation continued for months afterward. I'd been too cocky. Cockiness can get you into trouble, and I'd nearly had a taste of it.

Garth shrugged it off, reminding me of an old adage that his former boss had liked to use, "Good judgment comes from experience, and experience comes from bad judgment."

"Assuming you survive it, of course."

As we rounded Cabo Corientes, the air grew suddenly hot like a blast from a furnace. After a couple more days, we reached Zihuatanejo, where we'd planned to meet up with Ken and Cath from the boat *Felicity*. It was three days before Christmas. In the frenzy of preparations before we'd left Seattle, we'd given little thought to Christmas, so as soon as we arrived, we set off in search of *Velella*-sized decorations to make our first tropical Christmas feel festive. At a street stall, we spotted petite Christmas decorations that seemed designed for our limited space, and for $3, bought an eight-inch-tall, wire-framed Christmas tree perched on a wooden trunk, tiny hand-blown painted-glass ornaments, and a beaded garland. By bending the tree's top branches, I could wedge it onto the four-inch-wide shelf in front of a switch that I needed to use three or four times a day to light the stove. I added confetti I cut from silver wrappings, which had once imprisoned tequila-filled chocolates that I was happy to free. I draped a napkin around the base for a tree skirt on which I nestled the remaining tequila-filled chocolates, which we both felt an urgency to consume before they melted into a puddle in the stifling heat.

For me, Christmas isn't Christmas without decorated cookies and carols, so I arranged to bake cookies with Cath aboard *Felicity*, despite the heat. We had discovered a whole new category of hot that we'd rarely experienced in cool, rainy Seattle. Add to that an oven heated to 350 degrees Fahrenheit, and that was some kind of hot. Molding cookie dough that bore a close resemblance to soup into free-form holiday shapes taxed our artistic abilities and patience, as did trying not to drip sweat onto the cookies. Meanwhile, Garth and Cath's husband, Ken, jeered at us from outside, where it was much cooler. When we were done, Cath and I hosed ourselves down outside, while Garth and Ken ridiculed our flat cookies before popping them into their mouths.

On Christmas Eve, we and several other cruisers piled into a group of dinghies, intent on caroling at fellow cruising boats around the anchorage. Despite our (possibly alcohol-induced) enthusiasm, we found trying to steer six dinghies en masse in any particular direction as challenging as we did singing songs for which none of us could remember the words. But we were all very merry and spread our good cheer.

By the time the holiday festivities drew to a close, Garth was desperate for time alone with me. He suggested a side trip to Mexico City, which I'd visited on business but he'd never seen.

After hiking the dusty road to and from the bus station where Garth and I'd looked into the particulars of getting bus tickets, we were overheated. We ducked into Rick's Bar to cool down. Rick's Bar offered an oasis for northern sailors to escape the stifling tropical heat aboard boats that were insufferable when the air was still. Rick's offered hot showers, laundry service, a book swap, Mexican folkloric dancing performances, and, most importantly, a place with cool drinks where we could meet up with fellow cruisers. Afternoons featured tournaments of Mexican-Train-style dominoes among groups of tanned, lightly dressed expatriates, sunglasses strung around their necks, sporting Teva sandals and sun hats or ball caps with large back flaps to keep the sun off. Sailors who cruised Mexico certainly didn't look like your average tourist. At Rick's we congregated with our kind, swapping tall tales and tips on where to go, or troubleshooting the complex equipment that many used to recreate the luxuries of home. I coveted the sense of community Rick's offered, and we both loved the ice-cold drinks.

When we mentioned our Mexico City plans to our friend Ken, he asked if we would like him to look after our boat.

Garth replied, "It probably won't sink while we're gone." He slurped the last of his ice cold 50¢ Coke, "Though I appreciate knowing you'll keep an eye out."

"Do you need me to run your engine for you while you're away?" Ken asked.

"No, it'll be fine." Garth said, shrugging his shoulders.

"Don't you run your engine every day?" Ken leaned forward.

"No." Garth sat back against the cool chairs. The fan whirled slowly overhead, drying the sweat off my back.

"We need to run our engine for an hour or two every day to keep up with the fridge and keep our batteries charged," Ken said.

"Two hours *every* day?" Garth said, his baritone rising into soprano range. Garth shook his head. "No, our boat'll be fine, really. But thanks for offering."

As we rowed back to our boat later, Garth said, "Can you imagine listening to the engine drone for two hours *every* day? Guess all that fancy stuff takes power to run."

🌴

We'd looked forward to having friends and family visit us, but because *Velella* was so small, we knew our visitors would need to stay in a hotel. Coordinating visits for a moving target was complicated, since we had to identify a location—in a place we had never seen—where we could anchor safely, that was easily accessible to hotels, restaurants, and an airport. And then we had to guess how long it might take us to sail there.

"So, Dad, when do you think you'd like to visit us in Mexico?" I remembered asking my father by phone before we had left Seattle.

"Oh, I don't know. How about sometime in January?" he'd replied.

"That sounds great, Dad. Keep me posted."

We stayed a long time in Zihuatanejo, thinking that might be a good place for him to meet us. But, as January in Zihuatanejo came and went, and he hadn't answered any of my emails, I decided to call him. We'd been in Mexico for three months and only planned to be in the country for another two.

My dad is a veteran world traveler. He travels light and could fit in at a four-star hotel or a fleabag motel as the situation might require—and often does, since he doesn't plan ahead. Mom had been the planner. In fact, he tries so hard not to be too much trouble that it's hard to pin him down enough for it *not* to be too much trouble. But I eagerly anticipated his visit so I could share with him the cruising lifestyle he had inspired.

When he answered the phone, he was happy to hear from me, but he hadn't yet made any plans.

What a surprise. I sighed, knowing I'd been foolish to assume he might arrive any day.

In the six weeks we'd spent anchored in Zihuatanejo, we'd watched a crew of twenty men painstakingly dismantle a cement building with hammers and crowbars under a scorching Mexican sun, something that'd take a wrecking ball half an afternoon in Seattle. Anchored in such a fertile environment for so long had produced an entire ecosystem on the underside of *Velella*, despite our hand-application of $100-a-gallon toxic paint that had come with four pages of health warnings in microscopic type. It was time to move on.

"Well, if you're going to visit us in Mexico, you're going to have to do it soon, because we're leaving the country at the end of March," I said. I imagined his gears clicking on the other end of the line in the silence that followed.

"And Mom's coming in mid-March," I added, acutely aware that double-booking them wouldn't work. After mom left, Dad bitterly contested the divorce. Her remarriage several years later to a former neighbor added to the awkwardness. But the final insult came when Dad's widowed father married Mom's mother, which—in a form of cruel irony—turned his ex-wife into his step-sister.

Even after all these years, whenever I mentioned Mom, Dad's face would darken; whatever we'd been talking about would be forgotten, replaced by a pregnant silence or a cutting remark. But his hesitation this time was brief this time. "Yeah, Okay. Let me look at my schedule," he said, setting down the phone.

I pictured him relaxing on *Charisma*, his aptly-named forty-seven-foot Valiant sailboat in Hawaii, where he lived. Since he'd retired from the Navy several years before, I had trouble imagining his schedule was tight. My pay phone was no longer in the shade, as it had been at the start of my call, and sweat trickled between my shoulder blades. I began to get agitated, knowing how much Telemex might be charging for this call and wondering how much time was left on my Latadel calling card. Many things were cheap in Mexico, but telephones calls weren't one of them. Planning ahead to call the U.S. might have saved me a bunch of money, but my strategy had been basically *not* to call.

Dad came back on the phone, "How about in two weeks?"

That meant mid-February. I did a quick calculation and decided that if we wanted him to come, we had few options.

"That's when my friend Julie will be visiting, but I think we can make it work," I said, sighing and trying not to let my frustration show. "We'll be in Melaque then. If you fly into Puerta Vallarta, you can take the bus down from there. I'll email you bus details. Send me your flight information as soon as you get tickets."

"Sounds good," he said.

I hung up, wondering if he'd actually read any of my emails. Regardless, I dutifully checked Julie's travel details, researched buses between Puerta Vallarta and Melaque—a mid-sized Mexican beach town—and emailed him the information from an Internet café.

"So is your dad coming?" Garth asked when I returned that afternoon.

"Ah…well, it looks like he might meet us in Melaque in about two weeks, at the tail end of Julie's visit."

"Might?" Garth rolled his eyes.

Dad likes to "wing it." Like me, he has an innate confidence that everything would work out. I never stopped to think much about what it must have been like to be on the receiving end of that: my hosts wondering when and if I might show up, how long I might stay, and what else I might anticipate fitting into my visit. Garth and my mother liked to point out that it might prove less stressful to plan in the first place. But I always thought part of the fun was being open to opportunities. Now I was on the other side with the extra complication that we were also on the move.

In early February, after a series of day sails and stops, we reached Melaque in Bahia de Navidad, a few days before Julie was scheduled to arrive. Our guidebook noted strong surf in the southern part of the bay, so we anchored behind a modest hook in the rocks that protected the northwest corner. On the southern edge of the bay was a shallow lagoon leading into the commanding Grand Bay

Hotel and Resort, a mega tourist complex, featuring several fancy restaurants, a twenty-seven-hole golf course, a 200-slip marina, and ambitious plans for further development. While tempting, a protected slip in the marina would have cost every penny of our weekly budget for a single night.

I'd emailed my father details about how to find Julie's hotel, suggesting he stay in her second bedroom, but I'd never heard back from him. The afternoon that my father was supposed to arrive, we made a feast in the kitchen of Julie's cabana, but when dinnertime came and went with no sign of him, we ate.

After dinner, Garth and I headed for the bus station. We waited for the next bus from Puerto Vallarta. And then the next one. And the next. I was worried about him, wondering if he'd missed the flight or gotten lost. We asked around in our halting Spanish about bus arrivals but found the answers confusing. I described him to a disinterested ticket clerk as best I could, then drew a map to Julie's hotel, and posted it near the counter. At 2:00 a.m., we finally gave up, deciding to get some sleep.

I shouldn't have worried. I'd forgotten how independent and resourceful a traveler my dad could be. After he and Mom split up, he was stationed in Italy as the head of the naval dental clinics in Europe. He'd jetted all over Europe and become a master of its history, classic art, and literature, which made him the ultimate tour guide when we'd visited. He'd committed to memory the schedules for the London theaters so he could garner a last-minute half-priced ticket to all the latest shows. I'd been impressed with the depth and breadth of his knowledge and experience and it fanned my own passion to see the world.

A dental meeting had taken him to South Asia years ago. Afterward, he'd sent his dress uniform home and then backpacked through India. We'd planned to meet afterwards to ski together in Colorado. At the airport, I'd received a cryptic message indicating that he'd be delayed twenty-four hours. When he'd finally arrived, I'd learned that he'd suffered through food poisoning, which he'd passed off with a wave of his hand. Like any successful traveler, he knew how to make the best of whatever situation he found himself in. But his fluid approach didn't work quite as well when bringing together two parties on the move. Especially when one of them didn't communicate.

The following morning, a shout from the beach caught Garth's attention. It was my dad, empty-handed. When we caught up with him, we learned that he'd jumped off the bus the night before—never actually reaching the bus station—and immediately booked a room for the night. Clearly, he hadn't read my emails. I always looked forward to his visits, perpetually forgetting the challenging logistics of his previous one.

Trying to forget my irritation, I suggested we get something to eat. As we sat down at a table in an empty beachside cantina, a violent wind burst across the water, sending placemats and plastic flowers flying. Wind blew the froth off the tops of waves that scurried in multiple directions like frightened geese. Out in the bay, *Velella* was bucking like an unbroken colt.

Garth studied *Velella* with a troubled look. "I think I need to go out there," he said.

"Yeah, I know," I sighed.

"I should at least let out some anchor chain, but I might need to stay out there."

I nodded. *Blasted weather,* I thought. *Once again, weather trumps all plans.*

We hurried to the far end of the beach, where our dinghy was nestled beneath a scattering of spindly trees that swayed in the wind. Garth took in a deep breath and looked at me, his mouth pressed into a thin, straight line. "Ready?"

I nodded.

We each grabbed a handle on either side of our light, flat-bottomed inflatable, lifted, and slowly walked towards the water with dread. My dad, a seasoned sailor, could see what we were facing. He watched silently, chewing his lip. About five yards from the water, we stopped and studied the waves, looking for a trend. We'd noticed the biggest waves often came in groups of three, but even the smallest ones were bigger than the largest ones only an hour earlier.

"Now," Garth said. We rushed forward together and set the boat down in the water. I stood in the thigh-high water and held onto the dinghy, keeping it as straight as I could while Garth jumped in. I gave it a shove as Garth put the oars in the oar locks and pulled with all his might. I stood in the water, watching his slow progress. With each oar stroke, he barely hung onto his position against waves that seemed intent on driving him back ashore. Water droplets from the oars danced in the breeze and splashed onto his back. What normally might have taken him only five minutes, took twenty. Finally he reached *Velella* and climbed aboard.

After Garth let out some anchor chain to dampen the motion of the boat in the waves, he stood brooding on the foredeck. I rejoined my father above the tide line and watched while Garth pantomimed an exaggerated shrug, flinging his arms out to the side. Then he pointed down. Clearly he was worried about the boat and wanted to remain aboard. My dad and I set off down the beach, with a quick stop at his hotel to pick up his bag, and on to Julie's hotel.

A few hours later, Garth arrived in dripping swim trunks, his shirt plastered against his back. His Tevas squeaked and oozed water with each step. He'd obviously had a wet row. The wind had dropped, but the waves had grown.

"Mind if I take a shower?" he asked, with an edge to his voice.

"Nice day for a row, isn't it?" I said, grinning.

He disappeared into the bathroom while Julie and I began reheating leftover rice and meat from the night before.

Later that night, though we tried to time our dinghy launch, it just wasn't possible to get two people into an undulating rubber boat and get oars into oar-locks between breaking waves. We quickly turned sideways to the seas and flipped. Next thing I knew, I was tumbling though sand and foam and then chasing escaped oars on a moonless night. We arrived at *Velella* tired and soaked.

The following morning, the wind had diminished further, but waves still terrorized the shore. Before our dreaded row ashore to meet our guests, I wisely filled a dry bag with two sets of clothes, several plastic Hefty bags, and a quick-dry towel. Wearing only our bathing suits, we did our best to keep control of the inflatable kiddy pool we called a dinghy. We were swept onto shore, a tangle of arms, elbows, oars, and dry bags, wondering if it might have been smarter just to swim.

On shore under the trees, I quickly toweled off and pulled a loose dress over my damp swimsuit. Together, we trudged to the hotel, where we shed our salty clothes and rinsed, knowing we'd be reversing the process in the evening. I spent a distracted day walking around town, dreading our return to the boat in the dark.

That night, we managed to keep the dinghy upright, though we arrived at *Velella* nearly as soaked as we'd been the night before. A growing pile of salty clothes emitted a whiff of ripeness from under the dodger.

Once Julie checked out of her hotel, we all sailed to Tentacatita, a protected bay five miles away, for Julie's last day. Armed with large plastic garbage bags encasing the luggage, detailed instructions, and slightly diminished surf, Garth managed to ferry everyone and their (thankfully) minimal luggage out to the boat in a mostly dry state. Once in the warm embrace of Tentacatita's large tranquil bay, we felt like we could finally relax. Next time, I thought, maybe we'll splurge for a marina.

🌴

We gradually realized that weather had become our new boss. If we didn't pay attention, we paid dearly, so we had incentive to figure out her subtleties.

Garth and I became more careful about studying daily weather forecasts so we might anticipate when conditions would be favorable for the direction we planned to head, or know when it was time to pick a different destination, *before* it was too late to move.

We realized that ways to get detailed weather information had developed since Garth's days sailing around the world twenty-five years earlier: longer-range forecasts might help us anticipate approaching storms so that we wouldn't get caught with our proverbial pants down.

Ideally, anyway. Our learning process was slow. First we learned that these weather charts existed, and then we had to learn how to access them and interpret them ourselves. But in the meantime, we relied on advice from sailors who had access to this information.

For seasonal planning, we'd carefully study something called pilot charts, which we'd purchased before we left Seattle. Matthew Fontaine Maury, a nineteenth-century seaman who'd been injured in a carriage accident that prevented him from going to sea, developed pilot charts by examining thousands of ships' logs to see what patterns he could infer from weather phenomena they reported. Sorting through reams of data and turning that raw data into easily-referenced, visual cues must have been quite a task with quill pens by lamplight. The pilot charts that evolved from his work and their electronic progeny show typical wind speed and direction, currents, incidents of fog, storms, and ice for each ocean in each month of the year. Today they lend solid reasoning to the migration paths of vagabond sailors like us. While an outsider may think our wanderings were completely whimsical, our travels fell within certain seasonal parameters to help minimize encounters with adverse weather events that can make sailing a truly unpleasant experience.

The most notable of these events are *cyclones,* also known as *hurricanes* in the Atlantic and *typhoons* in the Western Pacific. Hurricanes or typhoons generally occur in the vicinity of the tropics during warmer weather months, usually summer time, which in the northern hemisphere falls between June and October and in the southern hemisphere between October and June.

The potential fury of them scares the crap out of experienced sailors like me and Garth, no matter how much old salts might strut and scoff at the idea. (If you'd caught these sailors during the worst of the blow or even shortly before, while they may have appeared calm and collected on the outside, I'd bet they were quietly grinding their teeth and popping antacids, possibly even checking their drawers.)

To avoid enduring one of these stomach-eating, insomnia-provoking, and potentially home-destroying catastrophes, Garth and I made a pact to avoid typhoon and hurricane-prone areas during peak season. That meant getting out of the northern hemisphere typhoon/hurricane belt—in our case, Mexico and Central America—before June. During the transition months of late spring, we would be safe in that narrow band along the equator which is generally free of typhoons and hurricanes, since, even though that is where they form, they don't yet pack much punch. That gave us roughly six months during which we could explore the South Pacific in the trade winds between the equator and New Zealand before we needed to worry about developing cyclones.

After five months spent sampling what Mexico had to offer, we felt compelled to join the great exodus across the western horizon. We aimed to celebrate our second (and third) Thanksgiving in New Zealand, which offered safe harbors and a lower incidence of tropical cyclones since it fell outside the tropics. From that goal, we worked our way backwards to estimate roughly how long we could spend in each country between the Marquesas—our first stop in the South Pacific—and Tonga, where we planned to leave for New Zealand. Depending on what Mother Nature would allow, of course.

Our first landfall in the South Pacific would be the Marquesas, a set of islands 2,800 miles away in the middle of the Pacific. The prospect of a three- or four-week passage filled me with awe. This was a whole new level of commitment, since with the wind behind us, we couldn't easily turn around if we changed our minds.

Since hundreds of boats were making this passage, experienced cruisers became instant experts, helpfully offering tips and seminars about how to prepare (at least for the trip *they* had experienced). Everyone worried endlessly about the weather and if our boats were adequately prepared. Even I forgot all the sailing I had done to get this far and that I was traveling with someone far more experienced than the new "experts."

Our friends consulted Garth, knowing he'd already sailed around the world, thinking he might have wisdom to impart on finding the fastest, safest route to the South Pacific.

Garth licked his lips and started slowly, "Well…" Everyone leaned forward. "First, I'm going to settle on a southwest course until the wind shifts and then I'll jibe back onto a southwesterly course until it shifts again and so on, generally heading in the direction of the Marquesas." He sat back and lashed his hands behind his head.

Everyone thought seriously about what he'd said for a moment. He cracked a sly smile. Gradually, they realized that he had revealed no great secret, just common sense.

During the last few weeks preparing for a South Pacific cruising season, the men discussed the finer points of equipment preparedness while the women scurried to stores to fill our boats with food, forgetting that people eat all over the world. We stocked up on American and Mexican brands we feared we'd never see again. Day after day, we returned to the boat with bags and boxes of groceries, and we spent hours trying to squeeze square things into round spaces and round things into square spaces. We hauled as many vegetables and fruits as we could reasonably carry without making juice on the way back to the boat, buying them in order of durability.

I spent hours carefully washing each banana, grapefruit, orange and apple with bleach to kill any freeloaders and gently stowing it in padded crates scientifically grouped and spaced to prolong its life, in the hopes that it might last through three weeks or more of constant jostling while poorly ventilated in the heat of the tropics.

Shortly before we planned to leave Mexico, our circle of sailing friends had a blowout party as though it would be our last. We stayed up nearly all night, joking about our imminent deaths. With a generous shot of liquid courage—I think our host skipped adding mixers late in the evening—we felt ready to sail off the edge of the map.

In the morning, we didn't feel quite so ready.

Eventually I ran out of excuses to keep us from getting on with it, other than fear, so on the last day of March 2001, Garth and I checked out of Mexico to head for the South Seas. We were among the first to set out.

SAILING OFF THE EDGE
OF THE MAP

With more assurance than Christopher Columbus could have ever dreamed of, Garth and I sailed out of Banderas Bay in flat water and light winds. Next stop, Marquesas, 2,800 miles away.

The boat ghosted along beautifully. On the new VHF radio my mother had brought to Mexico when she visited, we called Ken and Cath, our friends on *Felicity*, to tell them how ideal conditions were. We set a time and channel on which we could meet by short-wave radio each day. Since we had purchased a cheap, receive-only radio, Garth and I could listen, but we were mute over distances greater than twenty miles. Ken and Cath generously offered to start transmitting before they left port, though they could still talk to everyone else in person besides us.

Like DJs with a listening audience of at most two and possibly zero, they clearly felt foolish, urging us on though never sure whether we were actually listening: "Hello to Wendy and Garth on *Velella*, if you're out there listening. Hope you're having a great passage. Garth, you need to remember to talk to Wendy, since we can't. She needs to talk to people, you know. We just fixed the autopilot, and as soon as we fix the water maker, we'll be off ..." and so forth.

Slowly we sailed away from the Mexican coast. Rolling swell soon replaced short coastal waves. The land grew hazy and distant, and then disappeared completely. There was nothing to break the line between sea and sky. We were too far offshore for anyone to help us. I realized at a gut level that getting to land required perseverance and our own ingenuity. I chuckled when I remembered that when we had stocked our medical kit, the pharmacist—who supplied the north Pacific fishing fleet—suggested carrying Valium in case we panicked when we suddenly realized that there would be no way to get off for another two or three weeks.

We listened to a public sailors' radio "net" to hear discussions among boats traveling in our area, whether or not we knew them. While these short-wave radio conversations provided a sense of camaraderie and an irrational feeling of safety, participants could offer little but entertainment and suggestions if a boat got into serious trouble. Occasionally boats were within a day of one another, though trying to render assistance across two lurching vessels might prove unhelpful at best and possibly even dangerous.

We grew to know the voices and personalities of the participants in this invisible entourage. We had the know-it-all (who was actually on his way somewhere else) weighing in on conditions we faced and offering his opinion about anything and everything. We had a cheery host with an incredibly strong radio signal whom we were surprised to notice we were passing at a rapid clip. Despite a powerful signal, which made us assume it came from a large vessel, we learned later that it was a steel sailboat not much larger than ours, but distinctly slower since it was three times heavier. There were the radio hogs that, once they got on the radio, proceeded to dominate the rest of the discussion. We had folks with too much time on their hands that worried incessantly about little things, like whether customs would confiscate vegetables upon arrival. (After three weeks in tropical heat, I figured I might not want them anyway.) And then we had the fellow we probably could have heard without the radio, who continually shouted into the microphone "CAN YOU HEAR ME?"

As on a party line, everyone listened in on every conversation within range. We took solace in hearing the trials of others, struggling to remember that we had volunteered for this—that we actually had devoted significant resources to reach this state of affairs. One friend described how she burned her rear end when the oven gimbaled towards her while she was cooking naked. Another told of a diesel-infused blanket that permeated the boat and overwhelmed them with nausea. I roared with laughter when a third described the unrivaled stench of decaying potatoes within hours of discovering the same thing myself.

Other than the radio, without a social life, I felt as though I were in solitary confinement. With little but books to keep us company, we were desperate for diversions. At least I was. Garth could spend hours redesigning the mainsheet system. I longed for something more satisfying than another formulaic crime novel, courtroom drama, or spy thriller.

As we moved southwestward towards a featureless horizon, I trolled the airwaves for BBC programs, chasing a moving target of radio reception to keep up with world news: Russia's armed action against Chechnya, a U.S. spy plane in a collision with a Chinese fighter, George W. Bush withdrawing his support for the Kyoto Protocol on global warming, Sir Paul McCartney and his then-girlfriend-soon-to-be-ex-wife Heather Mills meeting U.S. Secretary of State Colin Powell about an international treaty banning land mines, Dell touted as the world's top PC maker, the release of *Bridget Jones Diary,* and the ongoing royal scandal of Princess Sophie. Back in Seattle, we'd been devoted listeners to National Public Radio. You might have even called us junkies, if you define a junky as someone who will listen through every hiccup of a pledge drive. We'd foregone TV since our twenties, but withdrawing from NPR had been one of our greater sacrifices. Now offshore, getting a decent signal was difficult, at best. At first, we felt like we were going cold turkey during a marathon-long rainy weekend at home. What we didn't realize at the time was that this news blackout would span most of our voyage. The longer we were away from shore, the more it seemed that we were in our own little world. The outside world began to seem less and less relevant.

We continued our watch schedule of three hours on, three hours off, alternating sleep to keep a constant vigil. Over time, we felt more rested. Rarely did we see a ship. At the rate a ship can travel, it could reach us within seven minutes of when we first spotted it, but after scanning an empty horizon for so long, it was easy to become so absorbed in books that we forgot to look around.

When the winds were light, we became more ambitious, taking on little chores aboard. I found myself cleaning the toilet for entertainment one day. Though never a highlight on my schedule at home, it seemed more interesting at the time than staring at the same uninterrupted horizon. Shortly after my cleaning session, the toilet stopped working, though it wasn't related. Garth spent three sessions dismantling it, trying to figure out what the problem was. As its most frequent customer, I had a strong interest in his project's success, so I volunteered to take part of his watch while he continued swearing as he hunched over the smelly receptacle.

At 11:00 a.m. each morning, I rolled out of the bunk groggily and looked in the can locker, wishing a gourmet meal artfully arranged on fine china would magically appear. Then I chose a can of chili or stew, slopped it into a pot for five minutes, and then into two plastic dog bowls. While I wished for culinary inspiration and the acrobatic prowess to produce it while jostling about, for the moment, even reheated canned chili tasted delicious.

Each day, I sorted through vegetables in the bin (what Cath called "V-Berth Farms") to identify the next candidate in the rotten vegetable parade. I extracted a certain warped pleasure from hucking a rotten potato overboard. Sometimes Garth would remark on the vegetables that went flying past as he ducked to avoid a direct hit or noticed the remnants of something oozing from the lifelines. The menu for dinner was usually dictated by what needed to be eaten first.

The wind seemed to come up every day as we approached the dinner hour. I started fixing dinner earlier and earlier each day until we were eating at about three o'clock in the afternoon. When I threatened to serve Powerbars one day, Garth suggested adjusting our course so the boat motion was less boisterous until after dinner. I wholeheartedly agreed, eyeing him suspiciously and wondering why he hadn't suggested it sooner.

Garth was in the middle of Michener's *Hawaii,* for the second time. A wave splashed overhead, dousing him and the book. He blew saltwater off his dripping face. Then he looked at the drenched book. I could see the thought pass through his mind. Then he hucked the book over the side. "Oh well, it was starting to drag anyway. He was still describing the formation of the islands."

I laughed.

As we approached the doldrums near the equator, the heat grew intense. Our progress was slow in the phantom-like winds. Each time thick clouds appeared on the horizon, we grew apprehensive that they would bring rain and bursts of wind or lightning and thunder, but most passed without incident. We flew our spinnaker to eke out some progress in the still, oppressive heat. I opened all the ports for ventilation in the suffocating interior.

Garth looked up from his next book late one afternoon and said, "There's another big black cloud heading this way."

"Probably doesn't have any wind. They never do," I said.

Garth shrugged and resumed reading. I went down to use the toilet.

In the middle of my being what you might call, "occupied," the boat lurched. Instantly, *Velella* was bowled over until she was practically on her side. I heard the sound of water gushing past the open portlights. Fighting a reluctant zipper, I rushed aft to close them. There were six, each requiring about seven rotations of a wing nut. My fingers fumbled in a panic.

Out in the cockpit, Garth had his hands full just trying to steer through the gust. He was practically doing a chin-up with the tiller.

And then the boat abruptly stood up. Through the hatch, I could see strips of spinnaker fabric trailing in the water behind us. Flashes of blue and white fabric undulated in the stern wave we'd kicked up. The pole that once held it in position took an abrupt right turn at the forestay.

Garth said, "Guess that one had wind."

We spent the better part of the next afternoon carefully removing anything useful from what remained of our spinnaker and saving the shredded blue-and-white fabric to make flags for each of the countries we would visit.

Several days later, spinnakerless and unwilling to endure the oven-like heat that running the engine added to already toasty temperatures, we sat awaiting an invisible breeze. On the morning net, Jordan of the boat *Queen Jane* stated his position over the short-wave radio. I compared his position to ours and noticed how close they were—possibly within VHF range. In such an intimate community, of course we'd heard of *Queen Jane's* crew, but we had not yet met them. *Why not a mid-ocean rendezvous?* I immediately started hailing them on the VHF.

Finally, after about an hour, they heard my call.

"*Velella*, this is *Queen Jane*. Hello!" Jordan replied.

"*Queen Jane*, *Velella*. Switch channels?" I said, remembering my radio etiquette.

"Why? Who the hell else is out here?" Jordan said.

Garth snorted.

"You've got a point. We haven't seen anything for weeks." After a momentary pause, I added. "I notice you're in the neighborhood," and told him our position.

"That *is* close. We don't have any wind, so we're motoring."

"Us either, but we're bobbing," I said.

"We'll probably catch up to you within the next hour."

No doubt, since our position was unlikely to change at the rate we were moving.

"We'll be here. Can't miss us. We'll be the white sloop off your bow."

As *Queen Jane* came within sight, over the radio, Jordan said, "I'll bet on that tiny boat, you might appreciate some ice and a nice cold Coke." He was right. The last ice-cold anything we'd encountered was weeks and about 2,000 miles behind us. As they came closer, we admired the perfectly varnished fifty-foot yacht. Their little boy ran along the side deck, squealing with delight at seeing another boat.

I stuffed books we'd finished reading into a dry bag. Garth deftly avoided side-swiping their pristine paint, while I tried to pass the bag across the water on the end of a boat hook without losing it overboard. After we successfully exchanged books for cold Cokes and ice, the crews of *Velella* and *Queen Jane* enjoyed rum and Cokes together, separately.

Our mid-ocean rendezvous was brief. As they pulled away, Kate and I continued conversing over the radio—discussing our impressions of *Angela's Ashes* in an impromptu book club of the air—until our signal grew frustratingly weak and crackly. The excitement of seeing and talking to other humans reminded me that, though we were out here on the ocean without anyone for miles, we were part of a community of sailors making the voyage westward.

We had little to indicate that we were making progress towards our destination besides a line on the chart. Our excitement grew as we reached the equator, that invisible line that divides the northern and southern hemispheres. Luckily, we crossed the equator at 5:00 p.m., a convenient hour for marking the occasion. To celebrate, we dressed in costume as King Neptune and a Sea Nymph and pulled out Almond Roca and blackberry wine friends had given us for just this occasion.

As we neared the equator, we carefully watched the GPS to note when we crossed. Suddenly Garth whined, "It's going back up!" The latitude numbers, which had been decreasing all the time we sailed south, were suddenly increasing again.

"Well, yeah," I retorted, "We're now in the southern hemisphere, sailing *away* from the equator."

Realizing his mistake, he stuttered, "Oh, uh, right."

I got a lot of mileage from that one.

Finally we reached a point on the chart where there was no denying that we were nearing the Marquesan Islands. Neither one of us wanted to say anything, fearing we'd get our hopes up and then jinx ourselves. I began watching the horizon carefully and felt proud—and a little relieved—when I spotted land just where I'd expected it to be. We compared the land characteristics with those on the detailed chart and calculated the number of miles to Atuona, the bay where we planned to check into the country. Suspecting we might not make it in before dark, and not wanting to dawdle all night unnervingly close to land while we waited for daylight, we slowed the boat for a more relaxed morning arrival. The extra hours let me finish sewing a French Courtesy flag to fly while we visited this French territory.

While I had been intimidated by the prospect of crossing 2,800 miles of ocean out of sight of land over three weeks, I discovered that if we took one day at a time, we could accomplish what I had once considered an impossible feat. While I was excited to explore new parts of this exotic place about which Garth had spoken so fondly, I found myself surprisingly reluctant to let the outside world invade our peaceful cocoon.

FRENCH POLYNESIA
PAUPERS IN PARADISE

In late April, after twenty-two days, twenty-two hours, and twenty-five minutes—not that I was counting, we made landfall in the Marquesas, one of three island groups that make up French Polynesia. When Captain Cook visited these high, volcanic islands in the eighteenth century, he found a population of 100,000 people, but he and his colleagues and subsequent visitors left souvenirs in the form of diseases in addition to nails, beads, and other trinkets. The Marquesans have been trying ever since to revive their decimated population—now numbering only 6,000 across six islands—and culture, with the help of descriptions and drawings preserved by none other than Captain Cook and his colleagues.

Like Captain Cook, we didn't exactly have a lot of street signs pointing the way, so finding land—*any land*—after scanning nothing but water world for nearly a month was exhilarating. We had just sailed 2,800 miles using a paper chart to tiny dots, that were barely visible in a vast expanse of blue. I too felt like an explorer who'd conquered the Pacific to discover a new world.

Of course that feeling vanished when we rounded the head of the bay to encounter a virtual city of boats. After three weeks of tranquility and complete privacy, we found ourselves parked in a row of boats like expectant customers awaiting a drive-in movie. Had this many others really just sailed off the edge of the earth, enduring weeks of isolation as we had? Unlike us, most had shortwave radio, limited radio email, and movies, so they hadn't completely disengaged, as we had. But still.

Before us stood the lush, green Marquesan peaks, typically shrouded in clouds. In our first few days, we experienced firsthand what made them so verdant. Rain showers abruptly interrupted the steamy tropical heat at frequent intervals. Puffy clouds strolled lazily overhead, bringing with them a perpetual threat of torrential rain—a curtain of water descending upon the landscape in some places, while twenty feet away, all remained dry.

Leaving the hatches open felt a little like playing roulette, but when they were closed, the heat was staggering. In the night, after closing the hatches and returning to bed during a squall, it wasn't long before I'd awaken in a pool of sweat. I became adept at stumbling out of bed buck-naked in a stupor, disengaging the stick that propped open the forward hatch, and perching on the cool toilet lid to wait until the squall passed and I could reopen the hatch. After several nights of that, we were functioning like a couple of zombies. So, using plastic clips that Garth had griped about buying at the boat show, he rigged a plastic tarp taut over the foredeck, low enough to leave the hatch open through squalls without the tarp catching the wind and creating a racket that would cost our sanity.

When we'd left Mexico, I'd warned my mother that she'd be unlikely to hear from us more than once every month or two when we would find an "Internet café."

"Internet café," I discovered, was a generous term, referring to a place where we could find an ancient computer with foreign keyboards that connected to the Internet at dial-up speeds. Typically, I would draft emails in advance on board on our decrepit, ancient laptop and save them onto a floppy disc. (Remember those?) Eventually we found computers that could handle thumb drives in the more urban areas, but this wasn't until several years into our trip. At the café, we'd download all incoming messages for later study. Then we could draft replies when we weren't paying by-the-minute. It goes without saying that general Internet surfing fell by the wayside.

We settled into even simpler and slower living than we'd experienced in Mexico. There was no Internet café or movie house where I could linger for hours in air conditioning for $2. There weren't even stores to explore. Our days were filled with hikes to Marae (rocky platforms of sacred ground) or a waterfall nestled into the craggy mountains, balanced with chores or a swim. Evenings we gathered in the cockpit with friends once the day's ninety-degree heat had finally started to dissipate and a light breeze drifted down the lush cliffs.

After three weeks on passage across the equator, despite wearing little to nothing, we'd somehow still generated quite a pile of laundry. Since engine maintenance required knowledge I didn't possess, laundry fell to me. I tackled the laundry by hand in a bucket on shore, fetching fresh water from a sink basin in the middle of a muddy swamp. Doing laundry became a social event, since every sailor had a pile of overripe clothes and a story to tell of the ocean crossing. While we soaped up, agitated, rinsed, and wrung our clothes, we gals (mostly) gossiped and shared stories of our passages to the Marquesas. A mini toilet plunger—this was another of Garth's discoveries from sailing around the world—surprised everyone with its effectiveness at simulating the agitation cycle of a washing machine. (Finding a way to dry clothes when it rained heavily for a few minutes every hour was another story.) Meanwhile, most of the guys were aboard their boats in various forms of physical contortion inside cramped, hot compartments, trying to fix complex equipment that had failed during the passage. With an engine that hummed efficiently and no complex equipment to fix, Garth read a book.

Cooking, cleaning, and laundering were aspects of this voyage to which I hadn't given much thought. I was amused to notice how we'd reverted to traditional male/female roles while cruising. The division of labor didn't always end up terribly even, but I found I liked some aspects more than I'd have guessed.

Doing laundry offered me the opportunity to splash in cool water in the scorching tropical heat, as well as a social outlet, as it has through the centuries.

Not all my friends seemed to enjoy it as much as I did. "I have a master's degree for God's sake," one girlfriend complained bitterly. I could get into a Zen-like state or sing along to Ella Fitzgerald blaring on my stereo as I soaped clothes in a bucket in the cockpit. Sometimes I even crawled with the clothes into the dinghy floating behind *Velella* like a child frolicking in a backyard wading pool. I'd discovered our dinghy was excellent at catching fresh water— fresh water we didn't have to haul. After a long session of hand laundry, my fingers would be ribbed, and my wrists would ache. Noticing that badly stained, size-XXL t-shirts took far more space, scrubbing, and wringing than my lightly soiled, size-four nylon surf shorts, tank tops, and sun dresses, I would call for back up.

"Okay, Garth, you're up, buddy." I'd chirp, adopting a game-show host voice, "You're the next contestant on *Laundering Right.*"

"Time to do a little hand wringing?" he'd reply if he were in an energetic mood, but usually I had to cajole him to break free of the inertia that gripped his horizontally-parked body; his energy level was inversely related to the temperature. At times I became resentful, particularly when I'd hear his snores through an open hatch while I toiled.

"Can you help me wring and hang up these sheets?" Sheets were the worst because of their unruly dimensions and tendency to hog the entire bucket. He'd look at me from where he lay on the bunk, then something on the book he was reading would reach up and grab his attention, and he'd be lost again to the world of words. Minutes would pass.

"Like sometime this century?" my voice would take on a tinge of irritation. I'd wait expectantly.

"Oh, all right," would come a reluctant reply, and he'd slap down the book he'd been reading and lumber out of the bunk.

Before we'd left for our cruise, time was always scarce. I gave little attention to meeting our basic needs, rushing through laundry, cooking, and even eating. At the end of a long work day, neither of us had much energy to cook, and we ate a lot of spaghetti because it was a filling, expedient meal. We'd even gotten into a pattern of dining out to such a point that restaurant meals no longer seemed special.

Now that I had time on my hands, I began to see cooking differently. With a fraction of the space and equipment, I expanded my culinary talents tenfold. If we wanted certain foods, I had to learn how to make them myself, by hand. I spent hours studying recipe books Garth had urged me to bring along—the massive binder of recipes he'd started in college and that we'd been adding to over the years, the *Joy of Cooking,* and my favorite, *Hot and Spicy.* I learned to make bread, tortillas, focaccia, pizza, pita pockets, quiche, and calzone and reproduce favorite restaurant dishes I craved. It became part of the fun.

I had been captivated by the Laura Ingalls Wilder books and the TV show as a child. The concept of self-sufficiency appealed to me. Of course, my family had teased me mercilessly over my obsession. My mother sewed me a prairie dress, apron, and bonnet—"Laura Dingall"-style, as my family nicknamed it. Photos of me watching the TV show dressed in my prairie attire and related jokes haunted me into adulthood. Yet here I was, living a prairie-like lifestyle, although a tropical, sea-based one.

Despite the heat, I'd power through a marathon cooking session. Reasoning that the boat was already hot, I'd prepare bread dough, and while it was rising, I'd whip up a batch of cookies. Since the bowls were already flour-coated, and the measuring cups sticky, I'd go on to roast flat bread on the stove top and then finish with fresh tortillas that we'd inhale in a single sitting. I spent hours dripping in front of a hot oven or cast-iron skillet.

Back home, family and friends had often celebrated Garth's homemade pies and cheesecakes. Occasionally he would stir or offer culinary tips aboard, but he cooked far less than he had before we went cruising. He explained that it was because he couldn't stand up in the galley. I suspected laziness.

A few weeks after checking into French Polynesia, we moved *Velella* to a less-crowded anchorage. Instantly our empty anchorage filled with a flotilla of our closest newfound friends. We settled into lazy days of snorkeling, potlucks, movies, and games with other cruisers, often forgetting that our pristine anchorage was in a foreign country. At sunset, we studied the horizon for a green flash. Once the vision of this natural phenomenon danced before our eyes, we realized that if we hustled up the white sandy beach, we could experience it again. Our days blended together like an endless tropical vacation.

One afternoon, a man in an outrigger invited the ten cruising boats in the bay to a goat roast on the beach the following day. The next morning, from aboard *Velella*, I heard the entire saga of the hunt and the unlucky goat's struggle echoing from the cliffs surrounding the bay. That afternoon, cruisers descended upon the beach in inflatable outboard-powered dinghies, armed with salads, chocolate brownies, and bug spray. Eight Marquesan men laid out banana leaves and then covered them with rice, steamed breadfruit, barbecued chicken, and goat. Our self-supplied serving dishes, plates, and silverware looked incongruous next to this native feast. We cruisers marveled at the rich flavor of the goat jerky as we chewed and chewed and chewed, until one by one we quietly slipped a mouthful into the sand behind a nearby coconut palm.

"Marinating in some of those Marquesan limes could soften this goat right up," *Velella*'s resident *non-chef* remarked with a smirk.

We had little in common with these Marquesan fishermen and their quiet lives, but music transcended the impasse. Before dancing firelight, we serenaded one another, trading traditional Marquesan songs for soft-rock hits of the 1970s like John Denver's "Country Roads" and Cat Steven's "Moonshadow."

In the Marquesas a strange mixture of modern and rustic coexisted. Marquesans in villages were keen to trade, looking to cruisers as a source of supplies. Sometimes the sheer numbers of cruisers overwhelmed tiny villages.

One day a young man paddled out to *Velella* with a stalk of bananas and several coconuts resting in the bottom of his outrigger.

"Echangez?" he said. ("Trade?")

I nodded, then went below to fetch a bag of clothes I'd set aside for bartering. One by one, I held up candidates. His expression remained impassive. After a few moments, he shook his head and quietly paddled over to the next boat.

Evidently Marquesans had little interest in the stained, holey T-shirts that low-budget cruisers like us had to offer when CD players, DVDs, and music were the alternative on a nearby boat.

A few weeks later, we were in the village of Hana Vave on the remarkably photogenic island of Fatu Hiva, known for its towering rocky spires cloaked in thick green foliage. We'd spent $10 each to dine with a group of cruisers in the home of a Marquesan family. Ten of us sat at a simple wooden table on benches inside the three-room, prefabricated home, which the French Government subsidized as part of its colonial arrangement. Before us lay the remains of our feast: roast chicken, rice, poisson cru, green papaya salad, baked red bananas, and banana leaves wrapped around a delicious coconut cream-filled mixture of unknown ingredients.

We'd had to postpone the dinner twice because the Aranui had not yet arrived with frozen chicken, yet I'd noticed that chickens strutted across my path regularly. I wondered aloud why we needed to wait for the supply ship.

"We wouldn't want to eat the chickens," came the answer. "They eat the centipedes." They had a job.

Our host, Angela, was a merry Polynesian woman with a rope of wavy grey hair that reached to her waist. She sank into a plastic chair outside, now that her cooking duties were complete. Her youngest child, a toddler, jumped into her lap. She tickled him and smiled, then waved us outside to join her. The older children began to clear away the dishes. I went outside with the other ladies and sat on the door stoop, while our spouses remained inside with her husband.

I still wasn't quite used to this sharp division between women and men. In the Marquesas (and in fact throughout Polynesia), we rarely saw men and women together in the way that we cruising couples usually traveled—in twos, as though paired on our own individual versions of Noah's Ark. When we'd been invited to church, an important part of village life, we'd been faced with choosing whether to sit on the men's or the women's side of the aisle. Garth and I would settle on the women's side, where the children congregated. Ensconced in these communities, I felt like I'd returned to a bygone era with distinct divisions of the world by gender.

Under a starry sky, the tropical air thick with the scent of plumeria and papaya, Angela began asking about our lives. Her English was surprisingly good. Most Marquesans we'd met spoke little English, and their French wasn't much better. I'd looked forward to practicing my French, only to discover that Marquesans treated with disdain the language of the colonists. We and Angela were equally surprised to discover that she was the same age as most of us—mid-to-late thirties—because she looked far older.

Before Garth and I had left to go cruising, I'd worried that we'd be decades younger than the predominantly post-retirement sailors. But fortunately, because of the dot.com boom—the bubble only beginning to burst when we departed—a younger generation of sailors was out wandering the oceans. Though we were on a vastly different budget than many of our dot.commer compatriots, we appreciated the youthful energy of peers.

Angela asked us about our families, and we told her of parents and siblings scattered around the world. She shook her head. Then she rephrased her question: "But where are your children?"

"Children? We don't have children," one of us replied.

She sat open-mouthed in disbelief for a moment. It was a phenomenon she probably couldn't imagine. Then she looked deeply into our eyes and stammered, "But, why do you not have children?"

The answer was complicated for each of us.

Conceptually I'd always assumed I'd have children, but as the years stretched on, I'd never had the urge to turn that into reality. Garth shared my ambivalence. I came of age in the gap behind the baby boomers, in an era marked by Cyndi Lauper's anthem "Girls Just Wanna Have Fun," which expressed my own sentiments well. I thought that to have children, I needed to have my shit together, not stopping to consider that there was plenty of evidence to the contrary. That, combined with the thought that they might someday turn into teenagers, stopped me cold. There were so many exciting things I wanted to do in life, and I hadn't yet figured out how kids fit into that picture.

One by one, friends would announce they were expecting a baby and still I lacked a yearning to join them. Over time, the news would spark in my mind the chorus from Queen's song "Another One Bites the Dust." I hated to be such a pessimist, but I'd seen countless friends excitedly announce their baby news only to disappear soon afterwards into diapers and tricycles, baseball coaching and dance lessons, rarely to be heard from again. I saw how harried they'd become, rushing to daycare and soccer practice after pulling a forty-plus hour work week, with not a moment of down time, unable to finish a complete sentence. The life looked unappealing, but I didn't see another way, at least in current U.S. society. And so we waited. And time had marched on.

Over time, our social circle shifted towards predominantly childless individuals or couples—people who were doing interesting things that took them in a different direction. We'd gradually found ourselves part of a subculture of people who Kurt Vonnegut would identify as "genetically insignificant." Sometimes you find you've made a choice, whether conscious or not, because the options have shifted while you were making up your mind.

I thought about what we childless wanderers must have looked like from the perspective of this Marquesan woman, whose life was centered around family and community. Lonely. Disconnected. Meaningless. But the frenzied way of living we'd left had often come at the price of family and community. Deadlines and multitasking eclipsed opportunities for meaningful connection. In a way, leaving it behind, we'd rediscovered community. Within a few short weeks or days, I'd bonded more closely with my fellow travelers than with many people I'd known for years. Someone not faced with the same challenges or opportunities probably couldn't imagine making the choices we had. We tried to explain, but how could we explain something we didn't quite understand ourselves?

After several months in the Marquesas, we headed westward for the low-lying atolls of the Tuamotus. Thanks to the invention of GPS, we had a much better idea of where we were than Garth's family had back in 1974 when they'd been navigating by the stars using a sextant. They'd decided—probably wisely—to give the "Dangerous Archipelago" a miss. Spotting a clump of palm trees on the horizon is challenging under the best of circumstances; doing it while leaping off waves in low-visibility rainsqualls is another.

When I took a Celestial Navigation class the last six months before we departed, it had been hard to take sun sights off the flat, sandy beach at Golden Gardens when our safety hadn't been part of the equation. I would struggle to remember all the niggling details about declination and refraction so I could get a good sun sight. With that, presumably, I could calculate our position, a reliable "fix"— provided I didn't introduce math errors into my formula. I'd squint into the lens of the sextant and fuss with the knobs trying to bring the star down to the horizon until my eyes began to water or some smart-aleck would walk by and say, "Figure out where you are yet?"

Still, even with the luxury of GPS and a rough idea of the tidal flows, we were nervous. Off the reef pass of Fakarava against a lee shore, we encountered high winds and periodic white-out squalls and I wondered whether we were about to make a fatal mistake.

"I'm not liking this," Garth said, studying the pass as we drew closer.

"No. It doesn't look good," I said, catching Garth's eye and nodding in the direction of an approaching squall. The coconut palms had been nearly invisible until we were within a mile of this reef. As reliable as the GPS was, it wasn't always spot-on with our paper charts, which were often based on surveys done some time ago, courtesy of Captain Cook or someone from an equally bygone era.

Adding to my sense of unease were radio reports from boats pinned inside of a nearby atoll in high winds, afraid to move because of how difficult it would be to navigate around coral heads made practically invisible in choppy water. Though I'm generally not a worrier, I sometimes wondered whether it might be better not to know about all the things it hadn't yet occurred to me to worry about. Perhaps it would be better to just deal with the facts if and when they presented themselves.

The squall sidestepped our path, and we drew closer still.

We faced a critical decision. Should we try to go in despite the danger or sail on? I'd been reading about Fakarava and listening to radio reports from friends telling us how lovely it was. The pull was as strong as the danger. I struggled with the decision of what to do. I usually was inclined to "go for it" without considering the consequences. Garth was much more cautious. I suppose he had reason to be, after experiencing the joys of being shipwrecked.

Just then, a sailboat appeared in the pass. Its exit demonstrated that it could be done, though the way it leapt out of the waves, flashing a bit of keel in our direction, gave me pause, as it was a much larger boat during what was *supposed* to be slack tide.

"Well, should we give it a try?" Garth seemed bolstered by the appearance of this other boat.

I shrugged, trying to suppress my natural inclination to underplay the dangers. "You sure you want to do this?"

"What the hell. Let's go for it." Garth compensated for my caution, taking a firmer grip on the tiller and steering for the pass. I held my breath, and we traced the sailboat's reverse track, wrestling against the wave motion to stay in the center of the unmarked pass as it curved into the inner lagoon.

We made it through safely, surely showing as much or more of our own underside.

Our reward was snorkeling that same reef pass for days on end, our dinghy loosely tied to my waist in tow behind me while incoming current swept me past parrot fish, sharks, and moray eels as though I were on a Disney park ride.

We cut our time in the Tuamotus short to reach Papeete, Tahiti, in time for Fête. After the solitude of the atolls in the Tuamotus and a light-wind, three-day sail, we entered the busy pass of Papeete harbor, ducking a high-speed ferry, a Korean fishing boat, and a small inter-island supply ship. Instead of tying stern to the main quay as Garth's family had done, we headed past the airport to where we could still anchor for free. Port Control required us to obtain clearance to pass both ends of the runway. Within seconds of gaining permission, a plane whizzed past our mast on its descent to the tarmac.

As soon as we set anchor, I learned that most Fête festivities had ended before we'd arrived. Fête did not begin July 14, but rather culminated on Bastille Day. My hopes for watching the famed dance competition that pitted the best staccato-rhythm Tahitian dancers against one another were dashed. When my family had been stationed in Hawaii, I'd swung my skinny seven-year-old hips as fast as I could to a pulsating beat, trying to mimic the Tahitian-style dancing that had fascinated me at the Hilton Hawaiian Village and the Polynesian Cultural Center. In my mind, I was as graceful as they were. In actuality, the shag haircut that my mother had foisted upon me, along with my floral one-piece Speedo and buck teeth completed an unromantic picture.

Instead of watching the astronomically priced dance finals, I spent a tortured evening within earshot of throbbing drums, wishing I could afford the *steak frites,* the scent of which taunted me from a nearby *roulette,* as the food trucks along the quay were called.

I did manage to catch the tail end of a crafts fair, where I splurged on a finely carved black lacquer Marquesan paddle I coveted. I justified the souvenir's $75 expense on grounds that it had another use—propulsion. We weren't too late for the free outrigger canoe races and my personal favorite—the fruit carrier's race, in which Polynesian men wearing nothing but lava lavas and leis raced through city streets carrying fifty kilos of fruit lashed to a roughly hewn tree limb. My feet hurt just watching.

🌴

With each stroke I struggled to row our flat-bottomed inflatable dinghy forward in a strong cross-breeze, but it felt like I was trying to propel a kiddy wading pool in a gale across the open sea. I only had to reach our boat, anchored a quarter-mile away among several others in water normally as clear and tranquil as a swimming pool. Today it looked more like a whirlpool. Flags taunted me with the futility of my task as they flapped noisily in the howling wind. Between each stroke, I drifted sideways downwind. *Pull, pull, pull,* I thought, trying to coach my overtaxed muscles to counteract the force of the wind. With nothing to break my rapid descent downwind, I imagined where I might end up if I paused for even a second. Would I be able to grab the pilings of the over-the-water resort a mile away? Did the airport runway stick out far enough to slow my progress? Or was I headed for the outside reef, sure to puncture my inflatable like a pin on a balloon? How long might I be stranded on the reef until someone noticed? No one would be likely to hear my shouts over the noise of the wind, and I had no radio. Fueled by fears of these consequences, I pushed on.

Normally I might avoid rowing ashore on such a day, but we'd planned to leave Papeete the following day so I could celebrate my birthday with friends in Moorea, and I needed to collect our mail before we left. As the wind was predicted to be strong, Garth preferred to stay with the boat, so I'd reluctantly set off alone in a building wind, hoping to get back before conditions got too rough. No such luck.

Merely collecting the mail sounded like such a simple proposition. Not in Tahiti, and not the way we did it. Despite Garth's assurances that sending mail general delivery worked just fine in the 1970s, I assumed that old-fashioned method couldn't possibly still work so many years later. Not believing him, I suggested my mother send our mail to the American Express office. When we arrived expectantly at the American Express Papeete office, we found it closed. We noted the office hours and returned at the designated time the following day, but discovered that American Express had sent our mail back to the post office.

"Ferme" ("Closed"), the sign said on a firmly locked post office door. We again noted the posted hours and planned our return trip.

As we had gone about our other errands, we'd begun to notice that Tahitian business hours followed schedules that could only have been inspired by a Frenchman after a bottle of wine. Some businesses opened only in the mornings. Some opened at 10:00 a.m., only to close two hours later for a long lunch (and probably several bottles of wine). Most had no hours posted, and we never did figure out when they might be open unless we happened to get lucky. Sometimes we just gave up. For essential stops, like the propane shop, we loitered in the vicinity doing periodic reconnaissance like a couple of cops on a stakeout.

When we returned to the post office the following day, a French postal clerk told us with a sniff that we needed to visit the *airport* post office. After wandering all over the airport, tired and hungry, we spotted a promising office—closed, of course. So we sat down on the cool concrete to wait. When the office finally reopened— late—we explained our quest to a rail-thin, dark haired woman who stared indifferently past glowing embers. As she pulled the cigarette out of her mouth, she furrowed her brow, emitted several smoke rings, propped her arm against her hip, and said, "But zis eez not ze correct office. Ze office over zere eez vare your mail eez," pointing her tar-stained fingers, "But eet eez closed for ze day." Of course.

After two weeks chasing our mail all over town, I'd finally gotten my coveted package. I'd ripped it open in anticipation to find…a few yacht-club newsletters. No note from my mother—not even a birthday card. *All this for a couple of dated newsletters,* I thought, as wavelets splashed my sore arms.

To ignore my protesting muscles, I imagined rowing in time to a metronome. *Stroke, stroke. Throw my whole body into it.* The soft dinghy undulated in the chop, making each wave a mountain to ascend and descend. Spray blew off the tops of the wave crests and smacked me in the face. Feeling a bit ridiculous, I looked around, wondering if I really was making progress. Bright sunlight danced off the aquamarine wavelets, and I'd nearly reached a group of boats.

Gradually I closed the distance to *Velella*. As I came alongside, I blew out of reach the moment my oars stopped pulling. Instantly, I was careening downwind in my little rubber raft. I lunged for the anchor chain of the boat behind us as I blew past. I nearly missed.

I clung to that anchor chain with a desperate grip, my heart pounding, while I plotted my next attempt more methodically, as Mr. Practical-Worse-Case-Scenario might. I planned to row up to the stern of the boat, where I'd have some wind protection, ram the back corner, and throw my arm around the back rail without having to worry about the oars.

I psyched myself up for another go. As soon as I let go of the anchor chain, the wind hurled me fifty yards downwind, and then another fifty, before I could get my hands back on the oars. Adrenaline shot through my body. Finally I got the oars pulling and made progress against the breeze. *Almost there,* I thought, closing in on the last 20 yards, trying to ignore my blistered palms. Just as my hand closed around the stern rail, Garth appeared from inside.

"Need some help?"

"Ah…no." I felt giddy with a sensation of accomplishment. *Maybe, next time I'll try general delivery.*

🌴

"Garth, there's some crap in the water up there," I said, pointing from where I stood on top of the boom. This late on a squally, overcast day, the normally brilliant cerulean blue water lacked enough light to reflect the white sandy bottom, leaving its surface looking dull and flat. It's hard to say whether that was easier than trying to steer into a setting sun and the blinding reflection it makes off the water. Since I had better eyes, I usually watched for markers and coral obstacles, while Garth steered our landfalls, but I still couldn't tell what I was seeing. Whatever it was took up a large portion of the narrow reef pass, and somehow, we had to get past it. Once we reached the main bay, we still needed to turn south for a mile before we would find shallow enough water for anchoring, which would be a challenge since we had maybe fifteen minutes of light left, twenty at the most. After that, we'd be unable to see where we were going.

As I studied the water, I noticed two distinct dark shapes.

"They're whales!" Two humpback whales lay side by side. I was thrilled, yet apprehensive. The narrow pass gave us no choice but to pass close to them. They were much larger than *Velella*. When we came within twenty yards, they continued their slumber, unperturbed. My anxiety melted away, and I longed to linger and watch them. Then I remembered that we were racing against a setting sun.

In the morning, they were gone.

In late August, shortly before we set sail for Rarotonga, in the Cook Islands, we stopped to load up on fresh fruit at a roadside open-air market near Vaitape, the town center of Bora Bora. Lining the road were several long tables piled high with luscious fresh papaya, bananas, and pomplemousse, shell necklaces, and t-shirts. Behind the tables plump, bronze-skinned women in loose floral dresses chatted idly. The crowns of plumeria blossoms that ringed their heads gave them a regal air. Passengers from the cruise ship had just been through the market. I eyed a pomplemousse, a large, green thick-skinned honey-flavored grapefruit, but as I picked it up, I noticed the price: 500 cfp, the equivalent of $5 U.S. Ouch.

We'd already eaten through the fifty pomplemousse we'd picked at a farm on Hiva Oa in the Marquesas and another twenty we'd craftily collected a few weeks before in Bora Bora. (While waiting for friends to select souvenir t-shirts, we had noticed a tree laden with pamplemousse and asked whether we could pick fruit that looked like it might otherwise go to waste.) "Sure, pick all you want," came the fluent-English-speaking proprietor's answer. So Garth and I had picked everything within reach.

As soon as our friends completed their purchases, one of them had joined in the game, asking Garth to lift him so he could reach the higher branches. Meanwhile, our amused friends from other boats had snapped photos of our budget-driven spectacle. Now those juicy pomplemousse, which had become a breakfast staple and a cool, soothing snack for us, were all gone.

"We can't afford this," I mumbled to Garth. We'd noticed that subsidies in French Polynesia inflated the cost of everything, and our dollar didn't go far. We'd sneered at dirty shacks posing as restaurants only to discover that we couldn't afford even the cheapest item listed on the menu boards outside.

"Well, it's only a few days sail to Rarotonga. We can manage," he said.

"Yeah, you're right." I said. I reluctantly set the pomplemousse down.

"Are you from the yacht?" the vendor woman asked. I looked up at her, then at the cruise ship anchored in the harbor and shook my head no. I pointed at the cruise ship and waved my hands back and forth to signal, *No, not that boat.*

"No, no." She paused. "From the *yacht?*"

"Little boat …petite bateau de voile," I said, remembering to add a snippet of my French. I was starting to realize that when I used the word "boat," people didn't understand what I meant. Even our little *Velella* was considered a "yacht" by many outside the U.S., though it hardly evoked what I associated with the word "yacht."

She nodded. I smiled. She smiled back, then picked up a bag and began loading it with papayas, bananas, and several pamplemousse.

"Oh, no, no, no." I said, knowing we could barely afford a single item on the table, much less the whole lot now in the paper sack.

She pushed the bag towards us. "It's okay," she said with a smile, nodding towards the bag.

I realized then that she intended to give us the bag containing what must have been 3,000 CFP ($30) worth of fruit. The generosity of people we'd met in our travels astounded me. Stunned, I reached into my pocket and produced a 500 cfp note, the original price of the single pomplemousse, and handed it to her as I grasped the bag. A warm, gracious smile spread across her face.

"Merci. Merci beaucoup," I said.

"De rien," she said with a big smile. ("It's nothing.")

"Nous irez a Rarotonga, demain," I said. ("We are going to Rarotonga tomorrow.")

"Ah, oui. Je sais," she said with a beaming smile. She'd overheard our conversation. "Bon voyage!" she waved after us.

THE DAY THE WORLD CHANGED

On our second day sailing from Bora Bora to Rarotonga, in the Cook Islands, I was a couple hours into my watch. At 8am I turned on the morning net, as usual. We had twenty-knot winds on the beam, so I bounced around a bit as I tuned in and placed headphones on my head so I wouldn't wake Garth, asleep on the bunk only three feet away. The steps I leaned against groaned as I struggled to keep my balance against the motion. Garth is a good sleeper and didn't notice the extra noise amid the steady rumble of water against the hull and creaks of the lines that positioned the sails.

The morning net opened as usual.

"Good morning, this is Jim, from the sailing vessel the *Also II* and this is the 'Rag of the Air.' The weather forecast from Nadi for September 11, 2001, is as follows: A high pressure system sits at…" With a grease pencil in my grasp, I prepared to draw in the locations of the weather systems on a laminated map of the South Pacific.

"Break, break," a gravelly male voice interrupted.

"Go, break," Jim said. No one dared interrupt a broadcast with "Break" unless it was important.

"Yeah, Jim, I just heard some alarming news about terrorist action at the World Trade Center Towers in New York. I think everyone might want to tune into news to hear what's going on first hand. Over."

"Can you tell us what's happening? Over." Jim asked.

"I don't have all the details and apparently the situation is unfolding, so it might be better for people to just listen for themselves. Over."

"Well, can you tell us what you know? Over." Jim said.

"Apparently, two airplanes have flown into the World Trade Center Towers and the towers have come down. Over."

After moment of silence, Jim clicked back on again. "My God," he said.

"Break." Another voice cut in.

"Go, break."

"I've got a list of radio frequencies and times for BBC broadcasts. Over."

"Go ahead," Jim said. The man then listed times and frequencies. I tried to copy the information down as quickly as I could. Jim closed the net, and I clicked off. I stood up and peered out the dodger windows for a quick scan of the horizon to see if there was anything to worry about. Brilliant blue skies and puffy white clouds floated above a wavy blue horizon for as far as I could see. The water glittered, and a flying fish skipped over its surface.

I ducked back below. My thoughts raced. *Two planes, New York City, terrorists.*

Since it was almost the time for Garth to come on watch, I woke him early.

"Garth...."

"Hmm?"

"Garth, are you awake?" I said, as I gently touched his bare shoulder.

"I guess," he mumbled and rolled over onto his back. He rubbed his eyes, then looked over at me with squinty, unfocused eyes.

"I've just heard some really big news. Are you ready to listen?"

"Yeah, go ahead," he said, rubbing his hand across his face and around the back of his neck.

"There's been a terrorist attack on the World Trade Center towers."

"Huh?"

"Apparently, two planes flew into the towers and brought them down."

He sat up and rubbed his eyes again. Then he looked at me askance. "Someone's been reading too much Tom Clancy." He scratched his head.

"I'm serious."

He stopped moving.

"Wow. How can that be real? I just read that in a Tom Clancy book."

"I know. So did I." And I remembered how far fetched it had seemed at the time.

"This really happened?"

"That's what someone said on the morning net."

"Wow." He crawled out of the bunk and stretched. "Give me a minute, and then let's see if we can find some real news."

I went back on deck to check the compass, and then did a more careful study of the horizon. Still nothing within view but sunny skies and cumulus clouds floating by. Our floating world seemed just the same as the day before. Back below, I checked the GPS, wrote down the date—Tuesday, September 11—marked our position in our ship's log, and then plotted our position on the chart. A few minutes later, Garth turned the radio back on and tuned into the BBC station we'd been listening to most recently. Nothing. Our current location was twelve hours behind Greewich Mean Time. Just after 8:00 a.m. where we were meant that it was only 4:00 a.m. in the UK, the location of our news source. Since so few people lived in this area of the world, few stations broadcast within reception. Garth flipped through the dial to find a station that was currently broadcasting. Finally, one came in with a strong signal.

"The people of Mali want to offer our sincerest condolences to the citizens of the United States and those who have lost loved ones in this most terrible tragedy. I want the people of of the United States to know that we stand behind you and will offer any assistance within our capacity."

Another voice spoke. "We are most disturbed to hear news of terrorist attacks against the United States. Please know that our hearts hang heavy with those who have lost loved ones in this tragedy. We cannot tolerate such hateful violence and will do whatever we can to help the people of the United States to bring the criminals behind this attack to justice."

The smooth voice of the BBC correspondent came on. "Those were statements from the countries of Mali and Senegal. This is Julian Keane. You're listening to BBC World Service."

Another, somewhat patronizing voice announced, "This station is now closing. Broadcasting will resume at oh-seven-hundred Greenwich Mean Time."

Garth spun the dial to locate another station. I wished I'd listened better to the broadcast discussion. After a while, Garth gave up in frustration.

"I think at 0830 GMT, we can get 17827, but that's not for several hours. I'm on watch now. Maybe you should try to get some sleep in the meantime," Garth said.

"Yeah, you're probably right." I settled into the bunk, but sleep wouldn't come. I couldn't turn my mind off. I tried reading for a while, hoping that would help me relax, but my eyes wouldn't focus on the page. I stared at the patterns in the wood above my bunk for a while and thought about how far away that world seemed from us now. The World Trade Center was an important financial headquarters. This had to be a shocking blow to the U.S. and the world, but it seemed so unreal. Nothing had changed in our floating universe.

With 300 miles still to sail, we carried on sailing. We didn't reach Rarotonga until late Friday, and we only just barely made it into port before dark. Our friends, Drew and Vernita, on *Layla,* cheered our arrival. When we dropped anchor, they stood by in their inflatable dinghy to help guide us carefully back toward the concrete pier and squeeze into a space between two larger boats.

We were ravenous, and they were just heading out for dinner—Drew in search of a "cheeseburger in paradise"—so we tagged along. We shared our shock over recent events. Vernita started to tell us about how the Port Captain had let them watch TV news in a conference room, but her comments were cut short by the start of karaoke blaring over the speakers of the outdoor bar.

The next morning, I tidied the boat, then bundled and dropped dirty clothes at a laundry that Vernita had told me about. Then I headed to an Internet café to send off updates I'd drafted in Bora Bora before we'd left that would keep our friends and family informed of our location and latest news.

I never considered the incongruity of my glowing recitations with the sudden change in the world. Replies varied from a rare, "How dare you!" to the much more frequent "Thank God, you're reminding us that life goes on," and "It's eerily quiet. No one is going out. Everyone is glued to their TVs."

I tried to imagine it, but the concept seemed too out of step with memories of the bustling place I'd left. It was slow to dawn on me the enormity of what we'd missed.

In a conversation much later, my mother told me how eerily quiet it had been during the flight ban. Like most everyone we knew, she lived in an area where a steady stream of jet engines passed overhead at high altitudes. Like any low-grade noise you grow to incorporate into your sense of normal, its absence was sudden and unsettling. Yet since I'd left the continent of North America, airplane noise had become a rare phenomenon. During that same time period, I hadn't heard an airplane for over a month.

That afternoon Garth and I walked east along the concrete breakwater. A mound of flowers offered a flash of color against the bright sky and azure water. In the center was an American flag attached to a post ringed by a vine wreath. Below it sat a handful of heartfelt letters and poems addressed to the victims, their families, and the people of the United States. Heaping bouquets of purple and magenta bougainvillea, bird of paradise, irises, orchids, and a lone jar of sand containing several shells surrounded them. I felt the prickle of hot tears tugging at the edge of my eyes.

At the Saturday market, among tables of fresh drinking coconuts, bananas, peppers, eggplant, green beans, and black pearls, everywhere we looked, it seemed someone was collecting for the Red Cross to send money to the victims of the attack. How ironic that this modest country was collecting money for the richest nation in the world. Surely, I could afford to contribute. I remembered the twenty dollar bill stuffed into my change purse for emergencies. My spirits soared as I stuffed the bill into the box of a bright-eyed young Polynesian girl with an unexpectedly strong New Zealand accent. Our eyes met and her eyes sparkled.

It was months before I saw photographs of the airplanes plunging into the towers and the piles of rubble after the towers fell. I will never share the vivid recollections of my fellow countrymen and citizens of the world who saw it live. Because of that, I found it difficult to understand the reaction that followed. And I wasn't prepared for how profoundly it changed our world.

NEW ZEALAND SAILING FEVER

In our somewhat deluded state, we spent the next two months racing across the rest of the South Pacific, acutely aware that typhoon season loomed on the horizon and we needed to be safely nestled somewhere south of the tropics before it did.

We were admittedly nervous about the passage to New Zealand and studied the weather for weeks in preparation. Sailor lore states that sailing to New Zealand from the South Pacific islands usually involves battling at least one patch of rough weather. The key was to avoid getting pasted twice. But despite our fears, on this passage, we faced a deceptively tranquil twelve-day run.

When we reached Aotearoa ("the land of the long white cloud"), in many ways, it reminded us of Seattle (especially the *cloud* part). After more than a year a half in muggy hot weather, the cool temperatures and overcast skies felt familiar as did the clean-paved streets, tidy green lawns, and orderly rows of clapboard houses. But the similarity ended there. Our return to civilization felt more like returning to a relaxed America of the 1950s, a time when the backyard BBQ and community ruled supreme, except that the

Kiwis drove on the wrong side of the road, British style, and were nuts about sailing.

After a brief stop to check into the north of the country where customs confiscated the powdered eggs and lunch meats that I'd bought in the islands, we pushed southward to Auckland, the business capital, anxious to arrive before Christmas. Garth expressed an urgency to replace failed equipment, while I wanted to celebrate the holidays with friends there.

Though Auckland is sizeable, it lacked the frantic feel of a comparable US city. We appreciated the Kiwis' casual approach to life, a marked contrast to the uptight feel of downtown Seattle, Bellevue, or Redmond during the lunch hour—at least, we appreciated this approach until Garth and I arrived at the marine store to find a sign on the door that read, "Happy Christmas! We reopen January 15."

For two avid racing sailors like Garth and me, arriving in a country full of enthusiastic fans and home to many world-class sailors was thrilling. While we passed two South Pacific typhoon seasons in this safe haven, New Zealand would host the America's Cup, as well as stopovers for the Volvo Ocean Race and the Around Alone Race. We had followed these global sailing events from afar for years, so I was ecstatic to be at the center of the action while it unfolded. And through unique circumstances, we would become more than just idle bystanders.

A few months earlier, our friend Vicky emailed that she'd be in New Zealand when we arrived. We'd known Vicky for years from racing sailboats, but grew closer our last two years in Seattle when her job in the marine trade made her an invaluable source of discount boat parts while we prepared *Velella* for voyaging. I admired Vicky's uncanny ability to multitask at a high level, dispatching obstacles without losing momentum. Evidently her skills had impressed more than just us.

We'd missed another key development during our absence: Seattle Yacht Club had launched a campaign to challenge the Kiwis for the coveted America's Cup, which Team New Zealand had held since it bested Dennis Connor's team in San Diego in 1995. Vicky's vivacious personality and efficiency had come to the attention of the organizers for the One World Challenge, the Seattle-based campaign. They offered her a job as the personal assistant to the head honcho, syndicate head Peter Gilmour, a job that put her in the center of team training, boat preparation, and legal matters—in fact, almost everything that involved the team's campaign. Also on the One World team were fellow Seattle racers Jonathon and Charlie McKee. Knowing people on an America's Cup team that represented my hometown fueled my interest all the more.

Thanks to Vicky, we had a front row seat of the Volvo Ocean Race departure from the back deck of the One World Challenge base. The team base was ideally situated near the entrance to the Viaduct, the enclosed port area that housed the America's Cup bases as well as the Volvo contenders during their brief shore visit, where it had a commanding view of the shore side action. One by one, as the Volvo teams left the dock, cheers reverberated through the viaduct, which pulsated with fans waving team colors. I couldn't imagine anywhere else I'd rather be at that moment.

Once the Volvo Ocean Race boats left the viaduct, Vicky steered us to the beefy chase boat where she typically spent her days coordinating the team's two-boat testing. With wind in our hair and spray flying, we jetted out to the Hauraki Gulf. Near the start line, we skitted off waves, surrounded by thousands of sailboats, runabouts, and motor yachts that had churned the water into froth. Cheering fans lined the hills for miles. In the midst of this mayhem, contenders struggled to maintain a clear lane as stragglers criss-crossed their path. When the starting gun fired, our high-speed chase boat under full throttle could barely keep up with these speed demons once they crossed the line.

That evening after we returned to the base, we wandered over to the Loaded Hog, where the Volvo Ocean Race shore-support teams were having a "Thank God, They're Gone" party. The bar was filled with high spirits that rose into hoots and hollers when someone began announcing the Dumb-Ass Awards for the most classic equipment mistakes by support teams. One winner had failed to open the seawater-cooling intake, toasting an engine in the process. Another winner had attempted to swap unalike masts. The energy percolating through the crowd was infectious.

As we wandered around the bar, we heard snippets of conversation in myriad accents among groups of tanned, fit males wearing team clothing.

"Hey, man, I thought you were going to be on this leg," a husky voice said over to my left. His unlined twenty-something face bore reverse-scorch marks where his sunglass frames had shaded his temples.

"Nah, mate. I had enough abuse last leg," came the reply with a laugh. "Jimmy jumped in for me this morning."

"Those suckers can have the Southern Ocean," another voice piped in. Laughter rippled through the group. They raised beer bottles and clinked them together as we jostled past.

"I didn't think we'd get that boom repaired in time," another voice said as we moved through the press of bodies.

"I think I'm going to sleep for a week," said another.

I tried to imagine setting off for the punishing Southern Ocean with ten other guys. *They're the crazy ones,* I thought. But there were crazier ones yet. The Around Alone racers were tracing a similar route around the globe, but single-handedly. They, too, would be stopping in New Zealand during a break in the America's Cup action.

Down at the bottom of the sailing world, New Zealand felt like the center of the universe. The country was swarming with famous sailors and millionaires there for the races. This shiny new world dazzled me, and for a few short months, I could forget our tight budget and the daily inventory of boat chores.

Over the next months, Vicky and I (and sometimes Garth) caught Irish Dancing at a local pub, went gliding, and celebrated Pacific Island cultures at the Pasifika Festival whenever her hectic schedule allowed. She hosted a pool party on the deck of her building and invited us to share Christmas dinner with her and fellow team members.

Of course, I coveted any and every inside glimpse into the glamorous AC world. I scoured the newspaper for juicy gossip and became adept at spotting the sailors, designers, and syndicate staff. When I encountered two-time America's Cup-winning skipper Russell Coutts at our local grocery store, I nearly crashed my shopping cart.

While the technical aspects of these competitions intrigued Garth, I had the fever. Garth whittled away at the list of boat projects to prepare for our next sailing season. I baked chocolate chip cookies for the "hometown boys" to snack on during breaks in practice on the Hauraki Gulf.

One day when I dropped off a batch of cookies, Vicky invited me to lunch at the base.

Later, when I breathlessly reported my luncheon to Garth afterward, he teased, "You are such a groupie."

It was true.

🌴

While I was busy being an adoring fan of the practicing America's Cup teams, Garth, eager for a new challenge, set about building us a brand new dinghy. He'd had enough of trying to propel an undulating flat bottomed raft that refused to row straight. Garth obtained a set of plans for a two-part nesting, sailing dinghy and identified a boat builder willing to lend his empty shop for Garth's project. Building a nesting dinghy meant that we'd end up with a decent sized dinghy, because the two halves could fit stacked on *Velella*'s foredeck, and, therefore, would take up less space when stowed. A dinghy that could sail gave us even greater range and a fun diversion when we lingered in protected bays. And it would turn rowing into a pleasure rather than an exercise in frustration. The two halves fit together with a tongue in groove and stayed together with the help of three bolts.

After Garth finished, I was so proud of his accomplishment that I told everyone we met about it and basked in the glow of their admiration, as though I had done it myself. I got a particular kick out of pulling into a bay, anchoring, then dropping each half over the side and, within seconds, turning two boats into one with the help of three bolts. Later, when we performed this feat before natives in canoes, they were deeply impressed. No longer would we spend a half-hour inflating the old gray Avon with a foot pump every time we arrived somewhere and then, before leaving, finding every possible contortion for squeezing the last bit of air out of it, so we could roll it and stow it below until the next stop.

Once the dinghy was complete, Piero, an Italian single-handing sailor who was on a tighter budget than we were, bought our old inflatable Avon for as much as we'd paid for it at a swap meet *before* we'd gotten a year-and-a-half's worth of use out of it. We even made a profit on the oars.

We named our new wooden sailing dinghy *Tasty Penguin* after our favorite New Zealand town: Russell. The Maori name for the town of Russell was Karororeka—which we could hardly pronounce, much less spell—translated loosely as "Tasty Penguin" in honor of the fine meal that a chief had tasted there. Something about that name struck us as funny, and the name stuck. Our dinghy's unusual name sparked all sorts of conversations, as well as countless odd looks.

Shortly after completing the dinghy, we sailed *Velella* up to Great Barrier Island, where there was a huge, protected bay surrounded by smaller inlets. In unsettled weather, its protection seemed nearly bomb proof.

After a short test sail one afternoon in our new dinghy, we were emboldened and decided to sail into town five miles away. The next morning, loaded with the week's garbage, money, a backpack full of grocery sacks, and a couple of cushions to sit upon, Garth and I set off for a day's outing. With the wind behind us and the sun sparkling on the water, we were off to a great start. A mile into our sail, the skies clouded over, and I shivered with the sudden chill of a cooler breeze. With upticks in the wind, we jetted forward in bursts of speed. I grasped the rail more tightly, wishing I'd worn something warmer.

"You know, I think the wind has really come up," Garth said a few minutes later. I looked around and realized that white spray was blowing off the tops of each wave.

"Yeah, I was kind of noticing that too."

"If it comes up much more, we're going to have trouble getting back." I nodded, knowing that once we turned around, we'd have twice the wind—the wind that was currently behind us, *plus* the wind from our momentum. We were on the far end of the inlet, but not yet out into the main part of the bay.

Garth continued, "We're still protected somewhat, behind the hill, but once we get past that, the wind is likely to be stronger, and we have no way to reef this sail." When he'd first talked about adding reef points to the sail, I'd thought he was being excessive. A nearby sail maker had wanted a fortune to add a reef to the sail, and I'd said no. Now I saw the need for reefing.

We sailed on for another minute or two. Garth broke the silence. "I'm turning around."

"Yeah, okay," I agreed, realizing it'd be a cold wet sail back already.

Decision made. But execution was another matter. Once we turned back into the wind, water sloshed over the rail, and the dinghy heeled alarmingly. The sail was deep, and there was no way to flatten it or spill any of our excess wind, which drove us sideways as much as forward. I knew conditions would be more intense once we turned into it, but the reality was even worse than I'd imagined.

"Whoa! We've got more wind than I realized." Garth stated my exact thoughts.

The distance to the boat seemed interminable, and our situation felt surprisingly precarious. We were a couple of miles from *Velella,* and our progress was painfully slow. Each wave stopped the dinghy like a brake. Water drove up over the bow and onto my face. The bag of garbage floated back and forth with the motion. I worried that it would float away while I was bailing.

My teeth started chattering, though I kept busy bailing water to keep up with the quantity that was coming in.

"How're you doing?" Garth asked.

"Oh I'm fine," I said, clenching my jaw so my teeth could stop chattering. I turned to give him a reassuring look.

"Your lips are blue."

"Yeah, I'm pretty cold."

Another puff of wind heeled the dinghy dramatically. I gripped the gunwales of the boat tightly, and when the wind eased, I resumed bailing. The boat felt pretty tippy, and I knew Garth had to concentrate to keep the boat steady. We fought every inch back. We reached *Velella*, climbed aboard, peeled off our wet layers, rinsed off, and nestled into layers of clothing we hadn't worn in ages.

Taking a sip of cocoa later, Garth said "I was really worried about you. You were already so cold, but you've no idea how close we were to going swimming."

"Oh, I knew just how iffy it was," I said. "By the way, I think those reef points are a fabulous idea."

🌴

I'd just returned from getting our propane tanks filled. Ever since we'd discovered that New Zealanders made a point of checking their inspection stamps and that the inspection on both our tanks had expired in 1984, we'd decided that I'd be more successful pleading ignorance without Garth present. We'd learned that getting the tanks retested cost nearly as much as purchasing new tanks—something we could ill afford. Plus new tanks no longer came in the size and shape that would fit into our cockpit locker. I worried we'd run out of refill options before we left the country, but since we needed propane to eat, I wasn't above begging.

"It's great to finally reach New Zealand after all these years," Garth said as I handed him a crescent wrench. "After my family's boat went on the reef in Fiji and we had to skip New Zealand, I've always wanted to see what we missed."

Our conversation distracted Garth as he connected the propane tank, a chore he normally hated. "For me, getting back to Fiji and to New Zealand were historic milestones," Garth said, "but I don't need to keep retracing the voyage of the *Vela*. I'm ready for something new."

He stuck his head down into the damp, mildewy compartment to push the tank all the way in. He reappeared, shuddered silently, then grabbed the wrench and went back in to connect the hoses. When he pulled his head out of the compartment, he set down the wrench and continued. "You know how we're using New Zealand to get out of the tropics during the hurricane season? We might be able to do the same thing with Japan—explore the country while we wait out typhoon season in the northern hemisphere. Don't you think Japan would be cool place to visit by boat?" His eyes were shining almost as much as the afternoon sunshine that had finally emerged from New Zealand's typically low cloud cover. Spring was finally turning into summer.

Recently, we'd met several Japanese cruisers who were sailing around the Pacific. That was probably what prompted the idea, but Garth and I shared an affinity for Japanese style and food. As a teenager, I'd become entranced by James Clavell's book, *Shogun* and the mini-series it spawned, learning the Japanese phrases and pronunciation that Mariko taught Anjin-san in the story. My father had an unaccompanied nine-month tour in Iwakuni in 1977—which meant my mom, sister and I didn't get to go—but he returned with paintings and pottery he'd collected. I had complemented the family items I'd inherited with porcelain and paper goods I'd acquired when I'd been to Japan on business.

He continued, "Hardly anyone ever sails to Japan, and I'd love to do something different."

"Hmmm." My thoughts whirled with a mix of conflicting emotions. People generally sailed the easiest, most logical routes for a *reason.* So why didn't anyone sail to Japan?

Garth shifted the second propane tank in the cockpit locker and continued. "We'd have to do some research to figure out exactly how to do it. The weather would be much more challenging than we've faced so far, since even though it's outside the tropics, Japan is situated in a pretty active typhoon region. But we could handle it."

Weather and lack of information was one concern, but there was another: if we sailed north, I would miss the community of cruisers, most of whom were migrating west to Australia at the end of the next sailing season—at least those who weren't going home or staying in New Zealand.

Many sailors, upon reaching New Zealand, decided that voyaging wasn't for them, and put their boats up for sale or arranged to ship them home. Many relationships didn't survive the pressures of living in cramped quarters twenty-four hours a day and the intense conditions that blue water sailing can entail. I thought of the times I'd run into a friend and ask where his wife or girlfriend was. He'd mumble something like, "Oh, she's flown back to the States." After a minute's pause, he would mournfully add, "To tell you the truth, we're not getting along so well. We're splitting up and putting the boat up for sale."

That thought got me wondering how Garth's and my relationship had weathered the change. I suppose our years of do-it-yourself home remodeling and sailboat racing had helped us work through differences in working styles earlier. Of course, we'd had our irritations and arguments. We were short-tempered in the oppressive tropical heat, and our introverted and extroverted styles often clashed. I wanted to go everywhere and see everything, and I'd get frustrated with Garth, who was often more inclined to lie around and read a book. *But split up? That was serious.*

One of our coping mechanisms for dealing with our personality differences was to travel in tandem with other boats. That let me explore with other sailors, which provided the stimulus and social outlet I craved, while Garth got the quiet time he needed.

And that was the rub about sailing to Japan. If we left the company of other boats, we'd lose a key pressure-release valve for our twenty-four/seven relationship.

"What do you think?" He brought me back to our present conversation.

"I don't know," I said. I also worried that sailing to Japan would lead to sailing back to the Pacific Northwest, a logical end to our voyage, but I couldn't imagine stopping yet. Even though this wasn't the easiest life, it was certainly exciting. And there was a certain allure and prestige to the concept of navigating all the way around the world, though I knew it no longer presented the same challenge as when Garth did it in the 1970s. The most straightforward route was now a well-worn path, called "the milk run," but sailing around the world held an appeal for me all the same.

As though reading my thoughts, Garth said, "I don't need to sail around the world again; I already did that. But I'll do it if it's what you want." He looked at me for a moment while I thought about that.

From New Zealand, the next logical stop for circumnavigating would be Australia, but Garth's description of his experience in the 1970s did not appeal to me. Anchoring in muddy river mouths like a series of rest stops, just long enough to sleep so we could make our way around this sizeable continent between cyclone seasons sounded like a chore. I'd had my fill of "Motel 6" cruising during our working years when we had to rush to fit a cruise into an all-too-short vacation schedule.

"I'm ready for a new challenge, and Japan would certainly be that." Garth began talking more rapidly, reading my silence as assent. "Besides, we could sail west through Asia from there, if you want to keep going."

That intrigued me. I'd seen a bit of Asia besides Japan on business trips, and the rich cultures had piqued my interest. As Garth stowed the rest of the propane locker, I pulled out a stack of articles my father had collected over twenty years, and I took out the Pacific Pilot Charts to study possible routes. The idea crystallized into a new goal.

And so began our quest to sail to Japan. Once we declared our plans, we met others who were going there—not many, but enough to reassure me that I wouldn't be completely bereft of company. Their willingness to share charts and information aided our planning and made it more tangible.

🌴

One April day in the marina, I vacated the boat for most of the day so Garth could change *Velella's* engine oil, a process that usually disrupted the entire interior of the boat and involved a litany of swear words. When I returned to the boat in the afternoon, Garth said, "You'll never guess who stopped by today."

"Who?"

"A couple came by, saying they wanted to interview us for Japanese sailing magazine."

I noticed a thick glossy magazine covered with Kanji characters sitting on the table. I picked it up and started flipping through it.

"Really?" I asked, impressed by the magazine's quality. "How did that come about?"

"So I was just sitting here, minding my own business, I was. Changing the oil, like I love to do," he said with a smirk.

"Yeah, and...?"

"And this Japanese couple knocks on the boat and tells me that they'd interviewed Jason and Tam about their cruise. Tam had told them we were planning to sail to Japan and suggested they might want to interview us, too." He had my attention.

"So did you interview with them?" I noticed a pile of oily paper towels on the galley counter and wondered why it hadn't travelled the last ten inches to the trash bag that hung near the sink. I imagined the mess captured for posterity.

"I told them I was kind of in the middle of something." He held up his arms as though they were coated with oil. His smile turned mischievous, "Besides, the official family spokesman was absent. Without you here, who would do the talking?" He poked me, and I cracked a grin. Then he added, "I suggested they return tomorrow at 11:00 a.m. I hope that suits your busy schedule, Madam."

Tomoko and Yuichiro arrived at eleven the next morning, as scheduled. Yuichiro, who had a camera slung around his neck, was obviously the photographer. He was surprisingly tiny; Tomoko outsized him. Their friendly, relaxed manner and ease with English suggested that they'd been in New Zealand for a while. They'd been covering the America's Cup since before 2000 when New Zealand retained the Cup, and their reporting would keep them in New Zealand another year until the competition ended.

Tomoko posed a few astute questions about our experience cruising and listened intently while I babbled nonstop, opening cabinets, sharing little tips and tricks I'd learned about food storage, cooking underway, living in a small space, and keeping cool in the tropics. Meanwhile, Yuichiro snapped photos from every imaginable angle.

Before they departed, Tomoko explained that the article would run in the November issue and that they'd give us a copy if we contacted them when we returned from cruising the islands in the fall.

After they walked away, Garth laughed and said, "They were probably wondering when you were going to take a breath."

Six months later, after we returned from escaping New Zealand's winter up in the islands, we contacted Tomoko and Yuichiro again. Tomoko suggested we come to the America's Cup Media Center and offered to take us out on the media boat to watch the America's Cup Louis Vuitton Challenger races, the elimination rounds that would determine who would challenge New Zealand for the America's Cup. Nine highly-funded professional sailing teams from nearly as many countries battled for the chance to race Team New Zealand for the coveted silver pitcher, named for *America*, the first vessel ever to win it. And we'd be in the middle of the action. I was ecstatic. When we arrived at the media center, Tomoko and Yuichiro treated us like royalty. They bought us breakfast and handed us a copy of the magazine with a six-page article featuring seventeen (!) gorgeous color photographs of us and our little boat. The wide angle lens made *Velella* look luxurious.

We spent the afternoon with them on the media boat, following so closely behind sleek America's Cup boats while they raced that even my instant camera without a zoom lens captured decent photos. Yuichiro's professional zoom lens captured shots that looked like he'd been sitting in the cockpit with the teams.

Afterwards, while Tomoko pointed out the bathroom to Garth, and I sat with Yuichiro out on the balcony, a parade of the most famous names in sailing walked by, starting with Mr. America's Cup: Dennis Connor, followed by Larry Ellison, Chris Dixon, and Bruce Farr in conference. They nodded acknowledgement to Yuichiro. I couldn't pull out my camera fast enough. Next to Yuichiro's elongated lens, my pitifully ancient point-and-shoot camera screamed "tourist," but I sheepishly snapped photos anyway.

Yuichiro, looking amused, casually asked, "Would you like to go to the press conference?" He didn't need to ask twice.

🌴

After the start of the Louis Vuitton racing, the Media Center became my second home. Through Tomoko and Yuichiro, I secured a front-row view of the racing aboard the Media Boat and became comfortable sitting among the reporters tapping away at their keyboards in the Media Center, watching the two-story, split screen that featured live TV feed from one race venue, along with Virtual Spectator for every other race, which gave a real-time overview of the racing action. Thus, at any given moment, I could monitor the races on the four courses, and, with the aid of Virtual Spectator software, have master knowledge of relative competitor positions and the wind shifts that gave one team an advantage.

Whenever TV coverage cut away to a commercial, the main screen would switch to a live audio feed from aboard the boat. As an amateur racer, eavesdropping on the professionals gave me a chuckle, because the dialogue so resembled our beer-can races back home.

"I think the wind might be stronger over there," a voice would say doubtfully.

"Do you think we should tack?"

"I don't know. What do you think?"

Sitting near me one day was a familiar bearded face with glasses that I couldn't quite place. Like me, he lacked the harried look of the typical reporter and had no laptop open in front of him. We smiled politely at one another as we watched the action unfold on the big screen. A more familiar face, Ed Baird, frequent America's Cup skipper and the lead TV commentator for this regatta, came over to speak with my mysterious tablemate.

"Evidently, my services are no longer needed," I heard the man say. At that moment, I realized that I'd spent the last twenty minutes sitting next to Doug Peterson, famous designer of *Luna Rossa,* for the Italian team, Prada, who'd been publicly fired only days before after a disappointing performance for the team. I strained to hear more, but the two moved out of earshot.

Two days before Christmas of 2002, near the close of the Louis Vuitton racing, I was upstairs on the balcony of the Media Center crashing the Christmas party. The atmosphere was relaxed, the food and champagne a delight. The Christmas party had followed the day's eventful race during which *One World Challenge* lost to *BMW Oracle.* The intervening press conference was a cross between a somber and a celebratory affair. One team's win at this stage of the game meant that the other team went home, game over. There had been nine challengers; now only two remained. This time my friends at *One World Challenge* were the ones packing up, marking the conclusion of the semi-final round. It wasn't the Christmas gift *One World* was hoping for, though the loss wasn't unexpected. Now only *Alinghi* and *BMW Oracle* were left to battle. One of them would challenge Team New Zealand for the Cup after the holiday break.

In one corner Ed Baird was speaking with Bruno Troublé, the organizer of the Louis Vuitton Challenger Series—the big honcho. I strained to catch the gist of their conversation without success. While their faces were quite familiar to me by then, and even mine to them—after all we'd been nodding acknowledgement of one another in passing for months now—I'd left the mystery of my identity intact, since the truth could hardly have been as impressive. A moment later I found myself inviting the famous America's Cup foremost female racing sailor, Dawn Riley, to a Christmas Eve BBQ with my fellow cruisers and began to wonder if the champagne had gone to my head.

My cell phone rang. It was Vicky. I could guess what was going on at the One World base at the moment.

"You want to meet across the street for a drink?" She was referring to the café on Halsey Street, where teammates stopped for coffee and gossip.

"I'm at the Media Center, and I don't have long before the last ferry to Bayswater. I don't think there's enough time. How about the Loaded Hog?"

"Sure. I could use someone from home to decompress with who isn't a part of this." For Vicky, this loss marked the beginning of the long process of packing up and preparing for what came next—what, she didn't know just yet. For Garth and me, what came next was obvious. During the break in the racing, we would sail to Tauranga to see the Around Alone race.

The Around Alone race tested the skill of solo sailors in an intense multi-leg race around the globe. Leg three concluded in Tauranga, New Zealand, during the lay period between the Louis Vuitton Challenger series and the final America's Cup races. As a trained naval architect, Garth was always interested in any and all opportunities to explore evolutionary boat design concepts—in fact, to look at any boat in any setting. I, of course, didn't want to miss anything that was a "happening" event, so we agreed to sail south to Tauranga in time to see the competitors arrive. We were particularly interested in seeing *Ocean Planet,* an unusual design by Tom Wylie, the same naval architect who had designed *Velella* twenty-eight years earlier.

I'd dragged Garth to a Christmas potluck at an Auckland sailing club, and there I'd met an American doctor living in New Zealand who knew *Ocean Planet's* skipper, Bruce Schwab. She'd invited us to join his shore crew. Almost instantly, I started receiving position updates by email directly from Bruce, who was sailing from Cape Town, South Africa, to Tauranga, New Zealand. His emails detailed the broken equipment he planned to fix during his shore stop, and I felt the thrill of being privy to inside information. The responsibility that came with that information hadn't yet dawned on me.

Halfway across the Tasman Sea, Bruce smashed one of his water ballast tanks in a mistimed maneuver. The mistake meant he needed to choreograph an elaborate and expensive repair during his New

Zealand stop. He asked the shore crew for more information about repair facilities at the NZ stopover.

Garth and I had hauled our boat to do basic boat maintenance in Tauranga our first New Zealand season. Since we knew the marina yard manager and were aware of shore-side facilities in the area, I thought I'd share what we'd learned, in case it proved helpful. When I finished drafting an email with all the details and contact information I could assemble, I asked Garth if I'd missed anything useful.

Garth ridiculed my naiveté, "Don't be silly; this is an around-the-world race. They're going to have huge crews of people to handle this kind of stuff."

Eager to be helpful, I sent the email anyway.

Bruce's appreciative reply indicated that he'd found my information useful, and I felt warm and fuzzy inside.

After the holiday festivities—during the month-long hiatus in America's Cup racing action—we left Auckland with ten days to sail 150 miles south to Tauranga before most of the Around Alone racers were expected to arrive. That seemed like plenty of time.

We squandered the first two days hiking to the top of Rangitoto, the 800-year-old volcano that formed the backdrop for America's Cup racing on the Hauraki Gulf, and digging clams for a fresh shellfish dinner. Though we had high hopes for gradually cruising the rest of our way south along the exposed but picturesque Coromandel Peninsula, those two days were the last of the favorable weather.

We spent several days waiting for gale force winds and driving rains to abate. Then, we could wait no longer. A forecast calling for light headwinds encouraged us to make an overnight run for Tauranga, but the strong headwinds that arrived instead created steep, choppy seas and a punishing sail. By the time we reached Tauranga after sailing twice the original distance, we were fried. Tensely holding my body in the same position for so many hours, sent my back muscles into spasms.

Fifteen hours later, still nursing an aching back, in the early morning hours from *Velella*'s cockpit, I saw a flotilla of boats flying Tauranga Yacht Club burgees venture out from the channel. There could only be one explanation at that hour: one of the Around Alone competitors had arrived. An hour later, *Ocean Planet* came in, under tow. One voice in my head told me we ought to head down to the marina to greet him. Another, yearning for more recovery time, convinced me he might want to sleep first. Before an hour had passed, our cell phone rang. The number that flashed on the screen was unusual.

"Hello?" I said.

"This is Bruce Schwab. Is this Wendy?" His tentative voice surprised me. Instantly I realized he was calling from his satellite phone, wondering where his helpers were. I felt a bit guilty, and then like a complete wimp. We'd only sailed from Auckland with stops. He'd raced *alone* from South Africa.

I told him we'd be there in an hour and rushed to get off the phone so the call wouldn't cost him any more money. We quickly dressed and rushed for the bus that would take us from our free anchorage to the Around Alone marina headquarters.

When we arrived on the docks, flags featuring the Around Alone logo flapped in the breeze around a surprisingly quiet marina. We weren't prepared to find Bruce alone, unshaven, and looking a bit lost. Where was the professional shore crew?

He showed us around the boat, answered questions, and patiently let me snap photos for a few minutes. Then he outlined his plan of action. He had less than a month to make repairs and get the boat ready for the next start. He was a man with a mission.

"First I want to strip all the sails and the interior stuff off the boat. Then I want to take off the boom and the pusher-vang struts, because they'll need to be repaired and coated. Then we'll need to jack up the keel so *OP* can fit under the Travelift to haul out." He stood there expectantly. Gradually, it dawned on me that *we* were the shore crew.

So what else could we do but set to work? The three of us took down the massive sails one by one and hauled them off the boat for a local sail maker to retrieve and make minor repairs. Then we slowly dismantled the contents of the boat's interior and carried them to a courtesy car provided by race organizers. I did a quick mental tally, noting that everything we were dismantling would need to be reassembled before the race start in a month's time—*after* the rest of the work was finished...a daunting task.

On the fourth trip to the car, with me hauling one end of a pouch of cooking equipment and Bruce on the other, I joked, "So, Bruce, do you have any other shore crew, or are we it?"

"Well, I think my rigger and shore manager are coming in two weeks. And probably some others a few days before the start." His dark brown eyes held my gaze. He wasn't kidding.

"So it's just us for the next two weeks?" I tried to suppress the alarm in my voice, but it came through anyway.

"Well, there are a couple of guys who are coming to take a look at the ballast tanks to provide an estimate for the work on that. I'll have to hire that out—unless you guys are experts at water-ballast tanks."

"Uh, no."

"Didn't think so. Not sure how I'm going to pay for it, but I'll worry about that later. That's what credit cards are for." He grinned and shrugged.

My mouth dropped open and I raised my eyebrows.

He continued. "I'm about $320,000 in the hole right now. Who knows where I'll be by the end of this thing."

Wow, I realized, *this guy really does need help.* He was more broke than we were. But, he was pursuing his goals with a burning faith that it would all work out.

As I worked re-gluing solar panels or re-bedding bolts, I answered questions from the public passing by on the dock. I quickly realized that everyone was a potential donor or volunteer.

Many barreled past, asking, "Where's the lady boat?" Twenty-seven-year-old Brit Emma Richards was the media darling who had captured the public's attention.

Among the folks who asked if they could come aboard for a tour were several cruisers we'd gotten to know while crossing the Pacific. As I showed people around the boat and explained the complicated systems that I'd learned about an hour earlier, I did my best Tom Sawyer imitation, encouraging them to join the fun of helping us help Bruce. Soon, Garth and I were supervising fellow cruisers (who fortunately knew about boats) and people literally off the street (who didn't) to tackle the tasks on Bruce's list. Some could help for only a few hours. Other agreed to stay on for a few days. We accepted all volunteers. The clock was ticking.

While some skippers had impressive corporate sponsorship, most were in the same position as Bruce—mortgaging everything for this dream of racing solo around the world and making repairs with the help of volunteers. If you'd have told me that I'd be working on someone else's boat for free, I'd have never believed it. Here I was, volunteering to repair someone else's boat when I dreaded working on my own. There was no doubt Bruce needed our help, and the camaraderie amongst the Around Alone skippers and the shore crews whom we worked alongside paid unexpected dividends. At cocktail parties and dinners, Bruce told stories and played classical guitar. And we were at the center of the action.

Before Bruce could haul the boat, we had to jack up the keel because it was too deep for the water under the Travelift. From our cruising friends who'd bought cars, we borrowed four manual car jacks. With them, in a coordinated effort, we slowly ground up this massive lead-ballasted behemoth manually. It was backbreaking labor. We were flirting with disaster without a safety line, since if one or more of the jacks had let go, the entire weight of the ballast keel could have come crashing down, taking who knows what with it. When the marina yard manager walked by and saw what we were doing, he shuddered and offered us the use of a hydraulic jack, free of charge.

Shortly after we got *Ocean Planet* out of the water, Bruce announced that he wanted to reshape the bow. Just the thought made me nervous. I lent him my calling card so he could call designer Tom Wylie to discuss his proposed modifications.

After an hour-long conversation, he emerged from the phone booth looking exhausted.

I asked him, "So what did he say?"

"He didn't like the idea, either."

I relaxed a little, thinking that this settled the matter. But not long after, I returned to the boat to find Bruce hacking the bow off *Ocean Planet* with a Sawzall. This man was over a quarter of a million dollars in debt. Until this moment, he'd had a perfectly acceptable boat. Now, with less than three weeks before he was to sail to the Southern Ocean, his boat didn't have a bow. And people called *us* crazy.

Bruce hired a team of local professionals to mold the bow into a more conventional Open-60 type entry. He wanted extra buoyancy for the Southern Ocean so that he wouldn't bury the bow into every wave. Two boot-clad Kiwis in shorts appeared on the scene to rebuild the bow. "She'll be right, mate," one said to me when he saw my worried look.

I'd heard that before from a Kiwi who hadn't sweated the details, but these two quickly demonstrated methodical precision. First they created a set of foam frames and then filled the area between them with foam parallel to the hull. Gradually they carved and shaped the foam to simulate the desired form. Once Bruce was satisfied with the shape, they fared in the hollows with epoxy, fiberglassed for strength, and then sanded using long boards to smooth the surface. I was fascinated to see the new shape take form. Covered with paint, the repair was seamless.

When famous sailor and race-organizer Sir Robin Knox-Johnston wandered through the boatyard, as he often did, he nodded appreciatively at the emerging bow and praised Bruce's bold decision. When I told him how much I'd enjoyed his book about his award-winning single-handed non-stop sail around the globe in 1968, he asked, "So did you buy my book?"

I stuttered, "Ahh, no. I picked it up in a lending library."

"How are we authors supposed to make a living if you don't buy the book?" he teased with a smile.

When Bruce's "professional" shore manager, Ashley Perrin, arrived from the States and saw the demolished bow, she wasn't quite as appreciative. When she spotted Garth, she laid into him, thinking he was responsible. He'd been in the middle of shaping the black carbon-fiber emergency rudders with a sander, so he was covered in black dust.

"I didn't do it," Garth pleaded, his sooty hands raised, looking like a chimney sweep. "In fact, I tried to talk him out of it."

Ashley knew better than anyone that Bruce didn't have the budget for the work. He owed her money, too.

After working nonstop for twelve days, Garth and I were exhausted long before any shore crew arrived from the U.S., but we still had much to do. With more experienced hands, the work went quickly.

Within a week of the start, we dropped *Ocean Planet* back into the water. A test sail would prove whether she was seaworthy. In a ripping current, getting off the dock and weaving our way past the other Around Alone boats produced a few anxious moments. With little time to make repairs, we were apprehensive that we'd screw something up. Hoisting the humongous main was a chore for a strong crew. I wondered anew how such a slight man as Bruce would wrestle these powerful sails in stormy weather. A few tacks and jibes in the harbor went without incident, and we celebrated our hard work at a crew dinner while furtively assembling encouraging messages for Bruce's halfway box between toasts.

Race morning in early February dawned warm and clear. We made sandwiches, donned shore-crew t-shirts, and wove our way through crowded docks swarming with media mania. From the foredeck of *Ocean Planet,* I could see thousands of people behind the roped area watching our every move as Garth re-spliced the lifelines, and we did last-minute checks. TV cameras and reporters swarmed the docks, conducting interviews. I nearly walked into the middle of a TV interview with Tim Kent of *Everest Horizontal* when I slipped through the crowd to wish him well.

I was thrilled to have played such an integral role, without having to endure the pressure that Bruce faced. Or the trip around Cape Horn. One by one, competitors left the docks under tow. (Race rules prohibited use of engines for propulsion.) Each received a traditional Maori-style sendoff to battle: a fierce Haka war dance in full war paint with bulging eyes and menacing tongues wagging.

When Bruce's turn came, we said our goodbyes and untied the dock lines. I hopped onto the tow boat with the rest of the shore crew while Garth remained aboard *Ocean Planet* to help coordinate the towing and raise the sails. Through a miscommunication, we released the towline early, giving Garth a firsthand view of the forces Bruce faced each time he unreefed.

At noon, after transferring Garth to the tow boat, Bruce and his competitors lined up for the start, and they were off. Reminiscent of the Volvo Ocean Race start, thousands of spectators lined the shores of Mount Manganui. Runabouts streaked across their path, churning up the water. We followed *Ocean Planet* for the next hour, waving and cheering while Bruce tweaked the sails. He looked miniscule on that sixty-foot boat.

Ultimately, we left him to sail his race. I thought of Bruce and the others sailing on towards the icebergs and growlers of the Southern Ocean as we settled in for a full night's sleep. Their next planned stop was Salvador, Brazil, around Cape Horn, 8,000 miles away.

After the Around Alone start, we hustled to Auckland to watch the final America's Cup races with my father. Dad was coming with some friends as part of a yacht-club-organized trip to see the Cup competition, and I looked forward to introducing him to the America's Cup scene. Not keen to repeat our waterlogged midnight row of Melaque, Mexico, I reserved a slip in Bayswater Marina for ten days to cover his stay. Then I discovered that Dad had gotten the dates wrong and would be coming a week later than he'd originally told us. He wouldn't arrive until just before we had to vacate our reserved slip. Too late. The slip was already booked.

"Dad's not coming until the eighteenth," I told Garth.

He stared at me for a moment. "You're kidding," Garth said, shaking his head, his eyes cast skyward. "Unbelievable. Here we go again."

And in a matter of moments, I went from being excited about Dad's visit to agitated. I wondered how I would juggle this one so that it wouldn't end up being his *last*.

Three days after Dad arrived, we vacated our protected slip in the marina and moved *Velella* across Waitemata Harbour to an exposed anchorage off Herne Bay near Dad's hotel. In calm conditions, we rowed ashore and left our dinghy tied to a tree to meet my father and his friends for breakfast. A lack of wind delayed the America's Cup races, so we spent the day poking around Auckland instead. Late that evening, when we returned to the dinghy, the pungent smell of decaying sea vegetation overwhelmed me. I was mortified to notice just how far the tide had retreated. Our dinghy was now a quarter-mile from the water's edge. We'd forgotten about tide, because we hadn't faced much tidal flush since we'd left Seattle.

Between the dinghy and the water's edge lay a soupy, clingy muck, across which we had to carry our new, 100-pound, hard dinghy. For the first time, I missed our light flat-bottomed inflatable.

"Oh boy," Garth said. "This is going to be fun."

From my first step below the tide line, mud that resembled a soiled diaper gooped around my ankles, gripping my Tevas. A sprinkling of pipi shells and rocks convinced me to keep my shoes on, but with each laborious step, gooey brown oozed between my toes. The mud released each shoe only reluctantly, and the strain threatened to pull my shoes apart before we reached the water. *Shluuuck, shluuuck, shluuuck.* The straps dug into the tops of my feet. Once we finally reached the water's edge, we set the dinghy down, removed our shoes, and tried to rinse them and our feet before getting into the empty floating boat—a feat that required several attempts in progressively deeper water before the dinghy floated *while* we were in it. By this time, our row to *Velella* was only 100 yards.

We might have faced the same problem the next day, but the morning's gale-force winds made it obvious there'd be no racing or rowing ashore. The same was true the following day. For two days, Garth and I stayed on the boat while my dad remained ashore partying with his friends, communicating periodically by cell phone, and hoping for better weather. Dad didn't seem to mind—he had friends and a rental car. Meanwhile, I chewed my fingernails on board.

We never anticipated spending so many days waiting, with racing cancelled either for lack of wind or a gale. Finally, after countless delays, the America's Cup races finally ended in New Zealand's humiliating defeat from massive equipment failure. The Kiwis lost the ultimate sailing prize to the team representing the land-locked country of Switzerland—in a coup led by New Zealand's own countrymen. We watched the slow demise of Team New Zealand from the public stands where a rowdy atmosphere turned instantly funereal when *Black Magic* proved to be a lemon.

Once again, despite fighting my inclination to "wing-it"—a trait I share with my father, but which Garth does not—we had endured another frustrating visit, held hostage to a hotel room at the mercy of Mother Nature. Boats demand we either be completely flexible or completely prepared, and, once again, we had been neither.

It came time to leave New Zealand shortly after the Cup ended in April 2003. Once again, we watched the weather closely, but this was our fourth passage between New Zealand and the islands, and we felt as though we'd gotten the hang of the weather patterns in that area of the world. The season before, we'd departed on the back side of a low, in a gale, hoping to catch a southwesterly push from behind. The tactic had worked reasonably well, though our passage had started a bit boisterously.

Hoping to follow the same approach, as summer turned to fall in the southern hemisphere, we watched for a telltale low to ride north for our second visit to Fiji. A low-pressure system looked promising, and so we left. The low quickly fizzled, but we'd already made our move. Soon a large high settled over the area. I thought of the North Pacific high that brought such steady conditions between Hawaii and the Pacific Northwest. The high-pressure system over New Zealand would block the lows and produce light winds, right? Since *Velella* excelled in light winds and flat water, we expected mellow conditions. So we kept sailing.

We couldn't have been more wrong.

The wind began to build and the waves turned sloppy.
"How bad can it be?" Garth said with a casual shrug.

HUMBLED:
THE GOOD, THE BAD,
AND THE UGLY

Pretty bad, it turns out. My charmed life among the rich and famous had come to an abrupt end. The good news about our passage to Fiji was that we arrived safely; the bad news was that we had to live through it.

Later, we heard a Kiwi proverb: "If it's over ten-thirty, it's going to be dirty."

The saying refers to the barometric pressure, which then was ten-thirty-two. We learned just what "dirty" meant: strong adverse winds funneled between two colliding weather systems, creating a "squash zone." The first six hours were pleasant, with bright sunshine and gentle winds behind us. And then we beat into twenty-five-to-forty-knot winds and fifteen-foot seas for the next eleven days, water continuously cascading over the boat.

In hindsight, we could have saved ourselves a lot of misery if we had diverted to New Caledonia. While we discussed it many times on the way, each time we carried onward, sure we'd already seen the worst of it. We'd promised to return to Fiji to see friends, and so we did. But after the pain that this stubborn choice inflicted upon us, it took us months to recover.

We weren't the only bozos to fall for the phantom weather trick, and we were not alone in our misery. I took small solace from the whining I heard on the cruiser's radio net from others making the same passage. Some suffered broken rudder bearings, others a broken forestay, ripped sails, lost solar panels, or even dinghies. We were relatively lucky.

But even though our boat remained intact throughout this rough passage, the details of our trip were ugly. Life was reduced to the barest essentials, a *food-in, food-out, sleep, survive, it'll-be-over-eventually* kind of existence. Even brushing my teeth felt like too much trouble. Whether we were sitting up with our eyes open on watch or lying down with our eyes closed in the bunk, we were always damp.

To prevent water getting into the boat, we had all hatches and openings closed tight, eliminating all ventilation. Clothes that got wet in the first ten hours remained wet for the next ten days, and began to mildew. We discovered leaks we never knew we had. Water could get in, but no moisture could get out, creating a humid, suffocating environment inside. Water accumulated on the floor near the toilet. It soon became evident that this was a seemingly endless supply of saltwater-based sewage.

Our routine aboard basically boiled down to:

1. Wake up (assuming that it had been possible to sleep through the jarring motion and the noise) and coat rear end with diaper-rash cream.
2. Pull on soggy clothes; try not to fall into something and generate a new bruise.

3. Slop something into a pot and heat it. Serve in a pot with a single spoon for both of us; rinse pot and spoon in ocean (carefully) and return to stovetop for next use.

4. Park in a saltwater puddle in the cockpit through regular dousings.

5. Remove soggy clothing at the end of the watch.

6. Bail sewage lake.

7. Disinfect hands; sponged down body with freshwater-dipped wash cloth; wipe saltwater sewage from feet.

8. Climb into a damp, smelly bunk. Attempt sleep on mildewed sheets.

9. Repeat every three hours.

The payoff for our valiant efforts was arriving in polluted Suva Harbor, desperate to run screaming from our own private torture chamber. Yet to avoid steep overtime charges, we waited another forty-eight hours to clear in. Unable to escape our fetid boat for another two days, we had plenty of time to discover all the items that had mildewed during the trip, and to realize how much water could come in through a tank vent that normally wouldn't be submerged.

FIJI: THE WARM EMBRACE OF BULA

"For being such a happy people, they sure have quite the collection of killing devices," I mused to Garth, thinking of the array of spears, clubs, and neck crackers we'd seen mounted in the history museum.

My walking encyclopedia replied, "Evidently, when the Europeans encountered Fiji, it was a time of intense feuding between tribes. Fijian people gained a reputation for being formidable warriors and fierce cannibals, though I found they could hardly be friendlier."

As I tried to catch the eye of the Royal Fiji Yacht Club bartender at the far end of the counter, he continued, "When my family was here in the Seventies, everybody was quick with a smile and a hearty 'Bula!' whenever we passed them on the street."

When the floral-shirted Fijian bartender came over, a smile lit up his dark face. I ordered a couple of 75¢ ice-cold beers. Around the bar sat several inebriated expats—clearly savoring not their *first* or *second* drink of the day, though the quantity was probably shy of double digits, since it was still early.

The Royal Suva Yacht Club didn't exactly fit the image that the name suggested. Though the building was clean and spacious, the 1970s-style padded wood-frame couches and coffee tables—ever popular in American church basements—gave it a more utilitarian air. Dining tables fronted slatted windows. Ping pong and pool tables offered diversions besides alcohol, as did a small bookshelf of dusty paperbacks.

The building sat on a tiny grass oasis at the head of a polluted bay littered with partially sunken hulks of ships that had failed to navigate the reefs that lurked just below the murky water's surface. Rusty-though-still-floating Taiwanese factory fishing vessels belched black smoke in close proximity.

This certainly isn't what the travel magazines and guides tout as a tropical getaway, I'd thought to myself as we dropped anchor a few days earlier. Still. I was enthusiastic to learn everything about the place where Garth had spent a profoundly formative year of his life.

Stretching from the land into the harbor were large plastic pontoons strung together to form a barely-floating pathway to the attached vessels. Though these were clearly designed with utilitarian runabouts in mind, a few fancy yachts treated these as docks, setting an anchor to add extra stability—an effort which probably doubled its original strength. Hence, derelict work vessels parked beside imposing pleasure craft.

We'd recognized one of them as we'd paddle around its anchor on our way into shore. Sailing magazines had featured multi-page spreads of its state-of-the art design and its plush interior along with its famous owner, Bruno Troublé, the America's Cup sailor and race organizer. Evidently, he too had sailed his new sixty-foot yacht from New Zealand not long after the cup ended.

Later, when we ventured towards a table for our first meal off the boat in ages, I noticed Bruno Troublé, the man himself, dining nearby with his wife and teenage sons, both of whom were hunched over and picking absently at their meals. My special access to the America's Cup Media Center had given me a close look at the power wielded by this man. Famous sailors and television personalities had followed him through the halls as he went about the business of running the Louis Vuitton Challenger series. Now, seeing his sons shrug and reluctantly offer the typical teenage monosyllabic replies to their famous father brought a smile to my face.

Garth looked at me with a quizzical expression. I nodded towards the other table.

"He may have lots of money and power, but he's still stuck in the same polluted harbor that we are." Sensitive to the possibility of insulting Garth's proprietary feelings towards Suva, I quickly added, "It's so fun to finally see this place that you've been telling me about for so long."

He took no offense, concurring "Well it ain't much, but I have a lot of strong memories here. It's sure neat to see it again."

Garth's memories naturally would turn our visit to Fiji's capital city into a tour of his life there the year after his family's sailboat grounded at Makaluva. I'd already noticed a series of photographs of Makaluva Island above the bar. Each picture showed its various shapes depending on how wave motion shifted sand around its reef over the years. That fateful night in September 1974, after days of being unable to get a sun sight to determine their exact position, a current had swept the Wilcoxes north. They discovered the discrepancy too late. After crunching hard onto the reef, the swell drove them onto it until the boat was on its side, filling with water.

It had become immediately clear they wouldn't be sailing anywhere soon, so they inflated the life raft, and, at dawn, made their way to the sandbar called Makaluva, a mile away. There, at the age of fourteen, Garth had lived "Robinson Crusoe-style" until the family was able to hire a salvage company to help them float the vessel off. Makaluva had since turned into a penal colony.

"A penitentiary is probably about all it's really good for." Garth sighed, disappointed that we couldn't explore the island as he'd hoped. "I lived on that desolate island for a week. It's a good thing we arrived with our own food. The bricks labeled "emergency rations" from the life raft didn't last long." His thick fingers bracketed the words with imaginary quotation marks. "Other sources of food weren't exactly what you'd call readily available." I'd heard the story many times, but always appreciated the understated, dryly humorous way he told it, imparting more vivid details with each retelling.

We ordered and then planned the next day's route. When our meals arrived, I dug into the steaming curry, which reflected Fiji's unique cultural mix. Despite being a former colony of Britain—known for its culinary blandness—Fiji inherited a rich spiciness from Indians who had come to work Fiji's sugar-cane plantations.

The following morning, Garth and I crossed the yacht club's gravel parking and past the yacht club "gate"—a metal bar across a driveway and a phone booth-sized guard shack with a thin, elderly Indian man sleeping inside. Just outside across the street sat a local prison—not to be confused with the one on Makaluva, which was a federal prison.

"Nice neighborhood for a yacht club, huh?" Garth grinned.

We hurried past a group of convicts and guards in a brush-clearing work party. The prisoners wore jumpsuits and carried machetes. The prison guards wore wrap-around skirts and wielded night sticks. I shot Garth an amused look and noticed he hadn't missed the irony.

As we came around a curve in the road, a banner announced the pending arrival of America's finest culinary export: McDonald's.

"There's goes the neighborhood," I cracked. Fiji's uniqueness could soon be lost to the pervasive homogenization overtaking the world's most far-flung locations.

Around another bend in a light industrial area, we came upon Princess Wharf. "Princess Wharf is where they piled everything we salvaged off the boat. Everything we owned sat there, in a soggy pile, like the debris it had just become."

I imagined how devastated the Wilcoxes must have felt at that moment. They didn't know whether they'd be able to rebuild their boat, or whether their dreams of sailing around the world were as shattered as the wood in the *Vela's* side.

A little farther up, Garth pointed to a promontory in the distance behind a chain-link fence.

"There's the government shipway, where we pulled the *Vela* out of the water. The hole covered half the port side." He looked at me for emphasis.

I shook my head, as though I were hearing it for the first time. A few steps further along, with a sweeping motion, Garth said, "This area is where we rebuilt the boat."

I tried to imagine Garth and his father closing the hole and reconstructing the interior in suffocating heat and rainsqualls without the resources of a marine store or even a hardware store.

"So much has changed since I was here," he remarked for the tenth time that morning. It had been more than twenty-five years.

"You're starting to sound like a geezer." I laughed.

"Yeah, don't I?" he marveled, and then he launched into another story about the kind of local woods they'd used to rebuild the boat.

Feeling awkward in the midst of busy shipyard workers, we trudged on towards town.

When we reached the bus depot, school-bus style vehicles idled listlessly. Passengers stowed burlap bags of taro root and taro leaves in the open compartment under the bus, then clambered aboard and rolled up the rain flaps, now no longer necessary since a recent rainsquall had passed. At the opposite end of the station, ten buses converged on the narrow exit simultaneously. Their impatient horns urged us onwards. We'd take many 20¢ bus rides during our time in Suva, but today we walked so we could take everything in.

A block farther along, the Suva public market, a huge two-storied concrete structure, bustled with activity. Ubiquitous blue tarps spilled out onto the surrounding pavement, covered with groups of bananas, coconuts, pineapples, taro, and breadfruit. Carefully stacked piles of carrots, eggplant, tomatoes, and peppers sat behind cardboard prices as did oranges and limes sequestered in plastic bowls. My heart skipped a beat at the sudden abundance, a marked contrast to some of the meager markets where we'd shopped.

"This is the best market in the entire Pacific. Looks just the same," Garth said.

More blue tarps lashed together stretched overhead to protect against a harsh tropical sun and frequent rain squalls. Behind each stack of produce, large, dark-brown people sat cross legged. Brilliant white teeth and twinkling eyes surrounded by a nappy halo beamed a warm welcome.

Inside the cool, dark building, the delicious scent of turmeric, cumin, cayenne, and coriander wafted into my nostrils. I spied Gulliver-sized bags overflowing with powdered Indian spices in deep vermillion and burnished gold. Bundles of dried kava hung above a vendor's stall, each wrapped to present to a village chief as protocol required. The abundance of choice and riot of color overwhelmed me.

Vegetables I'd never seen and seaweed shaped like bunches of miniature grapes intrigued me. A woman offered me a taste of the seaweed. We smiled at each other while I marveled at its texture and taste—remarkably like a tougher version of the salmon eggs I'd sampled in sushi restaurants back home.

I felt the urge to load up on fresh produce and seafood. Garth gently reminded me that we would be in Suva for several days, and we didn't want to lug our bounty around all day.

Beyond the market, we passed several low-rise 1960s-style buildings and more men in skirts. We brushed past men in bright floral (Bula) shirts and Indian shopkeepers in saris. Nearly every Fijian we passed greeted us warmly with a smile, a wave, or an enthusiastic "Bula!" The real charm of Fiji, its gregarious people, drew me in and brought a spring to my step as we continued down Victoria Parade.

I couldn't resist taking a quick glance in the food stores to see what was available. In addition to the typical Pacific island selection of corned beef and tinned mackerel, I spotted a pleasing variety of curries, dahl, and other ingredients for Indian-style cooking. Again, I was overwhelmed with the urge to stock up, until Garth pressed us on.

"Look, there's the old Carnegie library. Let's take a quick peek inside."

Evidently Carnegie's reach stretched this far. The moment I ducked my head inside, I could smell its mustiness.

"I spent a lot of time here, escaping the stifling heat. I was always hunting for a good book to read."

I tried to imagine its sparse, dusty shelves in the 1970s, which might make today's trading library at the yacht club look like an oasis of fine literature.

We moved past a derelict building. Its white colonnade edged around a grand verandah hinted of its former colonial glory.

Garth said, "Wow, that's the old Grand Pacific Hotel. That was built to house the Pan Am Clipper passengers. It used to be *the* place to stay. I always wanted to go inside, but after we wrecked the boat, we didn't have the time or the money to do things like that. What a shame to see it all boarded up." Quick to spot the irony, he added, "I heard the country of Nauru bought it when they were flush with money from phosphate mining. Now they're bankrupt. As usual Britain granted Nauru its independence once phosphate mining had run its course…with predictable results."

We continued past the national radio station, a small windowless building with antennas perched on the roof like a crop of freshly landed spaceships. Aboard *Velella* the previous season, we'd listened to the English radio station. There were also Fijian- and Indian-language stations. Garth joked that they were still playing many of the same tired songs that had been hits during his last visit—"Kung Fu Fighting," the Bee Gee's pre- *Fever* falsetto classic "Nights on Broadway," the Hughes Corporation's "Don't Rock the Boat" (always good for a joke on board), plus selections from Anne Murray, Neil Diamond, Glen Campbell, and Gordon Lightfoot. Each week featured the *National Quiz,* which pitted two schools against one another to answer simple historical trivia. Sprinkled throughout each day's programming were quaint announcements, congratulations, and condolence messages across the national airwaves, much like you might find in a small town.

Passing the radio station reminded Garth of the time his perpetually combative twelve-year-old sister angrily marched to the radio station to tell the DJ that she had correctly guessed the answer to the previous week's contest, despite his announcement that no one had. Garth could still remember the name of the DJ more than twenty-five years later: Yaminiase Nonovo. His descendants now hosted the programs.

During the peak of the day's heat, we reached Albert Park, where there was not a hint of shade. Afros bobbed across the rugby field. The cricket pitch was crowded with onlookers clad in t-shirts, shorts, skirts, bright floral (Bula) shirts, and dresses. Posters touting Suva's role as host of the upcoming South Pacific Games caught my eye. We'd heard ads for the event on the radio with a catchy theme song by the Tuvalu-based band, Te Vaka. While we had heard that funding was scarce for healthcare, sports did not seem to suffer the same neglect.

Not wanting to linger in the blazing heat, we pressed on down Victoria Parade in search of the house where Garth's family had lived while they'd rebuilt the *Vela.* Our route took us past the President's house, which had been the residence of the governor general appointed by the queen during Colonial times.

Fiji gained independence from the UK in 1970, four years before Garth's family arrived. Since then, its constitutional government, based on the British model, had been strained repeatedly by ethnic tensions between indigenous Fijians and a growing population of descendents from indentured Indian laborers. Indians made up roughly half of the population and formed the backbone of Fijian commerce, but a tradition of inherited communal land ownership left second- and third-generation Indian Fijians without the means to own or rent land. The underlying tension had erupted into what the media termed a "coup" shortly before Garth and I arrived in Fiji our first season, about which we'd have remained blissfully unaware except for our alarmed families.

I playfully snapped photos of the official guards, who looked cute but lacked an air of ferocity in their white skirts, and then we pressed on. Closer to the water's edge, the air cooled to a more bearable temperature. Victoria Parade became Queen Elizabeth Drive, and we shared a narrow walkway with girls in smart blue-and-white school uniforms. Finally, we neared the old house where Garth and his family had lived.

"There's the China Club." Garth pointed to a small, single-story cement building as we turned the corner. He swung his arm and pointed behind the building. "That's where they put the giant wok and cooked a huge stir-fry feast at least twice a week," he licked his lips and his mouth twitched a fraction, "while some musically-challenged band played Elton John's "Daniel" for the tenth time at ear-splitting volume." I snickered. Our pilgrimage to the Vela's Pacific landfalls felt complete when I rested my eyes upon the modest royal blue cement house that bordered the China Club property. This was the house where Garth's family lived for a year while they rebuilt the *Vela*.

"You can probably guess why rent was so cheap."

Our passports would expire within the year, and since many countries block entry to anyone with less than a year left on his passport, we decided to renew them while we had an embassy a short walk away. Coming around the corner, the fortress-like presence of

U.S. embassy shocked me. But 9/11 had happened, and in the post-9/11 era, even in Fiji, a U.S. embassy visitor was a member of an Al Qaeda sleeper cell until proven otherwise.

Inside, George W. Bush's clueless smile and Dick Cheney's sneer loomed over the guards and metal detectors that stood ominously at the far end of the empty lobby, erasing the warmth I'd felt when I first spotted the American flag. The area beyond was teeming with people seeking some form of visa to visit the U.S. The beacon of freedom and opportunity still shone brightly for many.

In the waiting room, we encountered Jesse, an effusive gal from Minnesota who was marrying a Fijian boy she'd met two weeks earlier at a waterfall. Their plans were to return to Minnesota to live, though he'd never been outside of Fiji. We nodded politely with frozen smiles, wondering how long a young Fijian might last in Minnesota.

I pictured this bright-eyed young man, brimming with enthusiasm for his trip to America, later finding himself buttoned up to his ears in a parka, shoveling snow on a frozen prairie. I imagined him working the counter of a fast-food chain—the best job he could find—all so he could pay the heating bill and make the next installment on his TV to help him through a long, icy winter. And for that, he'd given up playing with his friends in the waterfall that flowed through his lush tropical village.

At the front of the line, we navigated the bureaucratic rigmarole, and within a few minutes, an official suggested we return in two weeks to retrieve our new passports. And so we did—without incident, except for the intricately-carved Marquesan hair pick I lost for the danger it posed as a deadly weapon.

In the interim, we sailed south to experience more of Fiji. Our days were filled with steep climbs through fresh machete cuts we made in the jungle. Our labors in oppressive humidity with grimy sweat dripping down our backs typically culminated in an exhilarating swim beneath a gushing waterfall. We became connoisseurs of waterfalls, narrow streams plunging from great heights to wide cascades of water swirling around rocks.

At the edge of an algae-slicked natural water slide, I scooted forward until I could feel the pull of the water, pointed my toes, and let go. The rapid flow of the water flushed me down the narrow chute, whooping and hollering all the way. At the bottom, I plunged into a deep freshwater swimming hole surrounded by high volcanic rocks.

I returned many times and noticed how rainfall affected the waterslide's flow, appearance, and ride. As any whitewater rafter would tell you, each day, the river was a different animal whose mood depended on how much rain had fed it the day before. The more rain, the faster the ride. Fiji frequently obliged with torrential cooling downpours that sent us scurrying to the waterslide for the extra thrill.

I found the subtle variety fascinating and never tired of seeking the next, refreshingly cool reward for our sweaty treks through the jungle. I longed to see and do everything that was humanly possible. Yet Garth was beginning to grow weary of indulgent exploring for days on end. Often I sought the company of other cruisers for such ventures while Garth grabbed a few hours of solitude.

One afternoon, I returned to the boat flushed from swimming in a natural underwater cave where pumice that floated on the surface clinked against the glass of my mask. Garth rolled over and set down his book. He seemed mildly interested in my breathless rendition of my afternoon field trip but showed no interest in seeing it with me himself the following day.

At that moment I worried anew whether setting off on our own towards Japan would deprive us of a natural pressure relief valve that helped keep the harmony.

CHAPTER
11

VANUATU: NATIONAL
GEOGRAPHIC LIVE

In mid-September, we sailed for Vanuatu. A fellow cruiser had suggested we sail from Fiji to northern Vanuatu, then work our way south through the country so that we'd first see remote islands that were less affected by outside influences.

It was a promising idea, but we underestimated the magnitude of beating into trade winds. Beating into the wind in Puget Sound's flat water and light winds was usually fairly pleasant, but beating into waves that had built up over thousands of ocean miles was another. We assumed we could sail south when the trade winds weren't as strong, but the trades blew relentlessly on. Once again, we had failed to consult Mother Nature, and she had quickly exposed our naiveté. Our travels through Vanuatu were filled with rich interactions with the gentle Ni-Vanuatu people and the country's natural beauty, but punctuated by bone-jarring sails into steep waves that made *Velella* shudder in protest.

When we checked in with the northernmost customs office in Sola, the bank was closed, so we were unable to exchange money. No matter.

The customs officer, a shy, slender young man, suggested we pay the entry fee when we checked out of the country. And we soon discovered that since the copra trading boat hadn't visited these northern islands for a year, locals had little use for money anyway. They preferred to trade for items they needed rather than Vatu, the local currency.

For the next three weeks, we blithely traded clothing, soap, shampoo, shoes, line, fish hooks, sugar, and flour for fresh "vegetables," which I discovered usually meant bananas and drinking coconuts—which we loved once we finally figured out how to crack them open.

First we had to push beyond the shyness of the Ni-Vanuatu people. The Ni-Vanuatu are Melanesians, believed to have originated in Indonesia and Papua New Guinea. They are smaller and darker than Polynesians or Fijians and far more reserved. Shortly after we anchored inside of a water-filled volcanic crater on the faraway island of Uruparapara, several outrigger canoes appeared in the bay. They quietly paddled at a distance until we waved to invite them over. Unlike the Marquesans who'd developed rich tastes for cameras and CD players after trading with a steady stream of visiting yachts, these locals were happy to trade prawns for an epoxy-stained t-shirt—an island group in step with *Velella*'s budget.

One little girl paddled nearby most of one morning. We smiled and waved, but she wouldn't come over. When we asked a young man who came offering coconuts, he explained that she had eggs to sell, but was too shy to ask. Another day a tiny, cherubic-faced boy—who couldn't have been more than two years old—paddled alone to our boat and floated silently nearby for hours with big eyes that watched everything we did.

Anchored within sight of a spectacular twin waterfall on the west side of Vanua Lava, I was sure we'd found paradise. Below the thundering falls, a wide basin offered a refreshing swim, plus plenty of fresh water for our tanks and for laundry. And after a cool swim or laundry session, I could bake my body and damp clothing on the sun-scorched rocks. Nearby, crystal clear waters teeming with sea life and underwater crevices intrigued me, as did a host of bat-filled caves. The mild scent of sulphur in the air and occasional hissing steam reminded me that these geological formations were the product of a still-active volcano.

On our second afternoon there, a thin ancient native man dressed in the remnants of what could only have been a woman's discarded purple summer blazer paddled up and introduced himself as Patrick. His gray afro was closely cropped, and when his dark gaunt face broke into a friendly smile, he had several teeth missing. He offered to bring us prawns the following afternoon. Of course we accepted. For the next three days, Patrick arrived an hour before sunset with a modest, white-enamel-coated double boiler full of prawns cooked in oil. The first time he handed them over, he explained that they were from upriver, and his wife wanted to make sure they were cooked properly so we wouldn't be sick.

The prawns were a tasty treat. But what was even better was the time we spent with Patrick. Ostensibly, he was trading for prawns, but he seemed more interested in chatting. Our conversations had no great depth, but we appreciated the chance to just sit and talk. And as soon as the sun dropped to the horizon, he would paddle away with a promise to return the following day. Only with reluctance did we tell him of our plan to sail away. Our drive to see as much of Vanuatu as possible before typhoon season propelled us ever onward.

As we carried on southwards, between grueling waterlogged bashes into trade wind-whipped swell, we found several more heavenly spots. From one anchorage, in a friend's motorized dinghy, we wound our way upriver through a mangrove jungle past a bat-nesting area to a blue swimming hole. Halfway there, lily pads barred our way, but with a concerted effort, we cleared the rest of the way to our prize: all the cool, aqua-blue fresh water we could dream of, in a lush natural pool.

A week later, we pulled into the bay at Asanvari on the island of Maewo, where another waterfall gushed into the bay. Several sailboats were anchored here, including one that had spent most of the season. The crew had taken it upon themselves to advise the chief on the peculiar ways of sailors. With so many sailboats visiting each year, it seemed villages were perplexed with how to deal with this outside force. I yearned to learn as much as I could about the local cultures but remained wary of introducing change through my presence. We'd noticed that several villages had made efforts to cater to the needs of visitors for the greater good of the community by creating what they generously called "yacht clubs"—modest structures woven from palm fronds, where visitors could gather.

Shortly after we anchored, the chief paddled over and introduced himself. He told us of a dinner and dance performance the village was planning for the following evening in the "yacht club." The price was a fifteen hundred Vatu, about $15 each. Were we interested? *Yes.*

An hour later, a sixty-foot steel motor sailor pulled into the bay. Within minutes of putting an anchor down, yellow and red plastic kayaks hit the water along with the usual outboard-powered inflatable dinghy. Each carried a passenger or two, and they wandered in different directions. Several more people remained aboard. This was not the typical cruising couple we were used to seeing. Later, we learned it was an Australian charter boat that spent each season in Vanuatu touring with paying passengers.

Later that day, the chief returned and explained that the price of the dinner dance would need to be higher. We didn't quite understand the reason for the price change—something about needing to get more chicken from somewhere else, but Garth told him that we could not afford the higher price of 1,800 Vatu. Fifteen hundred Vatu times two was already a day's budget.

Vanuatu was proving to be an expensive country whenever cash was involved. We'd blown our budget many times already and were in danger of liquidating our account at this rate, yet I had my heart set on partaking in this cultural experience. I held my breath, hoping we'd find a solution to this predicament.

Chief Nelson's brow furrowed, and he thought silently for a moment.

"We are more interested in the dancing than the dinner anyway. Perhaps we could just come for the dancing," I said.

Chief Nelson pondered that for another moment. Then he snapped his fingers and, with his pointer finger raised, proposed a solution.

"Okay. Fifteen hundred Vatu. Dance and," pinching his thumb and forefinger together, "small dinner."

I imagined that meant no chicken, but I hadn't been expecting anything more than lap lap (bland starchy root vegetables and leafy greens baked in banana leaves filled with coconut milk).

"Okay," Garth said, smiling.

We spent the following day swimming and climbing the rocks that separated the cascading waterfall from the jungle, while passengers from the tour boat hired a guide to visit nearby caves. I yearned to visit the caves, too, but we were already splurging on the dinner and dance. And even I had to admit that finding the caves in the jungle without a guide didn't seem likely. Rumors that a crocodile had once eaten a cruiser in this bay were whispered among skittish crews.

Urban legend?

Who's to say?

Late that afternoon, we rowed ashore for the evening's festivities. Beside a sandy clearing next to the beach, we perched on logs at the chief's urging. Within a few minutes, eight male dancers came around the edge of a palm-frond building, chanting melodically, hopping on alternating feet and beating time with bamboo stalks. Their feather-trimmed, coconut-husk head dresses bobbed rhythmically, and nutshells strung around their ankles rattled in time to their steps. White war paint covered their faces and bare torsos. I was relieved to see woven mats covering their midsections instead of penis sheaths that some *Kastom* villagers wear—especially from this angle, about six inches away.

After the dancing, the chief ushered us inside the "yacht club" to a wooden table. As I settled onto a bench next to the table, I noticed a large kava bowl sitting in the corner with several bunches of kava root. Several young boys were chewing, and I wondered if they were preparing our kava by chewing the raw pepper root and spitting it into a bowl, as is customary. I had a certain reticence about trying the kava, given descriptions of its preparation. But, evidently the chief had been warned about Westerners' typical squeamishness, and several ladies wearing Mother Hubbard-style shapeless dresses came in carrying bowls of water, which the chief made sure to point out. While several men ground the kava root and mixed it with water in the low wooden bowl, others brought our dinners in a bowl woven of palm fronds. A string band, complete with a washtub bass and several guitars, played traditional songs complemented by strong male voices. I had the smaller dinner, sans chicken as expected, but Garth accidentally ended up with one of the more expensive dinners and had eaten half of it before he realized the mistake.

"Full tide or half tide?" the chief asked me, speaking of the level of liquid in a coconut shell. This was my chance to try Vanuatu's kava. Though we'd tried Fijian kava, Vanuatu's kava was far more potent, because it was made from fresh, rather than dried, roots.

"Half tide even seems like a lot," I said, and another woman offered to split it with me. Garth got a full tide. And then another. I took a sip. It tasted like muddy water, but with a subtle numbing of my throat, lips, and tongue, like a shot of Chloriseptic without the minty medicinal flavor. I felt a mellowness wash over me as I listened to the string band play.

As the tourists made a move to leave, Garth leaned over and whispered, "We can't leave yet." Usually he was the one prodding me out the door at the end of every party. "I don't think I'll be able to stand for a while." He looked extremely relaxed. "In fact, this Vanuatu kava is kicking my butt."

Garth and I beached the *Tasty Penguin* on the narrow island of Pentecost. I was curious to see this outlying island, famous for its tradition of land diving, which had sparked the bungee-jumping craze. Land diving from platforms built of sticks occurs on this Vanuatu island in April and May in honor of the yam crop. Now it was late September, and jumping out of season was just not done because the natural vines wouldn't have the right elasticity. (We heard that once the jumpers made an exception when Queen Elizabeth had visited, and someone had jumped to his death during the exhibition, but we never did find out whether there was any truth to this rumor.)

While we had no illusions of witnessing land diving, we did want to explore this less visited island culture where they lived much as they had for centuries. As we settled the *Tasty Penguin* under a pandanu tree, I noticed a slight, dark man stooped nearby, earnestly gathering pandanu leaves. He paused and looked at us impassively. I asked whether we could leave our dinghy on the beach. He spoke a few sentences, and while I recognized English words, I also realized that I had no idea what he'd just said. I looked at Garth. He shrugged.

Because the people of Vanuatu are widely dispersed among thirteen larger and seventy smaller islands, or are separated by thick jungle vegetation, Vanuatu has more than a hundred distinct languages, one for every 1,200 people. Whaling, the sandalwood trade, slave trading, and less-than-successful missionary work brought many Europeans through Vanuatu. Settlers from Britain and France, beginning mostly in the 1850s, created a system of joint rule and a duplication of nearly every government function and law—a model of inefficiency few can tout or would care to emulate. To communicate with outsiders, the Ni-Vanuatu people speak a combination of pidgin English and French, called Bislama, which uses a roundabout way of saying things to work within a limited vocabulary. So often instead of naming something, which would require a new word, in Bislama they'd just describe it. There are no verb tenses, and sometimes no verb at all.

Bislama uses English words derived from *want, belong,* and *got,* along with the French words *save* (from the verb meaning, "to know"), and *finis* (from the word *fini,* meaning, *"finish" or "done"*— used to refer to the past). Another useful word is *ia,* meaning "here" to signify *this* one or *that* one. Bislama simplifies complex language concepts like possessives by using *blong* ("belong") to describe relationships. Prince Charles is referred to as *nambawan pikinini blong kwin* ("number-one child belonging to the queen"). If I wanted to tell someone my name, I'd say, "Nam blong mi Wendy."

Some handy phrases we learned were: *Tank yu tumas* ("Thank you very much"); *Lukim yu afta, tata* ("See you later"); *Mi wantem sam...*("I want some..."); *yu save?* ("Do you know?") and *solwata, i kam up?* ("Is the tide coming in?")

Signs were easier to interpret because of the visual cues they often featured. Also, if we sounded things out slowly, we could often ferret out the words they meant to convey, with the added benefit of a good chuckle.

At a store in Port Vila, the capital city, we later found and purchased a handy Bislama language guide, as much for its practical use as its comic potential. The guide was called *Evri samting yu wannem save long Bislama but yu fraet tumas long askem (Everything You Ever Wanted to Know in Bislama But Forgot to Ask)* by Darrell Tryon. Some of my favorite discoveries were *hed blong em i no strait* ("the head that belongs to him isn't straight or he's mentally ill"), *Wan plen i fall down finis?* ("Has the plane already landed?"), and fishing company T-shirts that read, *fis i kilim i ded* ("He killed the fish dead"), not to be confused with *fis i kilim* ("he hit the fish").

At that moment, we had not yet learned Bislama nor acquired our handy guide. So Garth did his own version of Pidgin, which he'd perfected when his lack of French turned him into a deaf-mute in French Polynesia. He repeated the question slowly and loudly, pointing to the dinghy and pointing down as he said, "Here." The man spoke again at length, pointing in the direction of a small cut in the beach where a modest trickle flowed from inland.

Again I was clueless as to the message he was trying to convey.

After a moment more of our looking expectantly at him, he shrugged slightly, and then nodded slowly.

We tied our dinghy to a tree.

"Chief?" Garth said. Later we would learn that all we needed to say was, "Wan jif, yu save wannem ples i stap?" which means roughly "I want to see the chief of the village. Do you know where he is?" As in most Pacific island cultures, custom suggested we first pay our respects to the chief before wandering around a village. The man smiled and pointed inland, but said no more. He resumed his work. We tromped inland from the beach in search of the chief.

As we crossed through the bush, we spotted a pathway that cut past several huts made of palm fronds carefully woven into a geometrical pattern. Stones lined the perimeter of each hut, the surrounding area clear of brush. Outside each structure stood several narrow high wooden tables on which large utilitarian bowls and pots lay neatly stacked. Several basins of water perched on a rocky platform near what looked like a fire circle. In the clearing, narrow shrubs of yellow and pink glossy leaves brightened the scene.

Several young children flocked toward us. I guessed that they were curious about the rare presence of pale faces in their quiet village. They followed at a distance, peeking furtively behind tiny fists. Periodically they flashed brilliant, shy smiles, and their numbers quickly grew into a sizeable entourage. We gravitated towards an inland clearing, where we saw a bridge stretched across a river that was far larger than the trickle next to our dinghy on the waterfront.

"I think that man was trying to warn us about the river," Garth said, jutting his chin towards the water.

"I'm glad it's not raining," I said, noting the low water flow within its deep banks and remembering, shortly after our arrival in Vanuatu, rain so heavy that, with a tarp, we'd caught fifty-five gallons of fresh drinking water in twenty-four hours.

The children giggled when they heard us speak. Behind them at a distance an old woman looked over, pausing from clearing brush around her home. She looked tired, her frame slightly bent, her bosom hanging low under a thin, faded floral shirt. Wisps of white accented her closely-cropped, nappy hair.

"Chief?" Garth asked again. She pointed a crooked finger across the river and continued her work. We strode across a bridge made of sticks. Two older men approached as we reached the other side of the bridge. One was clothed better than the other, wearing a floral shirt that was almost a twin to one I had bought for Garth in Fiji only a month earlier. I guessed that he might be the chief and wondered if he had purchased the shirt in Fiji as we had.

He shook our hands, confirming that he was indeed the chief and asking where we came from. As we neared the beach, we pointed to our boat anchored offshore. He greeted everyone who crossed our path with a gracious command. Each had a gentle reserve that contrasted with the boisterous, outgoing amiability of the Fijians. All were slender with chiseled cheekbones, smooth skin, and clear chocolate-brown eyes that quietly took in every detail. Children followed us at a discreet distance, until the chief spoke softly to them with words we could not understand. Most ran back to where they'd first seen us.

A moment later, we sat down on a log that overlooked the beach and *Velella*. Her white hull sparkled in the afternoon sunshine. Evidently we'd completed the village tour.

"I was a boy during World War II," he began, in clear English. To have been old enough to remember events from World War II in 2002, the chief had to have been over seventy years old—much older than he looked, given his healthy smile. As he spoke, I noticed cloudy rings around his irises.

Until the Japanese blazed across the Pacific, sleepy Vanuatu had experienced limited contact with the outside world. The country quickly became an important South Pacific staging area for Allied war operations. I imagined what it must have been like to witness the sudden appearance of modern war machines without experiencing the intervening evolutionary years.

"One day," he continued, "I saw something in the sky I had never seen before. It was like a bird but noisy and big. I learned later that it was an airplane. Then there were many. And I saw many ships, all the same." He paused for a moment and brushed his hand through the rocky sand. He looked up and scanned the horizon.

"Once," he said, "Right here from where we sit, I saw a Japanese submarine hit a rock over there." He gestured towards the rocky point. "A ship came and bombed it until it broke into pieces and sank."

"Did you see any people?" I asked.

He shook his head. Then he gazed out over the water, lost in the memory.

Garth and I hadn't intentionally planned a tour of World War II history, but were pleased to note that our route to Japan would follow the trail of armed conflict in the Pacific. Our journey would trace the destructive path all the way to its aggressor, and Vanuatu marked our first war encounter.

He looked over at Garth and, with a worried expression, he asked, "Is this the beginning of World War III?" It took me a moment to guess that he was referring to 9/11 and its aftermath.

I took in a sharp breath. World War III? His question seemed so farfetched. Yet was it? I realized the responsibility he bore to advise and protect his village. From afar, the conflict associated with 9/11 made no sense. It seemed unreal. But so had World War II, at first. Where would it lead?

As someone who had endured weeks' worth of pledge-drives to get my fix of public radio news, I was surprised how little interest I had in listening to them now. The news seemed like little more than speculation and grim reports of senseless killing and destruction, irrelevant in this peaceful environment. Yet profound changes were happening that would affect our world for years, if not decades to come. In a place that looked straight out of a *National Geographic* photo shoot, I never expected to be considering the ramifications of global politics.

🌴

After a month in the country, we needed to renew our visas, so we headed back to Espiritu Santo, the largest northern island. To avoid paying anchoring fees off the crowded town of Luganville, we anchored in Palikulo, the nearest protected bay, and hiked two hours along the dusty road into town. Once a busy supply depot during World War II with as many as a hundred U.S. Navy ships and thousands of personnel, Luganville was the setting that inspired James Michener to write *Tales of the South Pacific.* Since then, Luganville had become a sleepy town populated with aging Quonset huts and the odd rusted war relic.

On our trek into town, we passed Million Dollar Point, named for the value of military equipment U.S. troops dumped at the close of the war after the local French-backed government refused to buy it, assuming they could ultimately get it for free. We jammed the "honesty box" with 500 Vatu each as demanded for a viewing and trudged down the rocky path towards the point. As we picked our way through scraps of barely identifiable rusted metal that littered a once-decent beach, with a smile Garth said, "Glad my tetanus shot is up to date."

I replied, "This is sad. I can't believe we just paid ten bucks to visit a junkyard." Our detour through Million Dollar Point was brief, and we carried on into Luganville.

Near that same point a few miles closer to town, under nearly a hundred feet of water lay *The President Coolidge*, a prewar luxury liner that had been converted into a troop carrier and which then had been inadvertently sunk by a friendly mine. While I would have loved to have gone diving, the tourist prices the scuba operations commanded far exceeded our budget. Plus we weren't yet certified divers.

But a week earlier we'd gotten a free taste of war history when we'd anchored inside a coral reef and snorkeled a sunken World War II plane that had crashed off the end of the runway. Hiking the following day, we tromped across what must have been the old airfield, because amid the lush jungle, we found ourselves suddenly baking under a blazing sun in a sizeable, unusually dusty clearing. Brushing away the cracked soil, Garth uncovered a hard surface: concrete. Almost as if to confirm our suspicions, within minutes, I spotted a battered airplane wing tip glimmering in the sunshine and a weathered Coke bottle from a bygone era.

In Luganville, once we'd checked in with customs, we loaded up on fresh supplies of papaya, tomatoes, cucumbers, cabbage, sweet potatoes, peppers, eggplant, and rice. Afterward we indulged in a cheap meal out at Numba Wan restaurant before heading back to the boat, this time splurging by splitting a 700 Vatu taxi with another cruising couple to spare our overloaded sweaty backs and blistered feet. The time to wander opened an infinite realm of opportunities that kept life ever interesting.

We had a pleasant beat in unusually flat water in light winds (5–10 knots) on our way into Lamen Bay. Outside the bay, our fishing line snagged something really big. Finally, we'd caught a fish. As Garth pulled the line in, I pulled out the gaff, the filet knife, quickly tossed the cushions below, and pushed lines out of the way so they wouldn't get blood and fish guts on them.

"Boy, this is really heavy," Garth groaned as he pulled against the line. As Garth drew our prize closer to the boat, he realized what we'd caught. "It's a shark," he said. I could hear the disappointment in his voice.

"A shark? Shit." I thought of a movie I'd seen years ago, when a shark they'd caught nearly pulled apart a small sailboat. In a moment of prudence, I said, "Why don't you just cut the line?

"It looks like the stomach is pulled out, and he'll die anyway. Besides, I want my lure back."

"For God's sake, it was only a six-dollar spoon you bought in Fiji."

"Yeah, but it's the principle of the thing."

I watched with dumbfounded amazement as Garth readied a line and pulled the shark close.

"What are you thinking?" I asked.

"Here, hang onto this," he said. Then he reached down and slipped the line over the tail and pulled it tight. The loop made a noose around the shark's tail. "Okay, you can let go." As the monofilament slipped through my fingers, Garth tightened his grasp of the line. He leaned down and tied the line off on the aft cleat, towing the shark backward.

The shark would have none of that. Water rushing backwards through his gills would kill him. He fought for his life, thrashing with mighty force. His muscles tensed and rippled under the gray taut skin with each thrust. And with every thrust, *Velella* shuddered. As the wind grew lighter, his force overtook the pressure on *Velella*'s sails. Soon, instead of us towing him backward, he began towing us backwards.

For the next hour, the shark battled against the forces of the wind, while I was acutely aware we were killing one of God's creatures. Yes, he was a shark with a killer instinct, which could tear apart our boat, given the chance. But he was simply doing what he had to do to survive. Meanwhile, we only hoped to subsidize our budget with some fresh meat, and he was meat we had little interest in eating.

When the shark finally stopped wriggling, Garth pulled him amidships and tied him off to a cleat while he readied the spinnaker pole—raising it to shoulder height. I watched, fascinated. Then, as though he'd done this hundreds of times before, he looped the line through the end of the spinnaker pole and clipped the other end onto a ring on the mast. The end result was that the shark hung from the end of the spinnaker pole out over the water—a safe arm's length from the side of the boat. When hoisted up to where his nose just touched the side deck, his fin extended above Garth's head six feet off the deck. This beast had to be nearly seven feet long.

Garth reached over with the knife in his hands, and ran it expertly down the shark's midsection. I chewed my nails, wondering when the shark would spring back to life. I gave a gasp when Garth reached his hand inside and pulled out its innards. They dropped into the flowing water below. We'd finally regained some of our speed now that we weren't dragging—or being dragged by—this hulking creature. Droplets of red blood trailed the water alongside us. Fresh blood called to sharks for miles, and I wondered whether another shark would be tempted to lunge for the fresh carcass, just barely within reach of the water, pulling spinnaker pole and the rig down with it.

"Shark meat will turn to ammonia if you don't clean it immediately," Garth said, showing no sign of concern.

"Are you crazy?" I asked.

"All right, so this isn't the smartest thing I've ever done. But I've got my lure back," he said with a devilish smile. I tried to imagine getting the lure out of that scary-large mouth full several rows of pointed sharp teeth. I'd let the *expert* handle it.

"What are we going to do with him?" I asked in horror. A ten-pound tuna had once fed us for lunch, dinner, breakfast, lunch, and then dinner again. By the time we'd digested all the meat, I couldn't stomach one more bite. And we *liked* tuna.

"Oh I don't know. We'll give him to the locals."

Easier said than done.

After a half hour, when the drops of blood stopped flowing from the fresh abdominal cut and the shark's impressive jaws, Garth slowly lowered him to the deck and deftly slipped the lure from his mouth. I needed to get the sails down, and we needed to anchor. I gingerly stepped around the unmoving, gutted shark, giving him a wide berth in case he was inclined to do one last shudder near my bare feet.

A friend had called on the VHF to invite us to her boat for dinner.

"You caught a shark?" she'd asked after I told her. "And you didn't just cut the line?"

"Yeah, want to cook it up?" I replied. I had no doubt she'd decline.

"Are you crazy?"

"Perhaps."

As we entered the bay, we saw a line of canoes sailing across the bay. In the last bay we'd visited, locals used sticks and burlap bags to create sprit or traditional (Sunfish style) rigs to sail long distances. Here they propped palms fronds on the bow to make use of the steady trade winds for a downwind run at the end of the day. Just as widely dispersed islands produced diverse languages, which Bislama helped to bridge, it also produced various styles of canoes. Some canoes had been completely dug out of a hardwood log, while others were topped with boards for height to prevent swamping. In more-prosperous areas, some canoes were even painted bright primary colors.

We waved over the first canoe we saw to offer them the shark. Between us, a turtle dipped under the surface. In the canoe was an older—probably married—couple. As they drew alongside, they smiled. I pointed at the shark. The husband's eyes grew big; then he gave me an apprehensive look. The wife shivered in mock fear, then giggled nervously. What I thought might be a generous offer was as much a liability to them as to us. But surely it could feed the entire village.

I pointed to the slit in its belly. The couple looked at each other a long moment. *Oh no, please! You must take it*, I thought, desperate. What would we do with it if they didn't?

Then the husband shrugged and stood up to maneuver this oversized monster into their modest canoe. Garth and I stood at either end—me lunging for the tail-end—and lifted the heavy carcass over the lifelines to their waiting hands. The canoe shifted precariously with the weight transfer. As they lowered it into the narrow canoe, there was nowhere left to sit. The shark was as big as the canoe.

"Hmmm," the man said. He carefully shifted his weight. The canoe skipped nervously. He reached down and grasped the gills to position the powerful mandible of the shark over the canoe's edge. They sat gingerly, nodded, and began to paddle.

The main reason for our visit was to swim with the resident dugong, for which Lamen Bay was famous. Dugongs are odd-looking, large, gray creatures, with a walrus-like head (minus the tusks) attached to the body of a large gray dolphin. Dugongs are most closely related to the manatee, found in Florida, although these species have a tail fin like that of a whale. The locals call them "cow fis" because they act like cows, grazing the better part of the day on tiny underwater sea grass, resurfacing periodically to breathe.

Garth had been skeptical, but the next morning, we swam with the dugong after all. He even let me touch his smooth-yet-bristly skin, which reminded me of Garth's often fuzzy face after days without shaving.

As we pulled into the bay below the towering volcano on Ambrym Island, I was surprised at how much shallower the water was than it looked. I'd gotten used to being able to tell the depth of the water by its color, but the black-sand bottom was misleading. Once anchored, I could see our anchor as though it were three feet from the surface. The narrow black-sand beach was a stark contrast to the blindingly white sand of the beaches we'd been seeing all across the Pacific. Coconut palms loomed overhead and the shore beyond was thick with lush foliage. The shoreline was dotted with the waxy red-based leaves of the bromeliad and the brilliant pink-and-yellow leaves of the croton. These plants had once struck me as exotic, sequestered as they were in the tropical section of my local plant nursery back home. Since then they'd become the new normal.

A copra drying shed stood nearby, its corrugated metal roof scattered with coconut shells that might soon find their way onto a trading vessel and ultimately turned into lotions sold in the fast-paced world back home...a world that now felt a million miles away.

Shortly after we finished anchoring, a lone dugout canoe arrived, steered by two young girls. They giggled shyly before they explained that they were selling finely woven baskets. I recognized the baskets from market stalls in the capital city, where they'd been priced at 1,500 Vatu (about $15). The baskets were made on the island of Ambrym. As I'd hoped, here I had a chance to trade directly with a craftswoman for a stained t-shirt—of which I had a large supply—rather than Vatu—which I didn't.

They explained that they didn't have any more baskets but would be making some to bring the next day and asked what colors I preferred. They pointed to various stripes on multi-colored baskets that were battered with age, and I selected purple and pink stripes, requesting two for gifts. They returned the following day, as promised, with baskets handmade especially for me, for the cost of a t-shirt.

A little later that same afternoon, an older man paddled alongside with a bamboo carved flute to sell. He carefully balanced his wooden paddle on the outrigger and then played his flute for me. The surface of the bamboo stalk was carved into alternating light and dark triangles. He asked for 200 Vatu (about $2), which seemed reasonable, so I readily agreed. Though he spent several minutes showing me how to produce sounds, I can't say I ever quite got the hang of it. Since I had bought the flute for Garth's mother, who had a talent for wind instruments, I figured it didn't matter whether I could play it anyway.

The man stuffed his 200 Vatu into a basket that looked just like the ones I'd ordered and went away happy. That $2 flute ultimately cost $16 to mail home, and though she loved it, my mother-in-law never did figure out how to play the thing.

We'd arrived in Ambrym with dreams of visiting its famous volcano, so we rowed ashore to see if we could arrange a hike to the volcano the following day. We met the soft-spoken Albert, who led us past the most impressively large banyan tree I'd ever seen and up a narrow winding path to Rantletvan. As we reached the village, we met Allan, who explained that we were too late in the season—the volcano was closed to protect the yam crop. Ambrym islanders still believed in black magic, and Allan explained that the volcano god would be displeased to have us walk through the yam fields so late in the season, which would cause the volcano to erupt and jeopardize the crop. We left Ambrym with our hopes crushed.

Months later, we ultimately did get to feel the excitement of standing on the edge of an exploding volcano in Tanna, the southernmost island of Vanuatu. The wind on our backs threatened to blow us into the molten crater that glowed beneath us. With each explosion, the earth shuddered and molten lava the size of a Volkswagen would launch in our direction. I remembered with amusement the comment from the guide friends hired the season before, during a particularly active volcanic period, "You go. I'll stay here. Too dangerous for me." Me? I was thrilled.

A week after we left Ambrym, we heard from other sailors that the fancy charter yacht had pulled in, and, for some reason, its passengers got to see Ambrym's volcano. Later that season, adverse winds blew volcanic ash onto the fields and ruined the yam crop. Maybe there was something in that black magic after all.

PART 3:

THE SEAS LESS TRAVELED:

ONLY THE LONELY

MELTDOWN IN THE SOLOMON ISLANDS

I noticed the numbers flash intermittently, then parts of numbers. I bit my lip. "The depth sounder is acting weird," I called to Garth.

He had just finished hauling up the anchor, and we were heading through a narrow reef pass.

"Yeah, so what else is new?" Never one to panic, he added, "Let's get through this pass; then we can take a look."

I brought my focus back to navigating through the second dogleg in the reef. I retraced the previous day's route in reverse; only this time, I didn't have to rehoist the sails in the middle of the hairy section.

Garth rinsed mud from the anchor off the deck with buckets of saltwater, working his way back to where I stood.

"Now it's gone blank," I said and cocked my head towards the featureless screen. When he arrived in the cockpit, I handed him the tiller. "I want to investigate,"

He nodded. By then, we were in the open waters off the island of Vella Lavella. The hot, sticky air was broken only by the breeze from our forward momentum.

As I ducked below, I peeled my oversized oxford shirt away from the heat rash on my chest that had plagued me since we'd arrived in the Solomons. I flipped the power switch for the depth sounder off and on. Nothing. We'd only just repaired the depth sounder in New Zealand a few months earlier.

I turned on the radios. Nothing.

Slowly, I went through all the switches to see if anything worked. Click…nothing. Click…nothing. Click…nothing.

Otherwise, everything looked normal. *Hmmm.*

"What have you found?" Garth asked.

No. It couldn't be. *Not again.* My thoughts raced to the last time something like this had happened: in French Polynesia, when the wire on the back of the battery switch fell off. (Yes, just fell off. Corrosion will do that, I've noticed.) Since there was no way for current from the engine to flow into the batteries, instead, it had flowed into everything else that was connected. Electronics don't like that kind of thing. The spike in voltage had fried our alternator. No alternator meant that we had no way to turn power from our motor into the electricity we needed for lights and radios.

Worst of all, in French Polynesia, we had lost our brand-new VHF radio, for which we had paid $150 and used for Two. Whole. Months. If you counted the impromptu "book club of the air" we had held with the *Queen Jane* at the equator, you could say that we had enjoyed just two or three *very* expensive conversations on that radio. While sailing 2,800 miles between Mexico and French Polynesia, there had been no one close enough to talk to. But before we'd even had time to grit our teeth about the wasted money, fellow sailors had loaned us a spare alternator and VHF radio, which allowed us to reach New Zealand.

In New Zealand, we'd bought replacements, but it was these very replacements (and more) that I couldn't get to work just now. Garth, ever "Mr. Fidget," brought me back to the present by snapping his toes—a talent that no else I know shares.

"Well?" he asked.

"Nothing's coming on," I replied, my voice low and hollow. I slowly raised my face to look at him.

"You're kidding!" he said, his voice rising an octave.

I shook my head. "I wish I were," I said, in a monotone. Our eyes locked as we realized how big a problem this could be.

After passing the tiller back to me, Garth rushed down to look for himself.

The "Oh, shit!" that soon followed confirmed my suspicions.

"How could this happen again?" he muttered. A few seconds later, he answered his own question, "The blasted master switch is sitting cockeyed. I probably knocked it when I was working on the engine last night."

"Maybe I knocked it when I cleaned the splattered oil afterward,"

"How it happened doesn't really matter," he said softly. He was right. It didn't change our predicament. We still had no navigational equipment.

Our engine had been regularly giving us trouble since we'd left New Zealand. Sometimes it would overheat and sometimes it would just quit. The day before, between the first and second dogleg in the reef pass, the engine had sputtered and quit suddenly. I'd been pointing out coral heads while Garth steered to my advice.

Then I'd heard the sudden silence.

"The engine died," he said.

I nodded and quickly hoisted the mainsail to keep our momentum and avoid getting blown sideways into the reef. We'd become adept at this kind of thing by now. Fortunately the wind had been behind us, and we had coasted easily into the bay while I resumed my vigil, watching for coral.

Once we'd anchored, Garth had sighed and pulled apart the engine, again. And that had left us with no time to explore, which had been the point of our visit in the first place. Today we were returning to Gizo to meet up with fellow cruisers for Thanksgiving.

Garth's eyes darted back and forth as he considered our present situation. He perpetually surprised me with his creative-yet-simple solutions to the most perplexing of problems. I waited expectantly.

Suddenly the energy drained from his body. "Ouch," he sighed with a heavy finality, slumping into a pose that resembled Rodin's *Thinker.*

In our previous electrical meltdown, we'd only lost a couple of things. This time, in addition to the depth sounder, we'd lost the speedometer, two marine radios, one of our two GPS navigation units, and even the stereo. Basically everything. We no longer had navigation lights, which meant we would be invisible to passing ships at night. All told, we had lost about $10,000 of equipment in less than ten minutes. Money we surely didn't have.

How could this have happened to us not just once, but *twice?* Mr.-Practical-Worst-Case-Scenario had even relocated the master switch so that it *couldn't* happen again—or so he had thought. I had expressed reservations about the new location and the quality of the cheap switch we'd found in New Zealand, but since he wasn't concerned, I wondered why I should be. Now it was obvious just how vulnerable the switch was. I felt like a fool. I longed for an *undo* command to take back the mistake, like I could on my laptop.

Stunned, we said little as we motored back to Gizo, where we had arranged to celebrate our voyage's fourth Thanksgiving at PT 109, a dive bar named for John F. Kennedy's sunken World War II boat, with the few other sailors in the region—though most of them weren't even Americans.

I wasn't feeling very thankful or celebratory just then.

We were able to navigate through the nearly invisible reefs and poor channel markers because we had just done it a few days earlier. Normally when anchoring I'd just look at the depth sounder to gauge the depth. This time, we used the Braille method—poking along slowly while Garth periodically threw a line with a lead pendant until it was taut and then calculating the water depth using the length of Garth's arm span—about six feet—as he pulled it in. Simple and effective…but tedious.

Anchoring wasn't as easy as it had been only the day before in Vella Lavella. The words from Dinah Washington's hit, "What a Difference a Day Makes," tumbled through my head, albeit with notably less enthusiasm than Dinah had sung them. I sighed, remembering that my memory was all that remained of our music collection.

Garth noted the irony that our boat, *Velella*, had found her undoing in Vella Lavella, a place we'd thought would be fun to visit just because of the name.

I thought of our last few disappointing days in Vella Lavella. We'd been excited to see the volcano. What we'd found after a long hike through a steamy rainforest at the head of a muddy river was a moonscape with steam vents of molten gray mud. Periodically, our sullen guide would yank me away from stepping on a newly formed vent. More than once, I'd felt hot vapor blasting past my skin as I'd struggled to keep my balance. Our day's highlight had been spotting two rare megapode eggs incubating alongside steam vents.

Perhaps it had been the smoldering temperatures. Or the omnipresent heaviness that lay in the wake of an inter-tribal civil war, which had ended only four months earlier (July 2003), and had left the economy in shambles.

Most likely, it was the feeling of being perpetually watched that had soured my attitude. The appearance of our boat in that out-of-the-way bay in Vella Lavella had caused quite a stir. Villagers had rushed their dugout canoes out to see us. But unlike smiling locals we'd encountered in every other country, most faces here wore a wary, haunted look. Was it shell shock? They watched us silently from a distance, which left me feeling anxious. Whenever one got tired, there was always another villager to replace him. After the first uncomfortable hour, we got tired, too, but there was no relief for us. *We* were the entertainment. I wished that our boat wasn't so small or so easy to see inside. In this unbearable heat, every stitch of clothing was one stitch too many. I longed to go naked so the heat rash on my body could finally dry out and heal. In this oppressive jungle heat, it wasn't hard to imagine soldiers during World War II dying of dysentery or skin infections without ever firing a shot.

In the middle of the night often in the Solomons, I'd awaken with an uneasy feeling. Outside in the cockpit, I'd discover someone paddling almost silently in the near distance. I found it incredibly creepy in the moonless darkness. I'd been perpetually on edge since we'd arrived in this country. The constant surveillance by unfriendly locals was unnerving.

Now that we were safely anchored in Gizo, Garth and I stared into space. A twelve-year-old boy paddled over in a dugout canoe so thin that he looked as if he were wearing it. The pale pink palms of his hands and bottom of his feet stood in sharp contrast to his midnight dark complexion.

"You are rich. You need souvenirs," he said. I didn't feel very rich just then, and the last thing we needed was a trinket on our tiny, overstuffed boat. I certainly wasn't in the mood to haggle over the price of a Noosa-Noosa. We shook our heads, hoping he'd realize "No" meant *no* and go away quickly.

I wasn't myself. In fact we were both cranky. The heat was smothering. Every time I touched Garth, his look broadcast at 1,000 decibels, *don't bother me.*

Oppressive low clouds, violent daily thunderstorms and rain squalls, suffocating heat, and crumbling polluted villages sapped our energy. Stagnant air left us without wind to sail, forcing us to motor—*If* we could. And the engine, only inches from where we slept (or tried to sleep), took hours to cool, if it ever did, leaving us lying in a puddle of sweat. Swimming offered no relief: Heavy coral bloom made the warm water look like egg-drop soup—inhabited by crocodiles.

We only had to pass three months in the Solomons until the weather would be safe to head north. Typhoon season hadn't quite ended in the northern hemisphere and was just beginning in the southern hemisphere. During the transition, the safest place to be, unless we were well outside the tropics, was in the vicinity of the equator. We'd been here only half that time, but already it felt like forever.

"When my family sailed around the world, we didn't have most of these things…" Garth tried feebly after a few minutes.

"Yeah, I know," I replied, appreciating his effort. "But that was before they had been invented," I ribbed him gently.

Our decision to take the little-sailed route northwards had brought us here, our first country off the beaten path, but we'd run into nothing but trials since we'd left our community of sailing friends in Vanuatu. We were lonely and frustrated.

And now this. Our choice had come at great cost. Would this prove the demise of our cruising life? No navigation lights, only a primitive way to guesstimate depths, and a spare handheld GPS to figure out where we were. No way to communicate with the outside world.

And no money or resources to fix it.

As it started to rain again, I wondered, *what are we going to do?*

CHAPTER
13

KWAJALEIN: U.S. TAX DOLLARS NOT AT WORK

The prospect of *working* for the *US Army*—the antithesis of the freewheeling lifestyle we'd been leading—sent shivers down my spine, but we were desperate. We needed a place to fix our broken equipment, and there weren't many options near the Solomon Islands. Replacing so many expensive items wouldn't be cheap, and a little income would do wonders for our depleted bank account, though we weren't sure whether we could get jobs.

Regardless, the lure of access to cheap American products that we hadn't seen in the past four years and the opportunity to get mail easily through the U.S. postal system encouraged us to sail for Kwajalein in the Marshall Islands, the site of a U.S. Army base. Fellow cruisers who had just visited had described it as a paradise that didn't include military jeeps or ugly camouflage outfits. We'd been skeptical until we'd realized they were talking about the same place where a couple we'd met in Fiji had told us they were sailing to find work.

"That's nice…Good luck," we'd replied distractedly when they told us their plans, never suspecting we'd be desperate to join them there less than a year later.

Kwajalein, the largest atoll in the world, is located in the middle of the Pacific, 2,400 miles from Honolulu and nearly 2,600 miles from Japan. A former volcano, ringed with coral, the island sits only a few feet above the ocean waves. For centuries, it was sprinkled only with a few palm trees and huts—until its strategic location qualified it as an ideal location for a World War II military base. In other words, it was a sand-spit in the middle of nowhere that only had value because someone decided it did. The land mass varied little from any other sand-covered, palm-lined thin stretch of rock we'd seen for the last few years, but for expatriate Americans with few options like us, it had a magnetic pull like neon lights to a gambler in the middle of the Vegas desert. Because we'd been away for years, this slice of Americana called to us like a siren, and we fantasized about Oreos and Fritos, "food" that we'd never held in much esteem when it had been readily available.

We left the Solomons in January 2004, armed with two handheld GPS units and a makeshift depth sounder (a borrowed sensor unit strapped to a wooden broom handle that deployed through a PVC pipe tied to *Velella*'s transom). We pointed northeastwards towards Kiribati, though we doubted we could actually get there in what were normally adverse winds. Howling westerlies from a typhoon to the south gave us an unusual push that helped us reach Kiribati in record time. A half hour after we arrived, the wind changed direction.

From Kiribati, Kwajalein was an easy 400-mile sail. Once we were sure that we could make it there, we contacted Bob and Robin, the cruisers who'd gone there to work, and they agreed to sponsor us. Without a sponsor, we would not be allowed to visit—or even stop there, unless we claimed an emergency. Their sponsorship would make them completely responsible for us during our stay, though they barely knew us. Once again the generosity of cruising fraternity impressed me. They assumed we'd pass the required background check and told us to arrive in Kwajalein three weeks later. (We later learned just how careful these background investigations actually were after a friend realized that she'd accidently transposed her Social Security number, and no one had noticed for over a year.)

We expected an easy sail to Kwajalein, but soon faced high winds and big seas. The aging stitches in the awning that protected us from relentless sun let go like a slow-motion dynamite fuse each time the fabric billowed in the breeze. I wondered if it'd still be in one piece by the time we arrived. Waves broke over the boat, perpetually soaking us and surprising us with their power. One wave punched out a dodger window, leaving a gaping hole with a vinyl square flapping in the breeze. Salt spray swirled in the wind, infiltrating everything with a pervasive, gritty dampness. Whenever I went below to double check our position on the chart, I was afraid a gush of saltwater would flood the cabin. Both of our floating harnesses inflated and then popped, leaving us without backups as we slogged the remaining distance between Kiribati and Kwajalein. I felt vulnerable and was anxious for an end to my misery.

Sure that we'd be spotted on radar the instant we came within fifty miles of the atoll, particularly in the post-9/11 era, we were surprised to find a deserted reef pass. Waves crashed against the outside shores with a fury of foam and spray. We threaded our way through the maelstrom into the protected waters inside. Ripples on the water shimmered aquamarine in the late-afternoon light.

Seeing nothing but a sandy beach and a couple of palm trees, we decided to have a quick bath before facing the bureaucracy of checking in. I didn't think our matted hair and smelly clothes and bodies would make the best impression. With no sign of activity and darkness falling, we cooked and ate a pot of spaghetti, and then fell into bed, exhausted. We relished a full night's sleep—together—though we half expected to awaken in the night to spotlights and guns.

In the morning, we continued south in gusty winds and chop to the main island five miles away. We'd been inside a military base for nearly fourteen hours, yet we still hadn't seen anyone. Gradually, huge radar domes and non-descript, boxy buildings, surrounded by a sprinkling of palm trees, appeared on the horizon. Large gray ships flying the Stars and Stripes signaled that we had arrived. Moored pleasure boats tossed on their mooring lines, and even full-keel sailboats rolled heavily in the confused waves.

"I'm not too excited about mooring my boat in this crap," Garth said.

"Yeah!" I nodded. I pointed out a break in the pier. "There's the end of the breakwater. Hopefully we can stay inside after we check in."

Uniformed men in a robust inflatable met us and escorted us in to a dock. As we tied up, they requested we step off the boat. Suddenly, we were surrounded by heavily armed cops. Bomb and drug-sniffing dogs clambered aboard unsteadily, toenails clicking unevenly as they tried to navigate the rocking boat. They lurched down our narrow varnished wooden ladder into the interior, led by gun-toting police handlers in buzz cuts and black street shoes. I wondered what the dogs would make of the mixture of sweat, spoiled food, and the ripening pile of saltwater-drenched clothing. If one of the dogs concluded something was amiss—though I couldn't guess what—and sat down, we were in trouble. In our dilapidated Teva sandals, stained t-shirts, frayed shorts, and damaged boat, we looked like the kind of riff-raff the Army would want to keep out—or seize.

We fidgeted on the dock, awaiting the dogs' verdict.

"Kind of rough out there, ain't it?" drawled the fit one, who looked like he was in charge. "We've had small-craft warnings for days now."

"I'm not surprised," Garth said.

"I'm Mike," The man offered his hand.

We introduced ourselves and shook hands, relaxing a little. A few other men, looking like campus police in shorts and baseball caps, stood at attention a ways off. This odd mix of official and casual was our first glimpse at the incongruity of this place.

Evidently we had passed inspection; the dogs reappeared, and the police didn't escort us away in handcuffs. Instead, they led us up the dock, as our friends Bob and Robin appeared.

"Welcome to Kwaj," Bob said, as we came closer.

Robin's auburn hair glistened in the sunshine.

"I was afraid we wouldn't be able to stay" I said with relief.

"We were starting to worry about you," Robin said, in her low Louisiana drawl.

"Really?" I said as we made our way inside a sterile concrete building where a number of overfed rent-a-cops stood around an official-looking desk. A few others were hassling a number of mocha-colored women, who were about as big around as they were tall—even in their platform flip-flops. Their portly bodies filled dark, polyester, shapeless dresses. Their faces wore expressions of boredom. Seeing the Marshallese reminded me that we weren't actually in the U.S., despite the abundance of American flags and Southern accents.

Bob, Garth, and I sat down and filled each other in on our travels since we had last crossed paths in Fiji, while Robin went to check on the badges that allowed us entry onto the rest of the island.

"I never thought I'd find myself looking for work with the U.S. Army," Garth shuddered, bristling at the thought of anything regimented that was not of his own making. His experience working for a Navy contractor early in his career had been more than enough to know that it wasn't for him. And while I may have grown up a Navy brat, since we often had the luxury of living off base, I'd had limited exposure to its more bureaucratic aspects. After the freedom we'd tasted voyaging, it'd surely be a shock for both of us.

Bob was wearing ripped jeans and beat up shoes. As Bob pushed his long hair out of his eyes, Garth added "We figured if you guys could hack it, we ought to be able to."

"Yeah, well it's easy money," Bob said "and by the time we got here, we were down to fifty dollars." He gave a casual shrug, though his wiry intensity was visible beneath the surface. "I'm working as a carpenter, and Robin's on the evening shift as harbor control. It's a living," he added unenthusiastically.

Finally Robin returned with our visitor badges, which meant we could pass through the chain link fence into "America."

As we rode past several non-descript buildings painted beige and brown Bob pointed saying "That's GSK, and there's FOM, where I know there are some open jobs." I began to wonder how I'd keep track of *where* everything was once I figured out *what* it was.

About a minute and a half later, we pulled up to a large building lined with windows. Out front were bike racks filled with myriad shapes and sizes of highly individualized bikes as rusty as the ones we rode.

"Well, that's about it." Robin laughed. "You've already seen most everything. This is the PDR." When I stared at her blankly, Robin clarified "the dining hall."

"Oh," Garth and I said simultaneously. We dismounted our bikes and stowed them in a couple of open slots and headed inside.

Bob added, "Of course, some people call it Café Pacific, but it sure ain't no café." During the lengthy check in, we had missed lunch, and were starving. We were surprised to find the place packed for dinner at 4:30 in the afternoon.

After months of struggling to make stir-fry without fresh vegetables or meat, we were easily impressed by the selection. We stared as if we'd just been released from a prison camp, failing to notice that nearly everything was fried or laden with fat. Every low-quality, cholesterol-infiltrated dish imaginable was on the menu—from chicken adobo and beef brisket to liver and onions, chili corn dogs and commercial-grade cole slaw—all in massive quantities. We heaped enormous portions on our plates just like the supersized folks who waddled in with us. When my eyes caught sight of the salad bar I nearly fainted. After coming from Kiribati, where "fresh vegetables" referred to a moldy cabbage or limp carrot, we furtively loaded a second plate like addicts in the presence of controlled substances.

We sat down at a long rectangular table unremarkable from any other in the large hall.

"This is the 'Yachtie' table," Bob said. "Everyone sitting here is either a sailor or works around the water. That's the teachers' table, the IT table, and the Hawaiian table." Bob pointed out. We nodded while we shoveled food into our mouths. The hall was filled with people who made the Michelin Man look like a Weight Watchers' success story sitting behind plates more over laden than ours.

Through the window, I watched a 300-pound man climb onto a bicycle, overflowing the seat as if he were sitting on a metal rod.

Though I'd made myself ill, I couldn't resist slurping the last of my root beer float.

By the time we left the dining hall, we had arranged to borrow a sewing machine to re-stitch our awning and dodger windows, had gotten access to the yacht club's wholesale account to replace our broken equipment, had obtained a list of job leads, and had been invited to a full schedule of social activities beginning with a yacht club happy hour the following evening. I could hardly wipe the smile off my face.

Despite its being a U.S. Army base, few people actually wore Army green. A tiny tropical community of American civilians tended by a cadre of Marshallese manual laborers gave Kwaj the feel of a country club, complete with a yacht club, golf course, and marina with rentable motor and sail boats. We could play a game of pool, ping-pong, or foosball in the game room, or get on the Internet for free. Two saltwater pools looked out over a palm-lined beach, and tennis courts stood empty nearby. Softball, volleyball, and basketball games brought cheers and onlookers in the afternoons. Since we'd hardly seen a movie in years, we were excited to learn that there were free outdoor movies in two locations, one of which was where Bob Hope had entertained wartime troops over fifty

years earlier. A dive club offered unlimited access to World War II
wrecks and pristine coral. A hobby shop offered tools and space for
woodworking, art, and pottery projects.

Sudden immersion in American accents and flags after so little
exposure for so long repeatedly gave us a start. As we made our
way on our rusty bicycles around the island of only 1,100 people,
inhabitants waved warmly. We discovered that no matter how far we
rode, we were never more than three miles from where we started.
We occasionally came across a golf cart—allowed everywhere *but*
the golf course—or a pickup truck along the road. A conversation
in the middle of an intersection could last twenty-minutes without
being interrupted. We could dial four numbers to call anyone on
island for free. Intimate schools and fire and police departments
reminded me of the fictional TV town of Mayberry. Most residents
expressed disappointment in the grocery, liquor, and department
stores, but for Garth and me, who had been shopping for four
years in stores that mostly featured competing brands of spam-like
substance, canned mackerel, and imitation Velveeta, the choices
were overwhelming. The tiny library, complete with written catalog
cards, took me back to a bygone era. Only the recent magazines and
newspapers from several U.S. cities hinted of modern times. I was
smitten, and even Garth was pleasantly surprised.

Given our situation, Kwajalein seemed well-suited for fixing
our boat, and our employment prospects looked promising. At the
yacht club happy hour, I was nearly hired on the spot for a new job
developing the company's internal website, while Garth seemed to
have his pick of several open engineering positions. With nearly
sixty days left on our visitor passes, we thought we had plenty of
time to complete the hiring process.

While the clock was ticking, we wrestled with a temperamental
sewing machine to repair our failing awning and dodger. We mail-
ordered new radios, spare oil filters, and fan belts. Laundry that
once took the better part of a day, now took a couple of hours in a
machine while I read a book. That left more time for BBQs, happy

hours, movies, ping-pong sessions, and other spontaneous social encounters. I could hardly have been happier.

After two weeks, the marina manager was pressured to move us from the dock out to the rolly anchorage. Then Garth got a temporary job updating building drawings for a private subcontractor. We were glad to have the infusion of cash to slow the hemorrhaging of our bank account while we replaced our broken equipment. Every night, the boat rolled heavily while we tried to sleep, and every morning, I rowed Garth in before dawn. After not working at all for four years, suddenly Garth was working six days a week on a few hours of sleep. And each morning, Garth splashed through waves on the way into shore and then shivered for the next ten hours in icy air conditioning.

"What have I gotten myself into?" he muttered one morning as I rowed him to shore.

One afternoon as I prepared dinner, I picked up a pepper and noticed a few holes. I naively imagined a cute little bird flying through the open hatch for a nibble, but when I mentioned it to Garth, he immediately said, "Oh, no! We've got a rat on board."

When I balked, he asked, "Didn't you see those huge rats scurrying around the garbage at the marina? One must have gotten aboard when we were tied up."

I thought of the uncollected garbage that overflowed the garbage cans while the marina manager surfed the Internet at dial-up speed. I finally believed Garth when I saw torn bits of plastic food packaging and those telltale little brown bullets.

We spent weeks trying to catch that damn rat. First we set a mouse trap with cheese. Each morning the trap sat unsprung, the cheese unmolested. Then we tried peanut butter.

Then one night, "thwack!"

Out of a sound sleep, I was immediately airborne when the trap sprang, a foot from our heads. I got up and shined a flashlight at the sprung trap where an ugly furry body lay. I did a little victory dance and went back to bed.

In the morning, there was no sign of the rat.

Bob and Robin suggested we visit Pest Control for a bigger trap. When Garth explained that he needed a rat trap, the Marshallese man said, "I set the trap for you, no problem. What house you live in?"

When Garth asked if he would set the trap on our boat, the man immediately handed over a trap and wished him luck. "Here coconut. You make fire under it and it smell very sweet. The rat, they like. They come. Smack!" he said as he clapped his hands together, nodded at the trap, and gave a toothy grin.

And so it was the next morning, just like the man said...except the sprung trap had no body in it, and the coconut was missing.

A few days later, Garth laid his hands on another piece of coconut, drilled a hole in it, and securely wired it onto the trap. "There's no way that rat's getting anymore freebies," his mouth stretched into a crooked grin.

Finally the trap sprung while the rat was still in it, probably trying to figure out why that coconut was so damn hard to get. Not taking any chances, Garth chucked the rat and trap over the side.

The time on our visitor badges dwindled down to days, and still we had no contract jobs. Each day we visited the Human Resources office. No contracts materialized, and no one seemed concerned. Yet on Kwaj, once visitors have been on-island for sixty days, they're required to leave and are not allowed to return for a year. We were rapidly approaching our sixty-day limit without any sign of the jobs we thought we'd secured. We weren't in a position to fly home at a cost of $3,000 and wait until someone got around to issuing a contract. The bored faces each day in the Human Resources office clearly indicated that they didn't care whether we got hired or not.

Frustrated, we prepared to leave, and I began restocking groceries. At least we had new radios and a newly stitched awning and dodger. We made a last visit to Human Resources. Garth was about to tell them to forget it. The HR manager's demeanor softened and she produced a contract for Garth. Yet, even if Garth had a contract, I would not be allowed to stay unless I got a contract also. And we had no intention of living apart while I sailed solo or flew home so Garth could work a job that wasn't even in his field.

We continued preparing to leave. Another visit to HR revealed that my contract had been jeopardized by a lost label on my urine sample. I imagined an unmarked bottle of urine cast aside—and, along with it, my job prospects. Finally after a few calls, the head of the IT division took the risk of hiring me to develop the company's internal web site, though I hadn't passed a drug test.

With our year-long contracts came two furnished dormitory rooms, generously described in our contracts as a "studio apartment." Yet, compared to our thirty-one-foot boat, we were tripling our living space. We had a choice room, with another one just across the hall. Since Garth and I still liked each other, we decided to share one room and use the other for storage. We brought *Velella* into the dock and moved our belongings off the boat, bicycle load by bicycle load. We had ambitious plans for a complete boat refit while we didn't have to live in the middle of it.

We started our new jobs, our world now reduced from open seas to a two-block radius. On my third day in cubicle-land, I opened an email from the HR manager in Huntsville that inquired whether I had received the job offer she mailed to my mother's house and whether I wanted the job. (*Um, I started working last Friday…*) I tackled my job with my usual zeal, working extra hours to learn how things were set up and understand the needs the website would be designed to meet. Bob, Robin, and even Garth marveled at my naïveté. Even my colleagues chided me about my industriousness. I slowly realized what was really expected of me: show up every day, reply periodically to office emails, and fill out my timecard. If I wanted to surf the Internet, fine.

But even if my colleagues considered the work optional, I took it on as a personal crusade, reasoning that the new website would improve life on island and the process of building it would polish my rusty web-design skills in my own personal government-retraining program.

Unfortunately, the U.S. Army doesn't have much need for naval architecture, so Garth figured using his skills as a mechanical engineer for buildings might be more satisfying than sorting packages at the post office. Maintaining systems in a harsh environment without materials or replacement parts was a talent that Garth had perfected. He was used to devising creative solutions out of necessity. Unfortunately, his colleagues weren't. Garth soon discovered that parts he'd ordered to provide solutions were unlikely to arrive before his employment contract expired. So he came up with unconventional ideas only to discover that his colleagues preferred to leave things in a state of disrepair rather than risk an unproven approach. Trying to fix broken air conditioning and kitchen venting instead of designing ships frustrated Garth's active mind, and he complained bitterly. Despite how unhappy he was at work, I was remarkably content.

Like *The Truman Show*, Kwajalein is isolated from the real world in a way that gives it a two-dimensional feel. A company town under the protective wing of the U.S. Army, the Kwaj community felt like a friendly small town with the undertones of a military dictatorship. Island politics reflected the personalities of the current Colonel and the senior management of the contracting companies. Real problems were eclipsed by pet projects. Yet the transient nature and interdependence of this tiny community meant commands were subject to interpretation. When the colonel-in-charge requested that a PA system broadcast bugle calls to remind everyone of Kwaj's military status, the system was perpetually broken because everyone tasked with making it happen hated the idea.

In true military style, rules were designed for nineteen year old soldiers lacking common sense. From the condescending public service announcements on TV, one might conclude that the military hired only morons. Then again, some of what I saw on island with my own eyes suggested common sense wasn't as common as I'd assumed. (Two males playing hide the salami at the kids' pool and a woman throwing a chair through her plate-glass front window after locking herself out spring to mind.) And, of course, the enforcement of rules was inversely related to how well-liked the violators were and their status on the island. A severe violation by someone of lower stature got him a seat on the next plane out, much like an unpopular contestant on *Survivor* voted off the island. One man came to work drunk and found himself sobering up on the afternoon plane back to the U.S., his belongings to follow by barge a month later. When the head of a large department was caught screwing his secretary on the family beach, she was on the next morning's flight, while he stayed for another year. Those who lived in dorm-style housing like us had their quarters inspected monthly for fire hazards and unauthorized cooking appliances. (Imagine, people might actually get tired of eating fried food in the dining hall and wish to cook a meal in a toaster oven or grill a steak on a George Foreman Grill. Nope. Not allowed.) Kwajalein was not a democracy, and contractors who didn't like it could leave, albeit with far more upheaval in their personal lives than quitting your average job. Every few days, new arrivals disembarked from the plane to replace those who'd left.

As we settled in, more of Kwajalein's oddities became evident:

- Due to regulations, after sailing 17,000 miles to get there, Garth and I each had to take a $25 class, two written tests, and three practical ones—to sail our *own* sailboat.
- When the need arose for a naval architect, project managers wouldn't consult Garth because, even though he was a certified Naval architect, he had been hired as a mechanical engineer.
- Every building was cooled to about forty degrees to mask a growing mold problem. When the air conditioning broke down, it didn't take long for the already fetid air to turn truly vile. (Incense and candles were prohibited, of course.) While the rest of us shivered and looked for any excuse to

go outside to warm up, the Marshallese showed up for work in parkas.

- The only private dining facility on the island, a dismal place aptly named the Yuk Club, was in constant use as a bar and for special events. After years during which chunks of concrete fell into the food prep area, the Health Department finally condemned the building, to heavy protests.

- Kwaj bicycles were highly individualized to reflect the personalities of their riders. Baskets, handlebar, and body modifications were combined with flower leis, toy bells, glitter, and flags, the likes of which I hadn't seen since elementary school.

- In a small community, you run into professional colleagues in all sorts of situations and—in the tropical heat—all states of undress. Some things you just don't want to know about the head of your department.

Ostensibly, the Army base was there to test intercontinental ballistic missiles—with Kwaj as the target. Yet if anything sophisticated went on there, I sure didn't know about it. Secret clearance must have been effective, because everyone had me convinced that we were all there for the diving and the cheap beer.

I hardly missed an event that I knew about. Alone or with company, I attended every high school choir and band concert. I learned to make stained glass, joined the community choir, went to the beach every day after work, and arranged ping-pong games, delighted with so many new free things to do.

I could hardly wait to explore the World War II ships and planes that met their ends at Kwajalein. After a nurse certified Garth and me in our own private SCUBA class, I searched for equipment so we could dive without borrowing. I found a small inflatable dive vest for $5 at the thrift shop. It almost fit, except that my tank hung cockeyed because my vest shifted whenever I moved around underwater. I was on a mission to leverage the cost of my certification and SCUBA-club membership any chance I could. Renting a boat for the entire morning and free air for two dives on World War II wrecks and untouched coral cost $13, a small fraction of what I'd pay anywhere else.

Garth found the pace of the social scene overwhelming, yet he was bored and frustrated with his job. Garth and Bob shared a lot in common. Both were achievers who were totally unchallenged on Kwaj and missed the tests that voyaging continually offered. While Garth saw his creative solutions go unheeded, Bob saw his fine wood crafting skills go to waste as he repaired rotting church pews and built picture frames for senior management to decorate their offices.

In the dining hall, the men commiserated daily, joking that they were just there to collect back the taxes that they'd paid the IRS over the years. Meanwhile they cringed as they watch their beloved boats roll and occasionally leap out of the water when the trade winds piped up. They grew anxious about the time they were wasting while their boats needed complete refitting. Before Garth and Bob could repair their boats, they needed a way to get them out of the water, but hauling a keelboat in Kwaj was a convoluted and expensive process that involved renting a decrepit crane and hiring a multitude of workers to stand around. It was not unusual to ring up a bill of $5,000 for the service while worrying about the boat getting wrecked in the process. And the crane had been broken for months. They watched enviously as others used the boat ramp, easily yanking their little runabouts out of the water after a day trip. The problem was that our boats were much bigger and deeper.

They couldn't buy or borrow anything to handle the job. Since Garth and Bob shared the same problem, it made sense to build a solution that would work for both of them and others in the same situation. They started measuring sailboats and gauging the depth of the water at the bottom of the ramp at all tides. They needed to find a way to build a trailer that fit vastly different boats, could be unloaded on land, and could be built from parts they could scrounge on an island atoll in the middle of the Pacific Ocean. That wouldn't be easy.

Despite common goals and motivations, Bob and Garth were opposites in many ways. This actually made them a great team for solving the problem. Bob was wiry and wily, while Garth was lumbering and deliberate. Bob had a knack for making connections and calling in favors, whereas Garth hesitated to ask anyone for anything.

They discussed what they might need to create such a mammoth trailer. Ordering parts was out of the question, so Bob scouted the island for materials they could use while Garth used his naval architecture skills to create a design. Garth came up with a list of what he needed; Bob came up with a list of what he could get. When the lists didn't match, Garth redesigned the trailer, and Bob went searching again and again and again. Dining hall discussions went something like,

"Bob, can you get me twenty feet of three-inch steel pipe?"

"I can't get three-inch, but I know they've got fifty feet of two-inch over at the metal shop, and the guy in charge would probably give it to me for a couple of tuna."

So Garth would redesign the trailer to use two-inch pipe. Together they scoured the junkyard and under bushes and took apart defunct machinery and old vehicles for parts. They even salvaged rusty wheel axles that had sunk a year before in an accident off the pier. Bob was astute at figuring out whether a carton of cigarettes, fresh tuna, or a six-pack of beer in the right hands might help to get parts or hunks of steel moved. They secured the help of a skilled welder who was wasting his talents repairing heavy equipment— like the crane—that should have long since been retired and was hungry for something more interesting.

After months of scrounging, they'd assembled the ingredients for a design that Garth thought could handle the job of hauling out all sorts of sailboats. They were finally ready to "begin" the project.

On the first day of building, Garth and Bob bicycled past the runway that covered most of the island to the welder's shop, where they'd consolidated parts. In an open field with not a breath of air, wearing long pants in 87-degree humid heat, Garth and Bob set about learning to use a torch to cut sheets of steel that were too heavy to move. Within two minutes of picking up a cutting torch, Garth saw flames leaping back towards his hand from a gas leak in the torch tip.

They had only just begun, and Garth was already bicycling to the hospital to get treatment for second-degree burns. Bob was as relieved as Garth and I were that he healed within two weeks.

Garth and Bob quickly learned how taxing steel cutting would be on their backs as they hunched over a huge sheet of sizzling hot steel, trying not to touch it.

Since most parts were salvaged from scrap, the financial investment to build the trailer was small. However, the labor to turn a rusty pile of useless junk into a sturdy vehicle that supported a keelboat that might weigh as little as 8,000 pounds or as much as 32,000 pounds was incalculable. The time invested in gathering parts, measuring, and designing (and redesigning), totaled about eight months. The back-breaking labor to build it took six sweaty months. Every evening after work, they'd grab a quick bite, and then head down to work until dark. Each weekend, they worked from sunup to sundown, just barely making it into the dining hall before it closed at 7:00 p.m. Meanwhile, I kept busy with the vast number of activities and socializing that Garth, even when not working, was too exhausted to appreciate.

Slowly this mammoth beast took shape, and the decisive moment arrived. Could it safely haul keelboats? To test its load bearing capacity before risking their precious sailboats, Garth and Bob hired a smaller crane to load 32,000 pounds of concrete blocks onto the trailer and then hauled that massive weight up and down the boat ramp. The trailer groaned under the pile of weights, but the test went off without a problem. Or so they thought. They planned to haul out Bob's boat, *Misty Dawn*, a 27,000-pound full-keel Block Island 40, the following weekend, when the tides were favorable.

As they adjusted the trailer to fit its first candidate, they discovered that they'd bent the frame during the load test. One pitfall of having the designer also provide the manual labor is that his laziness encouraged him to forego building one set of the reinforcements he had designed—bad idea. So, the day before the haul-out Garth and Bob spent a day straightening the trailer with a sledgehammer and a hydraulic press, then welding on the very reinforcement pieces that could have saved them the heartache in the first place. They were exhausted, and they hadn't even hauled the first boat yet.

The next day, *Misty Dawn* came out of the water smoothly with the help of a front-end loader and lots of friends. The trailer worked. Garth and Bob spent the next several days getting *Misty Dawn* off the trailer by painstakingly removing one frame at a time as soon as a support was there to take the weight in its place.

Our little *Velella* was next. Garth was so proud of his accomplishment that he wanted to drive the boat and the trailer all over the island to show that he knew how to get things done.

No need—news traveled fast on Kwaj. When his boss commented on the success of his project, Garth replied "Yeah, it's the only thing I've actually accomplished on Kwaj." They shared a laugh.

Before the week was out, Bob cleverly arranged to sell the trailer they'd begged, borrowed, and stolen to create to two friends for $10,000 with the condition that both *Misty Dawn* and *Velella* would be returned to the water for free. The trailer provided our friends with a lucrative new side business hauling out all the private sailboats on the island, and the pent-up demand ensured bookings for months.

Now the real boat work could begin.

I could barely contain my excitement. Of course I'm lying. As a connoisseur of life, I liked to cherry pick only the best parts, and boat maintenance wasn't one of them. Sanding and varnishing were the type of dreary repetitive tasks I dreaded the most. Kwaj offered plenty of far more pleasant diversions. I'd grown accustomed to finding ways to entertain myself while Garth wasn't paying attention to me in the company of other Peter Pan souls. Garth, newly energized by his success, became more focused than ever on fixing the boat so we could resume cruising. For me, the life I'd loved afloat seemed a distant memory.

It took all the energy I could muster to drag myself down to the boat to sand, varnish, and paint. My projects kept me inside the boat working in isolation, purgatory for a social creature like me. Surrounded by used sandpaper, dust, and dirt, I felt little connection with my home of five years. What kept me going was singing along to Bic Runga, Anika Moa and Chantal Kreveziak, as though I were a contestant on *American Idol*. I looked for any excuse to take a break so I could go outside and see who else was around.

With all the work to be done on the boat, Garth turned into a taskmaster, and, in my opinion, a bit of a drudge. Garth resented my lack of interest in the boat, and I resented his disinterest in me or in anything besides boat work. The divide between us grew. The great discussions we typically shared about history, philosophy, economics, and sociology ceased. His humor disappeared. So did mine. Our lighthearted banter was replaced by a prickly discussion of tasks and schedules, "shoulds" and "musts."

"Honey bunny..." he'd say in that tone I knew marked the opening of a lecture.

"Yes, honey bucket?" I'd reply, my voice dripping with sarcasm.

But he wouldn't miss a beat. "You know, you need to start varnishing the coach roof if you're going to get it done."

He was speaking of a job I dreaded, because I knew that I didn't possess the skill to do a good job, and for the rest of my days, the dribbles would haunt me. I preferred to let the fantasy persist that the coach roof would look splendid if only I had the opportunity to varnish it, rather than prove my ineptitude beyond doubt by actually doing it.

The pragmatist and the dreamer tiptoed around each other, hoping something would dissipate the tension and make us feel like a team again. We painted in oppressive heat, dripping sweat onto our paint surfaces mid-brush-stroke after carefully watching weather radar to find a dry period. Just as I was putting on the final topcoat on the cockpit—where on watch we have endless time to notice any and all imperfections—the heavens let loose. I let loose a quiet scream. Boats and boat work. A grumpy husband. All work and no play make life very dull indeed.

Still we made steady progress painting, varnishing, and replacing dead electronics so we'd be ready to leave Kwaj in February when the trade winds resumed to help push us westwards. We were required to give ninety days' notice before leaving. Garth gave notice at work with enough time to get *Velella* back in the water before his job ended. We discussed having me work until just before we departed so that we wouldn't be surprised by some silly new visitor policy that forced us to leave before we were ready.

As the hot, sticky doldrums and rain squalls gave way to trade winds, Garth got closer to his last day of work. He asked when I planned to give notice.

I'd been enjoying my job. I had a full social life. Besides, I still hadn't taken up pottery or painting. I hadn't collected any beach glass. I hadn't gone boogie boarding or water skiing yet. And I was apprehensive about setting off on a thirty-one-foot boat for twenty-four hours a day with someone I wasn't particularly excited to be around. I had grown to appreciate not having to worry about weather, not having to re-anchor the house in the middle of the night, being able to take a hot shower every day, the comfort of air conditioning, and having meals cooked for me, despite how bad they were.

After I gave Garth a vague answer several times, he started to worry. "You *are* going to go with me, aren't you?" he finally asked tentatively. Then he took my hands in his and said, "I'm sorry I've been so grouchy and distracted while we've been here. You know how I need to accomplish things or I just go nuts."

I thought of all those months during which he moped about not doing anything useful, followed by his single-minded focus on the trailer and then the boat. It had taken a toll on us. He went on. "I know we've had fun here, but how much longer do you really think you'd be happy here?" He had a point. Kwaj offered little but temporary diversions. "This place just saps my energy. Without a way to be creative, I can't thrive," he fidgeted, then looked up at me sideways, blinking rapidly. His bright blue eyes locked on mine, reaching across the distance. "Without you...cruising...everything...would be meaningless."

There he had me.

The next day, I gave notice, and so began the longest goodbye. I arranged the last dominoes game with the girls, the last ping-pong game, the last movie night, the last yacht club pot luck, the last sail on our friend's trimaran, and on it went. While I knew we'd miss the strong sense of community we'd had there over the past two years, by the time we sailed away from Kwaj, my liver was in serious need of a rest.

Two years after our meltdown in the Solomons, we were heading to Japan at last.

But, afraid that reaching Japan would mark the end of our cruise, I convinced Garth to sail to Hong Kong first.

CHAPTER 14

ON THE WARPATH IN SAIPAN

"**Y**our passports please."

A heavyset, dark man with his hands on his hips stood expectantly on the dock. A man next to him reached out his hand as though I were ready to hand them to him. *You have got to be kidding*, I thought. *Can't you see I'm a little busy?* We hadn't even finished docking yet. This was our second try, and it wasn't going particularly well. The engine had just died, leaving us with no maneuverability.

Our first attempt at docking in Saipan had been a disaster. Earlier that morning, we'd motored in shortly after dawn, barely sidestepping a squall that obscured the low reefs protecting the inner lagoon. Finally we'd found the entrance and passed through safely. As we approached the main dock, a black inflatable police boat had intercepted us.

"Follow us," a low voice said over a loudspeaker.

We fell in line behind them, and they led us to a narrow channel, for which our charts provided no information about the depth.

"How deep is it?" Garth shouted over the two engines.

"How much you need?"

"Six and a half feet …two meters," Garth answered.

"No problem."

We followed. The depth sounder read eight feet—not much margin for error. I watched for coral heads, but to me, it all looked shallower than we would normally risk. When I identified a channel marker, I saw Garth relax his grip on the tiller. During our voyage so far, the number of places where channels weren't marked far exceeded those that were. And often the ones that were considered "marked" featured nothing more than an empty Coke bottle inverted over a rod of bare rebar—a less-than-clear indication of which way to go.

Two men who'd been walking along a walkway that paralleled the channel stopped and watched us for a moment, then waved enthusiastically. I smiled and waved back while Garth focused on steering.

"Too bad you missed the fishing tournament," one of them called out. I gave an exaggerated shrug.

"Catch anything?" I yelled back.

"Two fifteen-pound wahoo," he replied proudly.

"Nice!"

Just then we struck something, and the boat lurched. We slammed forward, and Garth crashed against the dodger. When he got back up, his ear was gushing blood. He backed out until the channel was wide enough to turn around. It took the police boat several minutes to realize that we were no longer following.

"How come you didn't follow us?" A rotund man on the police boat said as he pulled up close to *Velella*.

"Because I hit a rock in the channel," Garth said.

"Ah. You gotta stay closer to the left side of the channel, so close you could almost reach out and touch the trees." His accent reminded me of the pidjin-influenced tones common among locals in Hawaii.

"That might have been helpful information to know," Garth said. "I naively thought the center would be safe."

The guy shrugged. *Not his problem.*

It had been maybe ten weeks since we'd painted *Velella* in the stifling heat of Kwajalein, and we already had a fresh gouge in the keel. Now, during our second attempt at docking, a dead engine left us drifting towards a rusty, corrogated-metal-faced dock. Hitting the dock could crush the hull as well as wreck the new paint.

And this bozo thinks I'm going to hand him our passports across the water?

"Can you please wait until we get settled?" I replied, as calmly as I could muster. Then to Garth, I said, "The engine just died."

He nodded from where he stood at the bow as though he wasn't surprised and quickly eased out the anchor.

I worried that the anchor wouldn't grab hold before our varnished wooden stern turned into splinters as it bashed into the corrugated metal.

"Can I toss you a line?" I asked the men on the dock.

One man shrugged. The other held his hands up, at the ready. I threw him a stern line, which he missed. He slowly gathered the line off the dock, and then held it in a clump, as though he were a statue.

These guys just don't get it, I thought.

The boat started to drift away from the dock as the anchor grabbed hold of the bottom. There was little Garth or I could do without an engine at that moment.

"Can you please pull us in?" I said. I didn't like being at the mercy of these guys, who clearly didn't have a clue about boats, but I didn't have much choice. I imagined where his help might lead— with him giving us a sudden yank—so I braced myself on the stern, ready to keep us from slamming into the dock.

Garth must have seen the situation unfolding, because just then, I heard him grind in some anchor chain. He rushed back to help me defend our home from crashing against the rust-streaked metal hulk they called a dock.

From that moment on, Garth and I worked together to hold *Velella* off against the wind and a steady surge of boat wakes until the other clearance officers arrived at their leisure. Our friend Brian, an experienced cruiser who lived in Saipan, had warned us we'd pay overtime if we arrived on Sunday. I imagined we were probably waiting for officials to arrive from their day off somewhere on the island. Light winds had delayed our arrival, but we didn't want to wait until Monday to clear in because I had arranged a visit from Kwajalein friends and my father arriving in two days. *How many times did I have to learn that boats and schedules were incompatible?*

Garth was too smart to say, "I told you so."

As the minutes dragged on, Garth and I wrestled to keep the boat from slamming into the dock as it shifted back and forth in the choppy waves. I worried I'd get my legs caught in a quick amputation. My muscles ached with tension. Garth's bleeding ear had finally slowed to a trickle, but he still looked like a victim in a slasher movie.

We'd been gone from Kwajalein less than twenty days, and I already felt like I needed a vacation from cruising. Our first landfall in Pohnpei, a week earlier, hadn't gone much better. Rain squall after rain squall had rendered the reef pass treacherously invisible and had nearly made Garth abandon Pohnpei for Saipan before we even got there. We quickly descended into a heated argument, during which I accused Garth of being a wimp, until he agreed to try again before aborting.

Finally, during a momentary sun-break, we had traversed safely through the reef pass, but then nearly wrecked the boat on a coral head inside until some kind soul took pity on us and led us through the unmarked maze of coral and ship carcasses to a safe anchorage.

After Pohnpei's officials charged us clearance fees as though *Velella* were a large ship unloading profitable cargo, we were dispirited and significantly poorer—a third of a month's budget poorer, in fact. A depressingly heavy mist loomed over Sokeh's Rock and the wreck-strewn anchorage. Wet clothing from our passage wouldn't dry, which meant that we had a clothesline of stubbornly damp items strung across the middle of our cramped interior. A brief visit to the commanding ancient stone-fortress city of Nan Madol and a frolic in a gushing waterfall nearby with an ever-cheerful Kapinga guide couldn't quite overcome our sour mood.

We'd come to Saipan lured by Brian's stories of diving and hiking on top of Saipan's already intriguing war history, but once again, we faced a harrowing arrival and budget-breaking fees. We were shocked to discover that checking in Sunday cost an extra $200 for "overtime" charges. When I learned the local greeting was, "Hafa adai," I grumbled, "*Half a day:* the amount of time it takes to check in, especially when overtime charges are involved," and I began to mourn what else we might have to forego to recover those funds.

Two such discouraging experiences in quick succession while we were still smarting from the Solomons meltdown and our arduously sweaty labors in Kwajalein restoring what we'd lost made me wonder once again if I hadn't outgrown my love of cruising.

🌴

Eventually the American captain of a nearby tourist trimaran helped to hold *Velella* off the dock until we could relocate. First, Garth tended to his ear wound, which proved to be a modest nick despite its initially prodigious outpouring. Then he turned his attentions to diagnosing the engine problem. A quick change of fuel filters appeared to appease our engine gremlins, and the engine ran smoothly while our new American friend, Fred, guided us into the protected inner channel.

A generous invitation to his house afterward for showers and a meal helped set us back aright. There we could check email and arrange to meet our friend Brian the following afternoon. Clearly, Fred understood the needs of a weary cruising sailor.

We docked *Velella* alongside a new pontoon featuring power, potable water, and free Wi-Fi. A tidy thirty-six-foot Japanese sailboat was also tied alongside, but no one was aboard. The pier was ideally situated inside a sizeable park, only a block from town. The park featured a small ironwood forest sprinkled with picnic tables along a sandy beachfront of sparkling azure water. And, within a few hundred yards of our boat, we discovered two intact Japanese World War II bunkers and a free war museum that detailed famous battles of the Pacific and Saipan's perspective on the war.

The "Seattle, WA" painted on *Velella*'s side garnered attention. I imagine few sailboats visit Saipan, particularly ones that have sailed this far. Within our first twenty four hours, visitors stopped by to offer tools, rides, and showers. Two perky marina staff, clad in smart blue uniforms sporting the marina logo invited us for a barbeque that evening. The temperature, in the high seventies, was much more bearable than the scorching heat of Kwajalein and drier than the clammy dampness of Pohnpei. Our situation was notably improved.

As the sun settled low in the sky, we joined a relaxed and friendly marina staff around a wooden picnic table laden with barbecued pork, calamari, and local Chamorro foods I didn't recognize. The men were swilling a fermented coconut drink called *Tuba,* which I found to be tasty when cold, but bitingly raw once it warmed up. One of the marina staff introduced us to the owner of the Japanese sailboat and mentioned we were from Seattle.

"Ichiro," he replied enthusiastically with a big smile. His eyes crinkled, and he nodded slightly, his thinning gray hair reflecting the low evening sunlight. He might have been in his early sixties.

I smiled back and nodded, having no clue what he'd just said.

"Ichiro," he repeated. "Seattle."

"Yes, we're from Seattle," I replied. The man scrunched up his face and looked up at the sky as though he was trying to remember something, but then shook his head and smiled again.

"Ichiro...Seattle," he said again, pointing emphatically at the Seattle written on our boat. I was still clueless about what he was trying to convey. I looked blankly at one of the older men on the marina staff, who spit in a cup, his teeth and gums stained red with betel nut juice. The Japanese man put his right fist atop his left and placed them next to his right shoulder; he swung them out in an arc and made a popping sound with his tongue. I cocked my head.

"Ichiro is a Japanese baseball player who plays for the Seattle Mariners," one of the younger marina staff explained. At that moment, the pantomime made sense.

"Oh," I said. I was embarrassed to admit that we'd been away so long, we had little awareness of what was happening in Seattle anymore.

"Base-a-ball," the Japanese man repeated with a heavy accent and a satisfied smile, now that he'd found the word he'd been searching for. He said nothing more and sipped contentedly on his plastic cup of Tuba.

One of the marina staff explained that though the man spoke little English, since he'd retired, he'd sailed to Saipan every year to spend a few weeks. Unfortunately, he would be leaving in the morning to return to Japan. I was disappointed, because I'd hoped to ask him about sailing in Japan. In the morning, his boat was gone.

A year later, we learned the sobering news that this Japanese sailor had never reached home. A month after we'd seen him, the same boat had been found off the coast of Japan with no one aboard.

🌴

To explore this area with my father had special meaning. When I was a toddler, my family had been stationed with the U.S. Navy on Guam, 100 miles south of Saipan. One of my few memories was huddling together with my family in our little house during a typhoon one night. Joining us in that impromptu slumber party had been Ethel and Kiyomi, two Japanese students who'd boarded with us. I imagined that, being back in this area again, Dad might flesh out details of my early history I'd been too young to remember.

I was ecstatic to reunite not only with my father, but eagerly anticipated a lively social gathering since Dad had often flown space-available on military transport to Kwaj while we lived there and naturally charmed all our friends. He had even spent days diving World War II B29s, Zeros, and sunken merchant vessels in Kwaj with Brian, while they both visited.

This visit, we would be docked at a protected pier with firm dates—at least from our Kwaj friends. My dad was again planning to fly space-available on military transport, so we didn't really know when he might arrive. Knowing my dad, we probably wouldn't have ever known anyway.

This time at least I was smart enough to suggest my father get a hotel room a block from the pier. Three people living on a thirty-one-foot boat could get a little crowded and the consequences to a marriage could be long-lasting. Garth appreciated my sudden foresight.

While we waited for my dad and friends to arrive, Garth and I pedaled through town on bikes Brian lent us. Hotels, restaurants, massage parlors, and poker rooms sprawled two blocks on either side of a five-mile-long road that ran the length of the west-facing beachfront. The building veneers showed signs of neglect, with peeling paint, partially-lit neon signs, and barricaded windows. These businesses served far fewer tourists than their volume suggested, evidence that the local tourism industry once flush with big-spending Japanese now barely made money on fewer, more budget-conscious Chinese and Koreans. Even so, a wide range of restaurant options reflected a diverse population of native Chamorro and the Thai, Vietnamese, Japanese, Korean, Filipino, and Indian immigrants that worked the tourist trade and small clothing factories dotting the island.

We biked the length of the straight beachfront park, past pock-marked World War II bunkers and rusted tanks. Scattered along the beach were "outrigger canoes" that demonstrated the impressive ingenuity that results from a scarcity of resources. Chamorros had molded the oddest assortment of raw materials into an amusing spectrum of "floating crafts." I hesitated to call them that, since the word *floating* struck me as optimistic. PVC piping or thick branches (shorn of their leafiest parts) stretched between dissected Jet Ski hulls and Hobie Cat pontoons to form an outrigger of sorts. Sometimes the main hull was a crushed Sunfish sailing dinghy or the dilapidated shell of a row boat. Occasionally we saw traditional wooden outriggers constructed of brightly painted plywood, which looked far more seaworthy.

This is what makes the tough sails worth enduring, I thought contentedly as I pedaled with a warm, gentle wind buffeting my face. *To experience things I'd probably never experience any other way.*

Our three Kwaj friends arrived the next morning as scheduled. After Garth and I capitalized on the shower facilities in our friend's hotel room and gorged ourselves to the point of embarrassment at the all-you-can-eat brunch in their resort hotel, we and our friends rented two cars for the six of us, with hopes that we'd see my father sooner rather than later. The next morning, I praised my unexpected good fortune when I spotted Dad pacing the dock, chatting on his cell phone, just after I awoke.

🌴

Our merry convoy grew quiet as we pulled into the serene, park-like setting of closely cropped grass. Only the occasional historical marker hinted of the death and destruction that had occurred here sixty two years earlier, when American soldiers seized the last Japanese command post and the aftermath. *So many lives destroyed because of unbridled ambition.*

A somberness settled over us at the tragic sites of Bonzai and Suicide Cliffs where Japanese settlers had jumped to their deaths. Parents had even shoved their own children over the edge to avoid capture and torture by American soldiers, which they'd been taught to fear. We'd learned in the war museum that following World War I, Saipan had become a large sugar cane farming settlement of more than 10,000 Japanese. Many stayed on through World War II, surely never expecting their miserable end. I stood at cliff's edge, where they'd spent their last moments. Below the dramatic drop-off, strong ocean currents swirled around jagged rocks. Above my head, white tropic birds rode updrafts. Souls of the departed, perhaps.

After our friends returned to Kwaj, on the weekend when he was off work, Brian showed us more than we'd have ever seen on our own. We poked around the remains of the overgrown Japanese air field, explosives bunkers, and the old sugar cane train. Together we tromped through machete-cleared paths in the jungle, red dirt caked to our Tevas, to natural and enhanced caves where soldiers and families hid during the fighting. In fact, Japanese soldiers had been found still living in caves shortly before my family's arrival in 1966, more than twenty years after the war ended. They were evidently unaware the war had ended. Inside these musty caverns, sake bottles, Japanese pottery, canteens, gas masks, gun shells, and even old bones lay much as they had been left sixty years earlier.

Brian introduced us to the local chapter of the Hash House Harriers, a worldwide affiliation of predominantly British expatriates who proclaim themselves to be members of "a drinking club with a running problem." Running the Hash was a hot, sweaty, but fun business, featuring serious "boonie-stomping" on a vertical course cut through the jungle not easily run by newbies like me and Garth or my lean, reasonably fit sixty-seven-year-old father. The course was conceived by two people who were the designated "hares." They marked the trail at the last minute with flour splotches on the ground. Sometimes those flour splotches proved to be false leads to divert pursuers and give the "hares" extra time to escape. The "hares" got a ten-minute head start, and then the rest of us tried to catch them. If we caught the "hares," they'd lose their shorts—literally.

Our hares escaped, not that *I* had any hope of catching them.

Once everyone arrived, panting, at the ending point just before sunset, the antics began. At a hilltop clearing with a spectacular view of the island and reef below, we experienced the Harriers' fraternal traditions. They featured songs and jokes, nicknames, and an initiation ceremony around a bonfire, along with impressive beer drinking. As FNGs (F'ing New Guys), we were prime candidates for initiation, which involved drinking or wearing (our choice) cheap beer from a stainless steel urinal. Another tradition involved contriving nicknames like "Drool Bag," "Donkey Dick," "Hand Job," "Happy Pockets," "Second Coming," "Vertical Lay," and "Max Cheesmo," which had me wondering what gem they might select for each of us. They toyed with pinning "Heini Kicker" on me since I'd clomped over an open can of Heineken—I swear that I'd been set up—but the name didn't stick. We escaped with our hardly-pristine reputations mostly intact.

On the way back to the boat, Brian ("Oly") told us that this troupe of jokers had recently helped the comrades of a fallen soldier locate where they'd lost their squad leader in battle sixty-one years earlier. Brian gave me a t-shirt that commemorated the occasion, perhaps to overcome my skepticism. The shirt read, "Operation SH3 Lt. Leary Memorial Run, July 9, 2005." The back depicted a captured Japanese flag the Japanese soldiers had autographed before they went into battle. English translations said,

"If you survive it is good; to die is better,"
"Walk your path without regret," and
"Die, I will die."

This story, along with recorded interviews I'd listened to in the museum brought the personal costs of war into sharper focus better than any history book.

On Sunday, Brian took us diving in a blue grotto, an oasis-like setting nestled into a deep chasm, where years of violent wave action carved natural passageways to the sea. We'd stopped our convoy here a few days earlier just to marvel and snap pictures. Dad, Garth, Brian, and I suited up from the back of Brian's truck in the parking lot.

Shouldering full dive tanks, we lumbered over to the entrance at the top of the abyss. We debated how many steps we faced until Brian confirmed that there were 120.

"I counted," he said.

Wearing what felt like twice my body weight, I descended the ladder-like steps with a precarious lack of balance, knowing full well I'd end up spastically sprawled at the bottom if I tipped over. Looking up the shaft from the bottom, I tried not to think about having to haul it all back *up*.

At the base of the steps, an undulating sea slammed water through a narrow cut between the mainland and a rock island, forcing plumes upward. We each timed a leap across the three-foot gap between crashing waves. Once across, I spotted sea urchins on the bottom twenty feet below me. Sunlight glowed through the blue like a light beam from the sea outside. The iridescent blue water called to me, and I leapt in.

Brian led us single-file through a narrow channel out to the sea. Coral-covered vertical walls loomed within arms-reach on either side. We traced the left edge beneath towering coral cliffs. As we rounded a corner, I instantly felt the strong pull of the current. We were in the ocean, immersed in the world of pelagic fish: tuna, mahi mahi, marlin, and sharks. I kicked to maintain control against surging waves that threatened to grab hold of my body and push me sideways into jagged coral.

Out of my peripheral vision, I noticed my father's position seemed to be changing erratically. He'd shared tales of diving in jeans and a t-shirt with double tanks stuffed in a backpack in the days before flotation vests and PADI certification. He railed against the organization's safety measures that he considered overly cautious, self-serving money makers. I wondered whether Dad was just being flaky or really having trouble.

Just then, I noticed Brian took a turn. After 500 yards outside, at the junction of another opening, Brian led us through a tunnel that snaked back into the cocoon of the grotto. In the shadows of a cave ahead of me, Brian and Garth stopped to admire a Napoleon Wrasse. When I didn't see my father after we'd reentered the grotto, I panicked. I imagined he'd been swept past the entrance. I pictured his bare skin nicked on the knife-sharp coral, spilling an inviting red-tinged bloody scent to hungry sharks lurking nearby. Had his cavalier attitude caught up with him? I gulped air carelessly as I craned my neck in every direction to locate him.

I found him where I least expected him: hovering above me, looking unconcerned.

🌴

My dad and I were eager to see nearby Tinian. Garth was just as eager for a day to himself. Most people visit the island to gamble, but we were more interested in its war history, when it secretly stored the two atomic bombs that ended the war in the Pacific. In the morning, Dad and I loaded Brian's bicycles onto the ferry with the vague idea that we'd explore war relics by bike until the return ferry.

Once we arrived, we realized just how naïve that notion was. As other passengers headed for the casino a few steps away, Dad and I stood straddling our bikes in the blazing sun surveying the abandoned sugar cane fields that stretched for miles. Sweat trickled downward between my shoulder blades. A heavy Chamorro man came up to us and asked if he could help.

"I was on the first rescue helicopter flight delivering diapers, baby formula and other supplies here after Typhoon Jean in 1967," Dad said, "but nothing looks familiar." It *had* been thirty-nine years.

"Really? I was born during Typhoon Jean. Bro, you might have saved my life." The man held up a fist as though greeting a fellow brother.

My father grinned.

I remembered the tales he wove of flying in Guam. He was a terrific storyteller; I never tired of hearing his stories. Like a skilled fisherman teasing a fish, he had a knack for delivery with pauses and gestures at all the right moments to keep a listener hooked until he'd spun a convincing tale of his bravery and cleverness. His stories were threaded with a rules-are-made-to-be-broken attitude that left me wondering how he'd been so successful in the military, a system built on protocol. Over the years, I'd heard how he'd learned to fly at the age of ten at a local airfield from retired World War II pilots who gave lessons to keep flying. As an eager kid in the 1950s, Dad would hang around the airfield doing anything to trade for flight time. When my family arrived in Guam in 1966 during a pilot shortage because of the war in Vietnam and rapid airline expansion, Dad's flight experience was valuable, and he was pressed into service. During Typhoon Jean, while the rest of us huddled in our base house, my father was on duty, helping to reposition and tie down planes to protect them during the worst of the storm.

"A wind indicator blew off at a hundred-and-sixty-seven miles an hour. The typhoon came in from the east, and we prepared for a direct hit by moving planes from Guam to Saipan. But the typhoon turned north, and afterward the C45 I flew north to Saipan was found two-hundred yards down the runway, upside down." *What a great story*, I thought.

The man nodded with enthusiasm, and I started to worry that with such an attentive audience, we'd never get beyond the parking lot.

Finally, Dad got around to saying, "We were hoping to see the atomic bomb bays and the war ruins."

The man shrugged. "Up the road is a store. Maybe they can point you in the right direction."

The island looked completely flat, yet on a bike I felt every slight rise. We slowly climbed the incline away from the ferry dock. Sweat pooled under my arms and dribbled down my back. I wiped my wet face on my sleeve. After a mile, we came across a convenience store at a sleepy crossroads, where outside, a couple of kids and a dog hung around an old white passenger van.

Dad and I looked around the store past jars of licorice, ice cream, and sodas, in hopes of finding a few postcards or a map. *No luck.* Finding the elusive bomb bays and getting to them by bicycle and back to the landing before the 3:00 p.m. return ferry seemed more and more impossible.

We grabbed a couple of Sprites from the refrigerator case. I pressed the cold can against my dripping face and rolled it down my neck. Dad stepped up to the counter and explained our interest in visiting the island's war history by bicycle to the Chamorro man at the cash register.

The man shook his head and said, "Everything is pretty spread out and not well marked. It'd be a long way by bike. Not sure you'd make it back to the ferry in time."

Dad and I looked at each other for a moment. *Our lack of planning might not work out so well this time.* Neither of us had any interest in gambling, and while a bike ride might be enjoyable, miles upon miles of abandoned sugar cane fields didn't offer the most riveting scenery. I couldn't bear the thought of missing what I'd come to see, and my father was loathe to disappoint his hopeful daughter. Dad chewed his lip, as though he were puzzling over the metallurgical properties of dental fillings.

The shop bell clanged, and a man poked his head inside the door to ask the storekeeper about plans for the next day.

Dad pulled out his wallet and began thumbing through it. After the man left, Dad paid for the drinks. In a jovial voice, he said, "So do you know your way around the war ruins?"

The storekeeper nodded.

Then Dad tossed out a grand idea: "How would you like to earn twenty-five dollars taking us around for a couple of hours?" Dad was banking on the appeal of offering a bored local an interesting diversion on this sleepy island. I took in a hopeful breath.

The storekeeper made a face that said, *Why not?* Then he called to a woman in the back, presumably his wife, and they conferred quietly for a moment. As they returned to the register together, he said," I'll do it for thirty dollars, so I can cover the gas."

"That sounds fair," Dad agreed, and they shook on it. "I'm Bob. This is my daughter, Wendy." A smile as wide as the horizon spread across my face. The Hinman tradition of "winging-it" would carry us through once again. Thanks to Dad's resourcefulness, I would get to see everything after all. I nearly hugged the both of them.

In the van, we fell into an easy rapport as we passed miles of jungle-covered fields alongside a straight concrete road. Grass jutted from jagged cracks in the worn pavement. I wondered if we were driving down the old war runway. Mike, our guide, confirmed that this was indeed the overgrown airfield used by both Japanese and American forces.

Dad launched into a story about how he and his fellow pilots turned an "unscheduled practice" for visiting dignitaries into an air show. "Anything to show off—a dipsy doodle for the USO tour folks visiting the troops in Vietnam." He paused to wipe the corners of his mouth with his fingers. "I took the comedian Danny Kaye on a helicopter ride. Glenn Ford, too, and lots of others I'd never heard of."

We jostled over a series of bumps and turned right into a road cut into the high jungle grass.

"One day, an admiral who'd always said that he didn't trust an airplane with a single engine requested a pick up for himself and a guest. We all wondered what was up." Dad suspended his long straight fingers in the air. Their flat, neatly clipped fingernails featured a perfect half moon of white at his cuticles. I often wondered where the Italian in me originated—the part that cradled the telephone in the crook of my neck so I could gesture with both hands. A few hours in the presence of my father reminded me. Giving the signal that he'd reached the climax of his story, he pursed his lips as though he'd tasted something sour, then parted his lips to reveal the prominent bicuspids that made his smile unique. "His guest turned out to be Bob Hope."

Mike didn't seem to have heard of Bob Hope. But I remembered his comedy show from my childhood and was impressed. I hadn't remembered hearing this story before.

Mike pulled into a clearing to show us an underground fuel depot, a power plant, and a radio communications building—several in better shape than twenty-year-old buildings in Kwaj, each surrounded by a narrow band of clipped grass and a marker briefly describing its historical significance. Yet true to Mike's word, no street signs would have guided us to them. At the air administration building, Mike told us that three Japanese soldiers had been found just after committing ritual Hara Kiri during the invasion.

Along the jagged coast, Mike pointed out another Suicide Cliff where most of Tinian's 19,000 Japanese sugar cane farmers had jumped to their deaths. In the Saipan war museum, pre-war photos of Tinian had shown thousands of tidy plots of land growing a broad spectrum of produce and sugar cane between sizeable Japanese towns. Mike told us that only about 3,000 Chamorros remained in what had become uncultivated countryside. Nearly all food was imported.

After weaving his way through a complex maze of barren roads, Mike pulled into another clearing where glass enclosures covered the two sunken cement pits we'd recently read about in the war books, *Enola Gay* and *Embracing Defeat*. Inside each pit, a sign perched on

a solitary easel offered a few photographs and a brief description
that identified Bomb Pit One, where "Little Boy" was loaded into
the *Enola Gay* before it devastated Hiroshima, and Bomb Pit Two,
where "Fat Man"—named for Churchill—began its deadly mission
aboard the B-29 *Bock's Car,* bound for Nagasaki. These modest
earthen coffins had hosted missiles that had changed the course of
history. I was wordless at the thought of the wrath that their former
residents had wrought and the threat that their brethren still posed.
At that very moment, the Middle East was torn apart and more
lives were being destroyed because of never-proven suspicions that
Iraq possessed "weapons of mass destruction." Proven or not, action
had been initiated and there was no taking back its damaging
repercussions. Why were we humans destined to repeat history,
however bleak?

On the ferry back to Saipan, Dad and I sat deep in our thoughts.
Mike had provided a pleasant but dispassionate glimpse into
Tinian's somber history as though it was far longer ago than his
own lifetime. Our voyage had featured a steady parade of contrasts
like this: frustration and delight, tragedy and humor. The most
powerful emotions that remind us of our humanity.

Our route from New Zealand had followed a path of World
War II destruction. After several suffocating weeks in the Solomon
Islands, I could vividly picture how jungle rot and dysentery had
plagued the coastal watchers stationed there during World War II.
I developed a newfound sympathy for these unsung heroes, who had
hauled heavy radio equipment through dense jungle looking for a
safe perch where they could spy Japanese ships plying "the slot"
and report them to Allies before the ships could bomb American
forces in Guadalcanal. I'd wondered what must have run through
the mind of the young lieutenant who would eventually become
President Kennedy, after his PT boat had sunk out from under
him. In Tarawa, thousands of soldiers lost their lives in an ill-timed
beach assault against gun emplacements that now served as latrines;
Kwajalein's silent wrecks of merchant vessels and sunken airplanes

now provided recreation for American divers, and its Marshallese inhabitants had become shuffling minimum-wage workers on a U.S. Army base. A history book would surely miss the irony.

Our first two landfalls since leaving Kwajalein had proved challenging. But such a rich experience of Saipan and its history reminded me why I loved cruising. I couldn't just choose the good parts. The contrast was what made me appreciate the simplest things in life, like a hot shower, a good night's sleep, a full belly, and nature's surprises in the form of a precious flower, a soothing waterfall, and fruit picked fresh from a tree. Without the contrast, every day would seem the same and I would take for granted the precious gift of being able to explore the world. Our Solomons meltdown had given us the chance to stop and reconsider what we were doing. Good and bad, I was glad to be back on the move again.

🌴

Our next stop would be Hong Kong. After my father left, with vague plans of meeting us there or in Japan, we prepared ourselves as best we could for what we suspected would be a difficult sail. (As if we hadn't had a few of those already.) We were leaving the predictable weather of the Pacific to head into the shallow, volatile South China Sea and a completely new monsoonal weather pattern near several major shipping centers. Sailing here would up the ante for us, in a new way.

Our route cut through the straits between Taiwan and the Philippines during the unpredictable transitional period as the NE monsoon gave way to the SW monsoon. We worried about bucking gale force winds in the straits where intense currents and tide rips would produce a wild ride. And we needed to make it through *before* typhoon season began. Yet nothing was bankable there; typhoons had been recorded in the area during every month of the year.

When the American captain had learned of our intentions to sail to Hong Kong, he'd said with alarm, "You're not planning to sail through the Bashi Channel, are you?" I could almost see his heart rate spike as he spit out the words, "I went through there in a large ship. The currents and wind were horrible. That was probably the scariest thing I've ever done in my life."

The Bashi Channel was exactly where we were headed.

CHAPTER
15

SLOW BOAT TO CHINA

The cliché *hours of boredom, punctuated by moments of sheer terror* is an apt description of our passage from Saipan to Hong Kong. The first twelve days featured mellow winds that were pleasant, though ever shifting, with mild seas. Garth absently whistled "On a Slow Boat to China" as the hours dragged on. Our greatest excitement was changing the clocks and readjusting our watch schedule to fit each new time zone as we sailed west. Until we reached the Bashi Channel.

At dawn, we arrived at the narrow slot between Taiwan and the Philippines in light winds and flat seas. Almost as though we'd crossed a barrier, the water color changed from intense blue to dull green. Within hours I felt a cold north wind funneling through the Taiwan Straits. Menacing black clouds lurked on the horizon. Here came the gale we'd feared. The title to one of my jazz favorites, Vince Guaraldi's "Cast your Fate to the Wind," flashed through my mind at that moment. We quickly added layers of clothing, battened the hatches, and downed hot chocolate to take away the chill until adrenaline kicked in.

As wind and seas built and we drew closer to Hong Kong, shipping traffic increased tenfold. Container ships, cargo ships, cruise ships, and every type of fishing vessel zigzagged unpredictably across our path. Then fog closed in, reducing our visibility to less than two miles while we battled gale force winds and boisterous seas that went from towers above to steep troughs beside us.

As the sun set, darkening our wet, undulating world, traffic posed an even greater threat. We relied on a hand-bearing compass to help us track the positions of ships on the horizon so we wouldn't be fooled by an optical illusion as we bounced around in the waves. Tracking shipping lights as waves rose and fell around and beneath us was nearly impossible. We ascended to great heights, and then dropped abruptly as if falling down an elevator shaft. Lights disappeared behind wave crests, occasionally shining eerily through a thin wall of water. Bioluminescence made each breaking wave flash like yet another ship. Garth counted twenty-six lights on the horizon; tracking them seemed futile. We resorted to emergency management, taking whatever evasive maneuvers were needed as each ship loomed over us.

Fishing boats, lit with strings of bright lights that made Christmas decorations at an American mall seem subdued, blinded us to the lights of far more dangerous container ships that could sink us in seconds without ever noticing. When the bright fishing lights disappeared abruptly, I knew we were in trouble. Mammoth container ships would appear out of the fog barreling down on us at twenty knots, leaving little time to react. I trembled in the cockpit, one hand on the tiller, the other on my million-candle-power emergency signal light, ready for quick action.

After each menacing hulk of steel passed, I'd breathe a sigh of relief until the next ship had me absorbed in rapt, quivering attention.

We endured two long, sleepless days until the wind and waves abated.

We steered along the mainland China shore hoping to avoid most major shipping routes. Though fewer container ships blasted past us, our coastal route put us smack in the path of ferries, twin fishing boats working in tandem, and tug boats towing modest container barges equipped with cranes for self loading. Still we didn't spot the high rocky islets around Hong Kong through the fog until we were fairly close.

As we slowly sailed through uninhabited islands in the mist, Garth tried to figure out why the engine would not stay running. He discovered the fuel tank intake line was clogged, and worked to resolve the problem as we approached landfall. In a narrow channel, when Garth had the engine pulled apart and was carefully siphoning fuel through the line, a steel fishing trawler that had been sitting immobile suddenly lurched forward across our track.

"Hang on, Garth!" I shouted as I maneuvered out of the way at what I knew was an inopportune moment.

"Ah shit," he groaned, looking up the companionway at me, sweat dribbling down his oil-smudged cheeks.

Anchoring in busy Hong Kong seemed unlikely, so we headed for Hebe Haven Yacht Club, a place our guidebook had indicated welcomed visitors and where we could find marina facilities outside the pulse of downtown. A racy sailboat sailed by, the first we'd seen in ages. Where there were sailboats, there would be fellow sailors and equipment to service our boat.

"Finally a vessel that can't kill us," Garth said with a wry smile as he shifted the engine into gear.

When we rounded the point into the inner bay of Port Shelter, the sight of hundreds of private yachts on moorings made me think we'd reached a boating Mecca. Visibility was still poor, and we could barely see tall apartment complexes hugging the high hills beyond. We pulled alongside what looked like a new pontoon. The place, clearly a center of activity, was surprisingly quiet on this weekday morning.

In contrast to Saipan, when officials couldn't wait for us to tie up before beginning their paperwork, in Hong Kong, we only had to check into their downtown offices within seventy-two hours. I imagined us navigating the busy streets, paperwork in hand, feeling a little like country cousins.

"And now for something completely different," I said as I gawked at the nearby buildings stacked nearly on top of one another like blocks. After years of living in unpopulated tropical islands, we'd arrived in a city with one of the highest concentration of humans on the planet.

"Toto, we're not in Kansas anymore," Garth said.

MERGING ONTO THE FAST LANE IN HONG KONG

W e'd survived our harrowing experience with fog, ships, and gales, but we had little time to reflect on our miraculous escape from what had seemed like certain death. My energy rebounded with the thrill of Hong Kong, a place I fondly remembered visiting on business years ago. Its pulse was irresistible.

Our second afternoon, Garth and I were inspecting a navy blue sailboat that was pulled up on a marine railway next to the efficient yacht club boat yard. Garth was pointing out design details and trying to guess what kind of boat it was. Garth carried a virtual inventory of boat designs in his head, and from several hundred yards away, he could usually tell me who designed a given boat, who built it, in what era—and could even guess what kind of rating it might have on the race course.

Occasionally, on a day like today, we came across a type he didn't know, which always surprised me. Beneath it a short wiry man worked diligently, his dark head cocked to the side as he taped the waterline for a coat of bottom paint. A moment later, he popped out from under the boat and wandered over to where we stood.

"Hi," he said, offering his hand after he wiped his dusty fingers. "I'm Tets."

We introduced ourselves.

"What kind of boat is this?" Garth asked him. I could tell by the way that Garth looked at it that he liked the lines of it and wanted to add it to his list of favorite boats.

"It's a Van de Stadt," Tets replied. He was Asian, but he didn't look Chinese. His name sounded Japanese, yet his accent didn't seem typical of Japanese people I'd met before. It was unusual to encounter a lone Japanese man in a foreign country, especially one doing manual labor. As I puzzled this mystery, Garth nodded and ducked his head for a closer look at the underbody.

"Did you sail to New Zealand?" Tets asked us. It seemed an odd question.

"Yeah. Why?" Garth replied.

"Did a Japanese magazine publish an article about you?" Tets asked. Because of his accent, it took a moment for his words to sink in.

"Yes!" I said, surprised. What were the chances of finding someone in Hong Kong who had read a Japanese magazine article written in Kanji several years ago? One in a million maybe? Tets listened attentively as I recounted the story of the Kazi interview and how it had won us a spot on the media boat to watch the America's Cup races.

He let me babble for a few minutes, and then he asked, "Would you like to go racing on Sunday? It's just a casual race, and we could use a couple more people."

"Of course!" Garth and I said, almost simultaneously. It was the perfect entre to the local sailing scene

Over the next few days and months, we saw a lot of Tets. He had a boat-repair business, and since Hong Kong was not a do-it-yourself place, he was working on several boats in the yard. Tets seemed as interested in boats as Garth was. As we got to know him, we learned that he'd lived in Hong Kong for over twenty years. He'd sailed there from Japan and had lived aboard with his British wife and four kids. When we learned that he'd been a naval architect designing yachts for Yamaha back in Japan, it was as though Garth had found a soul mate. The two of them spent hours discussing the finer points of racing, rig tune, and boat design. And since everyone knew Tets, soon everyone knew us too.

From that first race on, for the next eight months, we competed in nearly every event of the club season. Since Hong Kong expatriates lived a world away from family in small high-rise apartments or townhomes, most lived much of their lives in the company of friends at bars and restaurants. We had a full social life again. Too full, sometimes. I could hardly believe that most of these people worked all week, because by the end of a weekend of racing and partying, even this party girl was in need of a rest.

Initially we only planned to stay in Hong Kong a month or so. An early season typhoon quickly changed our minds.

🌴

"Hey, Wendy, take a look at this," Garth said. He was leaning over weather charts on the computer. Looking over his shoulder, I noticed a suspicious swirl in the lower right hand corner, just east of the Philippines. Then his finger migrated to the spot I'd just noted.

"Yeah, I see it," I said. That low pressure had the distinct shape of a forming typhoon.

"Let's hope for the best," Garth said. "But we should keep a close eye on it." I nodded agreement. When we left Seattle, we'd sworn that we'd avoid typhoon areas in season, yet here we were, and evidently, the season was starting early.

For the next few days, Garth and I closely monitored the weather charts on several Internet sites. We watched the system build in strength.

Seven different weather models projected its path to cross directly over Hong Kong—rarely did they agree so closely. The marina manager confirmed our fears by posting a scary looking weather map filled with warnings on the bulletin board between the dinghy dock and the sampan ferry-service dock. Mike Franco, the marina manager, made a point of warning every boat owner that a typhoon was heading towards Hong Kong and urged everyone to make preparations to withstand the winds. He emphasized that this one was packing the strongest winds he'd seen since a 1984 typhoon put boats onto the shores of that same protected bay.

The marina yard workers launched into a new sort of action. They began to pull runabouts down from the highest racks, where they were usually stored, and began the long process of strapping each boat to pad eyes anchored in the concrete parking lot, after they'd roped off areas to keep cars out. To minimize the number of dangerous items that might catch the wind, they launched any sailboats that were sitting up on blocks, even if they weren't finished, as long as they could float—assuming their chances of survival would be better in the water on moorings. They strapped down the metal containers that served as offices and workshops.

We were in a bay that was one of the most protected from all wind directions. Within that bay lay the tiny Marina Cove, which was even more tucked away. We briefly considered moving into a slip there, but found the fee to be outrageously expensive for a required minimum stay of three days. Then the marina owners announced that the marina was full. Not an option anyway. Our mooring was brand new and in excellent condition, so we placed our faith in it.

We were nervous, but there wasn't time to worry. We began our preparations first by buying enough groceries to last us for several weeks, and we filled our water tanks in case water supplies and facilities were compromised in the typhoon or we couldn't get ashore for some reason. Then we charged our batteries since overcast conditions would inhibit solar charging, and we might not be able to run our engine for days if the water were filled with debris.

Then we began slowly stripping the boat to prepare for winds projected to reach 90-110 knots or more. The most obvious thing to do was to remove a wind generator mounted on the aft rail that hadn't been working well for some time. Something designed to spin in the wind might be a major liability in high winds, especially if it came down while spinning. We had been already debating whether or not to keep this unsightly, loud, heavy beast that required work to get running again anyway; we concluded that its heyday was officially over. Since its bolts were frozen, we had to drill them out to dismantle it. That took us the better part of a frustrating day, but then a Scotsman gave us $50 cash for it as we were hauling it to the dumpster.

By Monday, forecasts were using the term *Super Typhoon*, and we were hearing reports of "phenomenal wave heights" and sunk/ missing vessels in the South China Sea, as well as deaths, flooding, and the destruction of thousands of homes in the Philippines. The general public remained blissfully unaware that Hong Kong lay in the path of a developing super typhoon, while we worried and tracked it for nearly six days. General forecasts predicted "showers and squally weather mid-week." Finally the South China Morning Post headlines and radio stations warned of the approaching typhoon. Suddenly, the Hong Kong Weather Underground turned to a subscription-only service, leaving us jittery without one of our favorite sources of information.

During those busy days around Hebe Haven, few stopped to chitchat. Everyone was focused on the task of preparing as best as possible. We worked nonstop for the next two days. We removed our awning and all other large objects on deck, and stuffed them into the V-berth. Next came the sails, which we shoehorned into our dwindling living space. The main sail became a three-foot-diameter, eighteen-foot-long cigar that stretched from the peak of the V-berth aft past our dining table, blocking access to the cabinets that held the first aid kit, our toiletries, and much of our food.

"I hope we don't have to live with this inside for long," I said.

"Hopefully it won't be more than a couple of days," Garth said. "If it is, we've got more serious problems to worry about."

As our eyes locked, I followed that thought for a moment and shuddered.

Back outside, we moved the halyards aft and tried to remove our dodger to reduce windage, but found the zippers frozen from corrosion. So instead we tied it down. Then we shored up our mooring lines and added back up lines and chafing gear. Finally, we placed diving masks within reach, just in case we'd need them to see in the driving wind and rain if we needed to go on deck during the blow, and we tied the tiller tightly to immobilize it completely. A million little details.

We'd done nearly everything we could think of for the moment. All we could do was wait until it got closer. We checked the weather map again. The typhoon was still moving directly for Hong Kong, yet the skies were a vivid blue and the winds gentle, concealing the furious weather south of us. With hours still to wait, we took a dinghy tour of the bay to assess the preparation of other boats that might break free and jeopardize our home. Then we rowed on to our favorite beach and hiked along the peninsula that protected Pak Sha Wan, our bay. We wanted to get some exercise before being stuck aboard for what might be days.

When we returned to the boat, we lashed the dinghy down tightly to the foredeck and stowed the oars and seat in the overstuffed V-berth. Then we braced ourselves for a strong blow, loose boats, and flying debris. We'd had offers from near strangers for a couch, but as long as there was something we might be able to do to protect our home, we felt compelled to stay aboard. We were nestled behind a well-secured marina pontoon that we figured would block most waves with only a few boats between us. We were close enough to swim ashore if necessary. I hoped it wouldn't be.

We waited nervously, checking the typhoon's progress using a Wi-Fi signal that barely reached out across the water.

At 3pm the typhoon number three strong wind warning signal went into force. The wind started to build, and we lost our Wi-Fi signal. Sampan service was cancelled. From our cockpit, we watched the marina staff remove the sampans from the water and tie them down. We were on our own, alone with our wits and RTHK, the radio station, which we relied upon for updates.

We felt the motion of incoming waves as the wind began to howl. The dock groaned like tortured wookies while halyards and sail covers flapped, and boats sailed around their moorings. During gusts, we heeled over as though we were under sail, heard the roar in the rigging. Through the windows, we saw whitecaps and horizontal rain. The roller furling headsail on the boat in front of us shredded as it came unfurled. I watched it from the companionway, wondering how long it could flap before the force of it drove the boat off its mooring into us.

As we listened, the radio reported tree collapses and falling items that injured people, cancellations of air, land, and sea transportation. A surfer in search of good waves was reported stranded on rocks after ignoring the warning. We expected conditions to deteriorate further, but then the situation improved, and we realized we'd seen the worst of it. Typhoon Chanchu, which means "pearl" in Chinese, came within 120 miles of Hong Kong for several hours, then tracked northeast. Winds reached gale force at times, but did not pack the punch we so feared. I felt like we'd gotten all prepared for a party that never happened. And now we had to put the boat back together.

"Looks like typhoon season has begun," I said.

"Yeah, I think we should sit tight." I nodded agreement.

🌴

I fidgeted at cliff's edge. Climbing up had seemed like a good idea at the time, but since I'd worked my way up here, I'd started wondering about the intelligence of plunging from this height into the still, deep waters below. Only moments ago, Nigel had climbed to this same cliff like a monkey, then thrown his body over the edge and returned to the surface without hesitation, so I knew it could be done. I just wasn't sure I could pull it off without killing myself. Now that I stood on the edge, my intentions to jump as Nigel did were clear. I couldn't change my mind without revealing my reservations.

The last thing I had expected to do in Hong Kong was go rock climbing and cliff diving, yet here I was looking down on three dark heads bobbing in the water-filled crevice of Luk Wu Gorge beneath a spectacular waterfall. Garth and I had only just met Nigel and Sandra, friends of friends, a few nights earlier. Nigel was a pilot for Cathay Pacific, and Sandra led youth adventures in Hong Kong. During dinner, she'd hinted about having me briefly join her team of leaders—taking kids camping, kayaking, rappelling, and running ziplines across canyons, and, of course, I'd been intrigued. Their invitation to go hiking introduced us to another side of Hong Kong.

The last time I'd been in Hong Kong on business—before the territory's handover to China—I'd rushed from skyscraper to skyscraper, from meeting to meeting, in a sea of bodies on the move. When I thought of Hong Kong, I'd always thought of a fast-paced city of high finance where seven million people lived in close proximity and scrapped for bargains at stalls stacked into rabbit warren-like mazes. It wasn't until my departing flight took off in daylight, the airplane wing nearly scraping laundry off a line, that I noticed how many islands made up the surrounding area.

Glowing reports of Hong Kong from friends who'd sailed there stirred those memories and rekindled my interest. And since our arrival, besides the typhoons and a full social life, each day we discovered more reasons to stay.

Over dinner, Sandra told us that Hong Kong encompassed more than two hundred islands, many uninhabited; more than a third of

Hong Kong's area was a nature preserve. Luk Wu Gorge was just one of many great hikes in Hong Kong.

"Woohoo, go Wendy!" Sandra shouted. Her Aussie accent jarred me back to the present moment. Could I get down from this wall without embarrassing or killing myself?

It's now or never, I thought and leapt over the cliff. I forgot to plug my nose, and when I hit the water twenty feet below, I was surprised by the force of water jetting through my sinuses. Yet I was energized by the adrenaline coursing through my body. I swam over to the falls, where I could feel the water pounding down on my head and shoulders and hear its roar in my ears. I wanted more of this.

After we lingered a little longer relishing the cool clear water, Sandra reminded us that the day was slipping away and we weren't even halfway. "We need to get a wiggle on if we want to make it back to the car by dark." So we packed up our water bottles and threw our shirts over our shoulders. We picked our way through boulders alongside the waterfall, slowly gaining altitude. When we reached the next plateau, we encountered another waterfall, equally stunning. May's dry heat had already evaporated the water from our shorts, and sweat prickled on my skin. I longed for another dip, but pushed on reluctantly. We navigated the flat edge of a narrow gorge, and then reached an area where we faced a choice between routes.

Sandra fished for her trail map and asked how tired we were.

"I think we missed the turn off. Oops! I guess we'll have to take the long way. I think that gets us back to the car," she said to Nigel who was looking over her shoulder. He studied the map and shrugged. I looked over at Garth. He grimaced. I laughed.

"Don't worry, we'll get there eventually, Garth," Sandra said with a wink.

After we'd been hiking a while, the route took a turn and headed steeply uphill. The foliage became less lush, the shrubs smaller. "Ah bugger," Sandra said, chewing her lip. "This is the route that takes us up and over, the one with lots of steps." She looked at Garth, who'd just finished wiping his shirt across his face. "Sorry, Garth!" she said, beaming.

We labored our way up stone and concrete-covered pathways, punctuated by thousands of steps. Sweat was dripping in my eyes. Garth lagged behind. When we reached the top, we turned to wait for Garth.

The panorama before me riveted my attention. High rocky islets sprinkled off the coast looked so inviting, as did the now calm South China Sea that extended beyond. Below us stretched the beach where we'd turned inland near the start of our hike and the little island that reminded me of Snoopy sitting on his doghouse. To my right, the High Island Reservoir, which holds Hong Kong's drinking water, shimmered blue in the sunshine. As we'd hiked past the alluring aquamarine waters of the reservoir earlier, Nigel had explained how it was formed by closing a narrow gap between several small islands.

"Almost there, Garth," Sandra joked as Garth panted his way up the steps. After Garth caught up, we paused a minute, breathing heavily, then continued. The path curved downward and Garth took the lead behind Sandra, gravity propelling his descent. Eventually the trail leveled off, then wound between rocky outcroppings. I stopped to snap photos, and then rushed to catch up. As I rounded a curve, I came nose to nose with a cow.

The cow paid me no attention and wandered into a nearby clearing. Along the trail, I noticed droplets of blood on the ground and realized that they must have come from the cow. I retraced a few steps, wondering if the cow were injured. When I reached the cow, I realized the cause of the blood. I yelled, "Hey, you guys, this cow is calving!" I heard nothing and realized how far behind I must have been.

When I finally caught up with everyone, they were rounding the final bend into the parking lot. "Did you realize that cow was giving birth?" I asked, in an awed tone.

"Really?" Garth said, sounding equally surprised at this discovery.

"Yeah, they're feral and protected so no one bothers them," Sandra explained. "They just wander wherever they want. Sometimes they create some interesting traffic problems, but they rarely get too far into the city." Sprinkled around the parking lot were several cattle grazing in the grassy parking strips between rows of cars.

We piled into their navy blue Volkswagen Golf and exited the country park as a double-decker city bus turned in. A mile past the park entrance, as though prearranged for our entertainment, we saw three cows standing in the center of a roundabout. A fourth was meandering its way across the street to join them. Cars swerved to avoid the oblivious cow.

"Amazing!" I said. "I sure never expected to see a wild cow giving birth in Hong Kong."

"We have wild monkeys, too," Nigel said.

Sandra laughed and said, "Just wait until you have to wrestle with a monkey for your lunch in front of a school class." She looked at me inquisitively and added, "So, are you interested in doing more of this?"

"You bet!" I said, hoping that she'd judged me a good candidate for outdoor leadership.

As we drove home, Nigel explained how land lease restrictions created the high density of downtown and protected country parks. Sandra bemoaned that sprawl was beginning to encroach on the wilderness areas in the nine years since the 1997 handover to China. Yet, the sprawl here paled in comparison to the epidemic of strip malls and box stores in the U.S.

Over the next few months, Sandra and I hiked to the top of 700-meter peak Ma On Shan and watched butterflies swirl around us while we sucked on our water bottles; we trekked the length of the peninsula that protects Pak Sha Wan, where *Velella* moored; we stopped to swim at Trio Beach and go sailboat racing in Port Shelter. Besides visiting temples, museums, and hiking around the world's largest Buddha on Lantau Island, we filled our days with outdoor activities which I would never have predicted. Garth and I invested in our own trail map, and, until the suffocating heat grew too unbearable, we explored other country parks sprinkled around the city, including the rugged mountainous park in the center of Hong Kong Island behind the skyscrapers.

After years in quiet Pacific Islands, the pulse of downtown Hong Kong came as a shock. Those first few months, we experienced sensory overload on a regular basis. The avalanche of merchandising was overwhelming, with neon signs that shouted messages at volumes we could scarcely ignore. Yet the lure of this fascinating place drew us out. The first time we searched for boat parts in Mong Kok, Hong Kong's industrial area, we gasped at the press of bodies on the street and fled back into the air conditioned oasis of the MTR station. We later learned that Mong Kok translates from Cantonese to mean "busy point." *No kidding.*

🌴

During the Northeast Monsoon, coal burning factories just outside of Hong Kong in Shenzhen filled the air with suffocating smog that hovered on still hot days. Some days, I couldn't even see the other side of Victoria Harbour from the Star Ferry halfway across the quarter-mile channel. The smoke burned my eyes, and my skin broke out worse than it had when I was a teenager. I could taste the metal in the air. When spring turned to summer, the weather pattern shifted to the Southwest Monsoon, and the heat and humidity steadily rose to unbearable levels. I couldn't decide which was worse.

When the heat grew too intense, Garth and I escaped into air conditioning as much as we could. After a night twisting in the sheets with the fan blowing directly on our faces from inches away, we'd awaken in a pool of sweat, feeling poorly rested and yearning for the cool oasis the yacht club offered. Each morning, we guzzled water and scoured the free *South China Morning Post* and sailing magazines in the club until morning traffic abated. Then we'd catch a LPG-powered minibus and an MTR train into town to visit a museum or gallery.

Garth and I probed every aspect of Hong Kong's evolution and fascinating culture, particularly when air conditioning was involved. We gradually realized that as Hong Kong marched towards modernization, residents had given little thought to history. On a highly touted walking tour, we repeatedly came across bronze plaques identifying places where some historical landmark used to stand, mounted at the base of a seventy-five-story edifice of metal and glass.

In a valiant attempt to revive Hong Kong's rich heritage, tourism officials created a museum to house every historical artifact they could lay their hands on. With entry fees at the price of roughly one U.S. dollar, we splurged to educate ourselves in the cool air of not only the Hong Kong Museum of Art, the Hong Kong Museum of History, the Hong Kong Heritage Museum, and the Hong Kong Maritime Museum, but more obscure ones like the Hong Kong Planning and Infrastructure Museum, the Museum of Tea Ware, and the Hong Kong Correctional Services Museum, which featured primitive torture devices and minutiae of how prison guard uniforms have evolved through the ages. Ironically, a prison the British had built in 1937 had been finished shortly before the Japanese used it to intern expatriates during World War II.

I imagined the subsistence lives of original villagers at the Law Uk and Sheng Yiu Folk Museums, as well as the Low Wai Walled Village. We solved puzzles in the Hong Kong Science Museum until polite staff gently tapped us on the shoulder to say, "Excuse me, but we are closing now. You can come again tomorrow."

I think if the tourism office gave an award for most-enthusiastic tourist, I would have earned it. Garth humored me for a time, even letting me drag him aboard the *Duk Ling,* a traditional Chinese junk that pretended to "sail" the waters of Victoria Harbor. Even after Garth lost interest and resumed working on boat projects, I carried on with my quest to take in every possible cultural experience in Hong Kong, often several times. I was a regular attendee of free classes in Tai Chi, Feng Shui, Chinese Tea Ceremony, Chinese Medicines, and even The Secrets of Jade Shopping, though I had neither the interest nor the funds to purchase anything.

Apart from my inability to speak Chinese, I could have run the tourism office single-handedly. When friends came to visit, I was prepared. I had done the research and then some. I set an itinerary: dine on Dim Sum at the Luk Yu Tea House, tram to the Peak, ferry to Lantau Island to see the world's largest Buddha at the Po Lin Monastery, shop for bargains among the rabbit-warren of stalls shoehorned into Li Yuen Street, and party into the wee hours at the nightclubs of Lan Kwai Fong. And that was just the first day. Our visitors included friends from Kwajalein and our friend Vicky, who'd since left New Zealand for Valencia, Spain, the venue for the next America's Cup competition. Though I imagined my father would be keen to revisit a place where, in 1971, he'd practiced dentistry in the Mandarin Oriental Hotel while his Navy destroyer tender, the USS Bryce Canyon, underwent refitting, my emails to him went unanswered.

🌴

After one steamy afternoon in the city, we noticed that a parking lot near the yacht club had been cleared of cars, and in their place a building was under construction. Perplexed by the bamboo scaffolding, I asked someone, who told me they were constructing a temporary structure to honor a local deity. Garth and I had already concluded that capitalism was the true religion of Hong Kong, though a mixture of Taoism, Confucianism, and Buddhism brought a rich cultural dimension to this bustling place. Because of Hong Kong's strong seafaring tradition, Tin Hau, Goddess of Seafarers—and, as sailors, certainly our favorite local deity—was honored everywhere. Before reclamation added real estate to areas once submerged, many temples had stood at water's edge; now their locations seemed somewhat illogical. Tucked into the tiniest pockets of space under a stairway or storefront indentation, were temples or miniature shrines to all sorts of deities, often with burning incense and carefully stacked bowls of fruit. It seemed as though locals had decided to appease spirits of the dead and any other potential deities, just in case.

The next day, the new structure was complete. Tin sheets covered the bamboo scaffolding and the sounds of musical performance wafted from its walls. I convinced Garth to duck inside for a listen. Inside, an empty line of folding chairs faced an elaborate red and gold set. On stage silk-costumed characters, heavily made-up beneath weighty black wigs howled like strangled cats. Inside felt like an inferno. You know the expression, "cat on a hot tin roof?" Well, we were *under* a hot tin roof. Two minutes of this Chinese opera was as much as I could bear.

🌴

June brought heavy rains that immediately explained the need for the impressive concrete retaining walls and deep gutters and trenches that we'd noticed lining every road. Spectacular thunderstorms packed a frightening intensity that made the ones we'd experienced in the Solomon Islands look like a warm-up act. A nearby boat lost all its electronics in a lightning strike, but fortunately we were spared.

During several torrential downpours, I carefully climbed into a dinghy filled with black rain to bail it, worried that the dinghy might sink if I waited until the rain stopped. I was shocked to note the distinct black scum line that had developed *inside* our freshly cleaned dinghy, clear evidence of the coal burning plants upwind in China that were the source of the poor air quality that stung my eyes and irritated my skin. Each week we moved *Velella* to the temporary guest dock to exercise the boat's engine, refill our water tanks, and wash the boat. And each week, within two days of scrubbing black tar off the cabin sides, I could write "Wash Me!" with my fingertips. Our once white dodger was slowly turning gray, with streaks of black where water dripped down the fabric. When I'd visited Hong Kong on business in June before the 1997 handover to China, I remembered clear, sunny, blazing hot days. Now, June days were still overwhelmingly hot, but rarely sunny. Was it possible such dramatic climate change could happen in less than ten years?

One morning after an oppressively heavy rain that pounded against the cabin-top all night making sleep nearly impossible, I went out into the cockpit, under the protection of our awning for a change of scenery. Heavy drops were falling into the milky, chocolate-colored water around us, which was filled with tree branches, plastic bags and other debris and flowing rapidly away from the stream at the head of the bay. I picked up a cushion to sit down. Beneath it, a foot long snake, an inch in diameter sat coiled into the space between stacked cushions. His suddenly-exposed head snapped to attention.

"Ahh!" I squealed and jumped to the far end of the cockpit two feet away.

"What?" Garth said.

"There's a snake!" I didn't know enough about snakes to know which were poisonous, though there were many in Hong Kong. I didn't feel like I was in a position to make subtle distinctions between colors and patterns of brown scaly skin that glistened menacingly in such close proximity.

"A snake?" Garth rushed to the companionway and took a peek from inside. I took in a sharp breath. Garth's sudden appearance close to the snake startled me. "Wow."

I twitched nervously, trying not to move, while Garth grabbed the end of boat brush from the V-berth and moved it slowly towards the snake. The open window over our bed sat below my feet, unnervingly close on one side of the snake, the open companionway a foot in the other direction. If he'd wriggled below, he might have hidden in any number of dark, cramped corners for a later surprise. The awning overhead posed another obstacle to getting the snake out of the cockpit without incident.

"Careful," I said, imagining all the possible scenarios: me getting bit, Garth getting bit, the snake slithering below. If he got inside our cramped quarters, how would we ever get him out?

The snake sluggishly wound his way around the pole. Garth gingerly flung him off the pole into the distance where we saw but couldn't hear his splash over the thunderous rain. Garth and I sat down on the cockpit cushions and watched the snake promptly wriggle back towards our boat, traversing the distance within a minute. He was intently targeting the rudder that hung on *Velella*'s transom, which had undoubtedly proved helpful earlier for climbing aboard.

When he got within reach, Garth poked at him again, lifted him out of the water, and flung him away again, further this time. As soon as the snake landed in the water he resumed his determined efforts to reach *Velella*.

"Guess he's found a spot he likes," Garth said, monitoring the snake's progress.

"Yeah, well, our dry cockpit sure looks cozy compared to that," I said, flinging a finger towards the sodden scene that lay beyond our awning.

When the snake got close a second time, Garth again pushed him away with his pole. The snake wriggled back in our direction once again, but was unable to overcome the rush of water against him. The tired snake clambered aboard a passing tree branch, riding it towards the opening of the bay.

"Whew," Garth sighed.

"Yikes," I said. "That was sure a surprise I wasn't expecting."

🌴

As summer gave way to fall, the weather cooled slightly— though it was still unbelievably hot for fall in the northern hemisphere—and Sandra officially invited me to join her company, exposing Hong Kong's notable expatriate population of school children to the great outdoors. If Garth and I hadn't been flush from freshly refilling our coffers in Kwajalein, we could have never afforded Hong Kong in the first place, but getting a temporary job leading youth adventures would help counterbalance the hemorrhage of funds, if only a little. Besides, then I'd have a perfect excuse for avoiding boat projects.

I'd expected I might work from time to time while we cruised, but before Kwajalein working had never been practical, and visa restrictions made it more difficult to work legally than I'd anticipated. After I filled out mountains of paperwork, my application was approved, and I got a work visa. Sandra had told me I'd need nothing more than a backpack (check) and "trainers" (hmmmn…) Though I wasn't a hundred-percent sure I understood what she meant by "trainers," since I didn't have any closed-toed shoes, I figured I might need some. I scoured the outdoor equipment shops alongside the stalls at the ladies market, and when I asked for "trainers," they steered me towards expensive trail shoes. I invested in the cheapest pair I could find. Soon I found myself practicing first aid, pitching tents on Tung Lung Island, scaling and rappelling vertical cliffs overlooking Hong Kong's many islets.

During the intensive staff training, I learned just how deluded I'd been when I told them I was fit. Harsh reality showed me that the "sport" of sailing, which, for me, typically involved uninterrupted hours of sitting on my kiester and drinking beer or reading a book punctuated by momentary flurries of action, did not quite prepare me to work in the company of ultra marathoners. In an instant, I felt positively geriatric.

During an adventure race, I was without-a-doubt the weakest member of my colleagues. I heaved and dripped in murderous heat, moving as fast as I possibly could, though I was clearly dragging down my team. With each step, my new trail shoes grew ever looser and my feet began bashing around inside the widening opening. I debated a stop to retie them, but decided it would cost too much time. I would pay for that decision for the next half year. In search of clues, we ran nonstop for miles, up and down hilly trails through underbrush, hopping over rock walls and bubbling streams.

At the end of the race, I opened my shoe to assess the damage. After my team suffered humiliating defeat, my bruised toenail turned black, loosened, and, as though dying a slow torturous death, finally fell off. Meanwhile, I still had to run as though nothing was amiss. (It took another six months for my toenail to return to how it looked before that blasted adventure race.)

Another day during staff training, suspended over a deep chasm on a zip line, I peered down on the waters of the South China Sea pounding against the rocks below. My safe return to the cliff edge from the middle of the line where I hung required pulling myself uphill hand-over-hand. My stomach growled, and I felt delirious with hunger. The distance seemed interminable. I cursed my habit of eating slowly. While my compatriots were adept at scarfing calories in record time, within seconds of returning to our demanding tasks, I'd realize I hadn't eaten enough to carry me through the afternoon.

The heat dampened my appetite, but I couldn't function unless I found a solution. A Powerbar™ taunted me from my backpack on the cliff, but it didn't do me much good now. Drawing on energy vapor and counting on adrenaline to ultimately fuel me to safety, I slowly worked my way up the line. When I finally stepped on terra firma at the end of the line, I resolved to keep a Powerbar™ in my pocket at all times. And to be more aggressive during our brief meal breaks. Soon I was elbowing my colleagues out of the way in the chow line.

Despite my anemic performance, I survived staff training. Not only did I get to go kayaking, rock climbing, rappelling, and running zip lines across deep canyons, I earned money for it.

🌴

On a sultry evening, a large group of us were sitting at a table outside Steamers Restaurant, a favorite expatriate hangout in Sai

Kung town. We'd just relocated for a curry dinner and pints of Carlsberg, Tetleys, or Beamish after regatta festivities had ended at Hebe Haven Yacht Club. The season finale merited a special outing.

Usually after the races, we ventured next door to one of the local Chinese seafood restaurants, called *dai pai dong*, to feast on seafood family-style at large plastic tables in an alley where restaurant owners washed dishes on the filthy concrete near our table. I was glad for my stomach of steel, because I'm sure that your average health department could fill a Tolstoy novel-sized notebook with health citations. And my mother would have been horrified at everyone's boarding house reach, dipping into communal platters with foot long chopsticks. But the seafood and Carlsberg were abundant and cheap, and group meals at the local *dai pai dong* with our racing friends replaced the strong community we'd left behind in Kwaj and within the cruising fleet.

A virtual United Nations sat at the table with Garth and me. One of my favorite aspects of Hong Kong was its international flavor, where well-traveled people from all over the world gathered together in this heavily British-influenced, technically Chinese territory. The people surrounding us mostly represented the commonwealth, if not the UK directly: Ireland, England, Wales, and Scotland, Australia, New Zealand, but also at the table were friends who were Japanese, Sri Lankan, and Indian. We were the token Americans. Our evening's conversation had run all over the map, but had just turned to politics, starting with American politics, which given the unpopularity of George W. Bush, we'd noticed was a source of continual fascination among people we'd met out traveling.

"How could you have elected that moron?" Murphy said. "Not just once, but twice?" He certainly hadn't been the first to express that sentiment. "Did you know he didn't even own a passport before he became president? Hadn't even *been* outside the U.S. In fact, only twenty percent of Americans even *own* passports. Or even have the faintest idea of geography. I bet if you asked them where China was, they couldn't even find it on a map." Murphy, a Kiwi, was one of the most hyper people I'd ever met. He never minced words when he had an opinion and usually fascinated me with his rapid-fire, blisteringly funny commentary on people and situations he encountered.

How could he possibly be a commercial airline pilot? He could barely sit still. He owned five sailboats, but he was too agitated to steer them in a race, so he'd arranged for Garth and others to steer his boat while he ran around the boat doing a little of every job, barking orders at everyone to "hop-to-it."

He'd just won the season sailing trophy on his thirty footer, *Wild at Heart,* and had strapped it to the hood of his Land Rover, like a fresh safari kill. Not even his dog pooping during the awards ceremony and the subsequent ribbing dampened his gloating.

Murphy was an equal-opportunity abuser, and we laughed at the cracks he made about nearly every nationality present, and many that weren't. Still, at the end of the evening, Garth and I were left shaken by the fresh reminder of how distant we'd grown from our own country.

🌴

Hong Kong's mixture of cultures from all over the world made it one of the most exciting places I'd been, and, for a time, I was tempted to stay beyond typhoon season. Yet the untenable heat of living aboard—or the shore alternative: cheaply constructed cell-block style apartment complexes streaked with pollution residue, with their maze of external piping and air conditioning units perched in each window—combined with acid rain fed by ferries and factories belching black smoke, ultimately convinced me to carry on.

🌴

For as long as I'd known him, Garth had always wanted to design and build his ideal cruising boat. As a young boy, he'd told me, he'd seen countless examples of ugly, poorly designed sailing boats and thought *I can do better than that,* and then set about training to become a naval architect. In a way, he'd been designing his dream cruising boat since he'd been a teenager sailing around the world with his family.

In fact, whenever we remained still for any length of time, his attention returned to designing a high-performance boat in which he could stand or sit comfortably. Each time we faced a new challenge, he thought about how his design might measure up in similar circumstances and would tweak it a bit, then run new calculations. He'd run ideas by me and ask my opinion, which I gave freely, never imagining I'd actually have to build the thing.

One steamy afternoon while I was pulling out the pressure cooker to make curried vegetable dahl for dinner, I broke the hinge on the pot cupboard for what seemed like the hundredth time. I looked over at Garth, who was reading a book. He'd seen me break it and grimaced. He tossed the book aside and sat up, bonking his head on the edge of the cabin sides in the process.

"You know, I'm so tired of fixing the same shit over and over again on this boat," he sighed, looking up menacingly at the wood above him and then rubbing his head. "And I'm tired of not being able to stand or sit up straight. Besides, I can't just keep hanging out. I need a new goal, and what I really want to do is build this boat."

His desire to build a boat was like a gnawing problem that I'd tried to keep at bay for years. Building the two-part nesting dinghy in New Zealand had dampened the urge for a time, but I knew it was temporary. In a fantasy world it sounded ideal to have a larger boat with features we couldn't find in any used boats we'd seen, yet even I was smart enough to know that the reality of building it wouldn't be quite so dreamy.

I had no interest in living amid boat construction. Living on the boat in the boatyard for even a week was my own private hell—a grimy, dusty, chaotic mess. Climbing up and down a rickety boat ladder to wash dishes or use the disgusting bathrooms that we found in boatyards was not my idea of "yachting," but I'd done a lot more of it than I cared to remember. Building a boat held little for me but the lonely prospect of becoming a boat widow. I wasn't being paranoid. I'd seen it before, when he'd built a dinghy for a friend while we were dating, built the *Tasty Penguin,* and then again when he built the Kwaj trailer. Each time, it had been tough on our relationship.

Shortly after we'd married, we met a couple, Dave and Candy, who were rebuilding their steel boat in a large warehouse, living in the tiny office space above, cooking on a camping stove. During a party in their industrial living space, I'd pulled Garth aside and quipped, "This is what our life would look like, shortly before the divorce."

Ten years later, we went voyaging on *Velella*. For years, we joked about Dave and Candy, still toiling in their Ballard warehouse wondering whether they'd ever go sailing again. A lifetime of fun, lost in sawdust and metal shavings. Last we'd heard they were just preparing to relaunch their boat. Meanwhile, we'd been out for six years, experiencing vastly divergent cultures, frolicking in waterfalls, and snorkeling in pristine aquamarine waters.

Sitting aboard in Hong Kong's scorching heat, Garth had been frustrated as a die-hard do-it yourselfer in a town full of people who hired out even the simplest tasks. We'd perplexed the yacht club staff, who expertly serviced member boats at modest prices. One worker couldn't help but wonder aloud why we did all our own work. Another asked how we could be "unemployed" for so many years.

Finally one afternoon, one of the yard workers stopped us, and, nodding wisely, said, "Ah, I think I understand now." As his face squinted into a smile, he raised a finger and said, "You work for *yourself*."

Getting the chance to discuss his design concepts with Tets, another trained naval architect, had refueled his desire to build a boat, though I don't suppose I could say it had ever really dimmed. Denying his dream was like trying to stop the tide.

Garth had talked with Tets and others about building it in China, others about the prospects for Thailand and the Philippines. None seemed promising, and Garth had expressed reservations about trying to supervise non-English speakers and the potential for cost overruns and mistakes. I wondered how we could afford to build a bigger boat. We could barely afford the upkeep on the boat we already had.

"What I need is an income and the raw materials. If I want to build a wooden boat like what we have, I need wood and marine parts. They really don't have any of that around here. The Pacific Northwest is a great source for wood; I have contacts, and I know marine suppliers for getting good deals."

"Yeah, I know a nice warehouse in Ballard that might be coming available," I said sarcastically, wondering whether Dave and Candy would divorce before their boat was back in the water.

"Yeah. That place would be perfect," Garth said, smiling at me. The sarcasm hung in the air for a moment. I shuddered, knowing how close it came to the truth.

A few days later at a fancy dinner out, complete with a rare indulgence of wine, Garth said, "I miss my family. You got to see your mom and dad several times because they came to visit, but I only got to see mine when we flew home from Kwaj."

"Maybe we should have flown home from Hong Kong in August when it was so unbearably hot."

Garth nodded, and we both turned quiet for a few minutes. Finally, he broke the silence. "We need to decide where we're going next, so we can buy charts."

We'd been over this ground many times. But every time, we'd reach an impasse and change the subject before we ever reached any sort of conclusion. We were terrible at deciding anything. We'd discuss possibilities endlessly, yet drag our feet on choosing a single course of action until the last-possible moment. Many decisions were made by default, as options disappeared.

"I want to sail to Malaysia and Thailand," I said. I feared sailing to Japan meant sailing home, and I didn't want to go home. Going home to me smacked of drudgery and paperwork. Every time we'd been on shore for any length of time, we were quickly buried in paper—marina bills, receipts, bank statements—that left my head swimming. I detested filling out forms, and shore side people seemed chained to them. I thought of my visits home, when my mother and I spent long hours handling business affairs. While I knew I needed to deal with those things, I resented how they drained the joy from our reunion, with endless lost hours trying to navigate through a rigid labyrinth of rules and procedures that didn't apply to our unusual circumstances. These experiences reminded me that outside our floating universe, I was just an anonymous account holder, whose disappearance would go unnoticed unless forms went unsigned or bills went unpaid. That didn't seem like living to me.

"And then what?" Garth said, bringing me back to our present conversation.

"I don't know, explore there for a while," I offered. Garth blew out a long breath.

"I can't just go to Malaysia and Thailand just to hang out. What about Japan?"

"Didn't you say we could do both?" I asked.

"That's what I was thinking originally. But after we wrecked everything in the Solomons and lost all that time in Kwaj working and fixing the boat...We've been away a long time. We've got some issues we need to deal with: the furniture that you inherited that's taking up space in your mom's house, the bill-paying that your mom is tired of handling. It's way more than she signed up for."

We'd finally set up automatic bill paying, but Mom still had plenty of business details to handle, and with all the traveling she was doing, handling our affairs was getting more complex. Garth had suggested hiring someone else to handle it when we were in Kwaj, yet I'd been afraid to make changes. Our arrangement felt like a house of cards. I worried that if I changed something, it would all come crashing down.

"What are you saying?" I said.

"I guess all I'm saying is that I can't just hang out forever. I need a goal. I think we need to wrap this trip up. We've got some things we need to deal with, and I'm ready to move on to other things, like building a boat, doing design work again, challenging myself technically."

"Doesn't sound like much fun to me," I said.

"There's a great saying I came across recently that said, 'Engaging work is more fun than fun,' or something like that. It's so true."

I thought about that for a few minutes, remembering times when I'd worked hard and had enjoyed it. But sailing wasn't always easy, and I couldn't think of anything else I'd rather do other than sail around the world. I imagined the harried pace of people back home. Right now that lifestyle held no appeal for me. I didn't see how I could live there again without getting sucked back into the frenzy. And for what?

With the help of wine, air conditioning, and candlelight, we pushed beyond the irritability of surviving oppressively hot weather and suffocating smog to discuss our future rationally. I relished the opportunity to reconnect with each other, something I felt like we hadn't done well lately in our short-tempered, overheated state. We talked animatedly late into the evening, discussing when and where we needed to travel to navigate safely around seasonal weather patterns.

The next morning after sleeping in, Garth said, "So we're going to finish sailing around the world in two years and then go back and build a boat in Seattle."

I'd had too much wine. I tried to remember how I'd agreed to such a thing. It must have sounded ideal at the time, in the heat of a brainstorming session, but in the stark light of day, it didn't sound terribly appealing to rush around the world on a schedule and miss so many areas I wanted to visit. I panicked.

"I didn't agree to that!" I blurted. Garth looked at me for a lingering moment and sighed. His shoulders dropped, and his energy level instantly dissipated. I too felt weary with the weight of my indecision.

Typhoon season ended in December, yet we still hadn't settled where we were going after we left Hong Kong. We'd start with the Philippines, but after that? We'd figure it out later. Garth bought charts for Japan, just in case.

CHAPTER
17

WALKING WALLETS IN THE PHILIPPINES

The South China Sea has a reputation for being a treacherous patch of shallow open water that can come to a boil in a hurry. Four days out of Hong Kong en route to the Philippines, we encountered waves whipped into a full froth and the motion on *Velella* wasn't pleasant.

I had just spooned our spaghetti dinner into the plastic dog bowls we used while underway. Gripping a bowl in each hand, I pivoted on my heel to face the companionway and a four-foot walk to where Garth sat expectantly, awaiting a hearty meal.

Just then an unexpected wave caught me off balance, and I dropped both bowls. They sailed across the width of the cabin, and landed with a muffled thud on the top edge of our fleece-covered cushions. Blood-red noodles and sauce splattered against the edge of painted wood above the seats and against the soft sage-green fleece fabric that protected our sweaty bare skin from the scratchy upholstery underneath. If I could have picked a worse place for this soupy red mixture to land, I couldn't think of it.

Gravity took over from there. The empty, tomato-stained bowls settled on the seats below, leaving a smudged greasy ring in their path, while crimson noodles slithered down vertical surfaces, as though they were unusually long worms writhing through soil. The slimy mixture oozed ever downward, dribbling track marks down the fleece and seeping into the crevices behind the seats where compartments stored charts, guidebooks, and the ship's log. Collateral damage in the form of splattered droplets that covered the nearby walls did not rest until gravity had been satisfied.

I stood frozen in a moment of disbelief. Then, regressing to early childhood, I launched into a full blown tantrum, albeit with a bit of adult language: "Fuck, fuck, fuck, fuck, fuck!"

Garth peered cautiously through the companionway at me.

"Damn it!" I stomped my feet. Though I wanted to jump up and down, I had to resort to stomping a single foot at a time, almost like a soldier on march, since I was getting jostled enough to know how dangerous that might be if I tried it. I picked up the empty bowls and hurled them into the sink. "Now, not only do we have no dinner. I have to clean all this crap up before it stains everything, if it's not too late already," I said, looking at the carnage. My stomach growled.

I flung my body onto the port side seat opposite, since the entire seating area on the starboard side of the boat was now occupied by a mess of gooey tomato slop. I put my head in my hands. I tried to cry, but tears wouldn't come. Finally I looked up at Garth with a weariness.

Sensing the storm had passed, Garth said gingerly, "Sorry. Didn't see those coming,"

"Ah, I should have known better," I said.

Garth astutely remained quiet.

My eyes drifted over to the mess again. What once looked so enticing now looked like recent indigestion. "God that looks disgusting."

"No kidding."

"So, how would you like a Powerbar for dinner?" I said, with a cynical edge to my voice.

"I was just craving one of those..."

The ridiculousness of the situation started to dawn on me, and we were both soon convulsing with laughter. After we'd laughed away some of the tension, I set about cleaning up the disaster I'd just created. I heaped noodles back into the pot I'd recently cooked them in, and then handed it to Garth to dump overboard.

"How am I ever going to get this clean again?" I said as I started to dab at the red-stained fleece.

"Wait. I have an idea," Garth said "You know that olive container? We could put the fleece slipcovers in there to soak until we get to the Philippines."

"That's a brilliant idea. We'd have the agitation cycle well covered by the time we got there." I grabbed the industrial-sized plastic olive jug, where we'd been storing rolls of paper towels. I loaded the fleece slipcovers with soapy water and tucked the container back up into the forepeak where it lived. This time the container was keeping the water *in* rather than *out*.

"You're so smart!" I said in my Adoring Girl tone when I finished.

"That's why you keep me around."

I wiped down the spaghetti-splattered charts and art supplies and chased all the wayward noodles I could find behind the seat backs—though more still lurked for later discovery. Then I served up our gourmet meal of Powerbars and nestled in next to Garth in the cockpit.

"What a fine meal, honey," Garth said facetiously as he crumpled up the wrapper.

"Except that you still have dishes to wash," I smiled.

"Maybe next time we should just skip the cooking part."

"Yeah," I laughed.

By the time we reached the Philippines, we both felt pretty beat up. When we'd left Hong Kong, *Velella* had been as well-prepared as ever, but after a rough crossing of the South China Sea, we had a slew of broken gear: a broken backstay, lifelines, and topping lift. A wave had punched through our dodger windows, shredding the fabric in the process. Though the spaghetti-stained cushion covers could wait, these other items demanded urgent attention, so we diverted to Subic Bay.

Three officials arrived at our boat to clear us in. As they lounged in *Velella*'s cockpit, their stomachs bulging over gold nugget belt-buckles, we completed paperwork and got our passports stamped. Then the immigration officer cleared his throat, shifted uneasily, and rubbed his hands as he told us that we needed to pay each of them fifty U.S. dollars.

Fifty *dollars* each?

Not pesos, U.S. dollars. The two others nodded in unison.

Our friend, Tets, who had been a delivery skipper for yachts to the Philippines, had relayed several stories about getting ripped off by officials there. "Subic Bay is the worst," he'd said. Even guidebooks had hinted that officials commonly demanded bribes. Little annoyed us tightwads more than knowing someone was trying to take advantage of us, to pilfer money we didn't have to spare. I glanced at the chunky gold-nugget necklace that hung around the neck of the immigration officer. Garth and I shared a long look. This had the rancid smell of a payoff to me.

Garth cleared his throat. Should we boldly declare that we knew we weren't required to pay this amount, or use delaying tactics? I eyed our passports, which the immigration officer had just set down, casually reached for them, and flipped through them until I spotted the visa stamp granting us ninety days. I set them below on the table.

Garth evenly explained that we would need to visit an ATM machine to obtain cash. The looks of disappointment that crossed their faces confirmed what I suspected. The wiliest of the three, the immigration officer, then drew a detailed map of how to reach his office so we could bring him cash in the next few days and promised he'd tell us how to reach the other offices so we could pay them. They looked doubtful. We nodded and smiled, indicating we'd stop by in the next few days, yet knowing that we'd already fulfilled our obligations.

A couple of weeks later, after fixing everything that had broken, we saw the immigration officer in town having dinner with friends. He didn't speak to us, but I could tell that he'd recognized us. Garth whispered to me, "We need to get out of here before his buddies pay us another visit." I nodded vigorously. We were ready to go. Subic, once home to a large U.S. Navy base, retained the sleazy remnants of sex-starved men on leave; strip clubs, prostitutes and skanky bars on dusty, crowded, litter-strewn streets, offered nothing in the way of charm to encourage a longer stay.

The next morning we awoke early, and Garth went to pay our marina bill while I readied the boat for sailing. Sarah and Clement aboard *Kuroshio*, the next boat over, had invited me for coffee, so I joined them when I finished. Garth tromped down the dock, fuming with anger. "This place is just one big rip-off."

"What happened?" I asked.

"It cost like ten times what I expected to pay—more than any marina in the U.S. that actually has facilities."

When we'd arrived, we pulled into the more derelict of two marinas, thinking it'd be more affordable. Where we'd stayed had no electricity, a serious garbage problem (which also meant a rat problem), and the most disgusting, broken-down, mildewed bathrooms I'd ever bathed in.

Garth's voice had a razor-sharp edge as he went on, "I think this crappy marina cost more than the resort marina across the waterway with nice docks, Wi-Fi, and clean bathrooms." With a jab of his thumb towards a boat on the end of the dock. He added "And on our bill were charges for water they used to wash every line, cleat, and fender on the boat and scrub mildew from every single item aboard." A Philippine-based Frenchman visiting our friends shrugged his shoulders, the universal symbol for *that's the way it is*.

With an attitude of disgust, Garth disappeared aboard *Velella*, while our friends commiserated and offered other discouraging examples of Philippine corruption they'd encountered. After a couple of minutes, Garth called to me from our boat, "Come on, we need to get out of here."

"Yeah, you're right," I said, reluctantly, and returned to *Velella*. Just then a small middle-aged Filipino man wearing a Western shirt, jeans, and cowboy boots strode authoritatively up the dock. He introduced himself as the chief medical officer and asked to come aboard. Garth gave me a look that said, *see what your dawdling cost us?*

He commented on the weather and asked us where we'd come from and about our visit so far. I could sense Garth's impatience as we chatted idly. After several minutes, he broached the subject that must have brought him there.

"We in the medical department provide a service to our people to keep them safe from disease. It takes resources to provide these services." He gave us an earnest look and continued, "You are from America. America is the wealthiest country. The Philippines is a small country with limited resources. But we do not need your charity." In that same roundabout way, it dawned on me that he was in the midst of an elaborately choreographed attempt to solicit the same $50 bribe his junior colleague had been unsuccessful in securing the day we arrived. For the next half hour, Garth and I listened with as much patience as we could muster to a seemingly endless string of repetitive, contradictory statements as his diamond ring glinted in the brilliant sunshine. We provided no hint that we understood the purpose of his visit, and he made no formal request. Possibly realizing that he was making no progress, he departed, saying without irony, "Enjoy your visit to the Philippines."

As the man walked away, Garth vented a stream of hot air. "This harassment isn't going to stop until we leave the country, is it? Who needs this crap? Why don't we just sail to Kota Kinabalu, Brunei, or Singapore instead? So what if we don't have clearance papers. We probably wouldn't be the first boat to arrive without exit clearance from the corrupt Philippines."

Our neighbors, who'd heard the exchange, said, "You're checked in. Come with us to Puerta Galera. We'll have fun." I stared at them, paralyzed by indecision.

"Come on; let's get out of here before his friends show up." Garth said. He started the engine. I untied the lines and jumped aboard, feeling like a criminal on the run from the law.

As we motored out into the bay, we debated whether to leave the country or head to another Philippine port. Perhaps it wasn't fair to judge the Philippines harshly from our experience in Subic Bay, but our friends hadn't provided much evidence for hope. Even the Lonely Planet guide wasn't terribly charitable, describing Puerta Galera as "something of a haven for foreign, alcoholic retirees."

Okay, there were a few arguments for staying: The weather had been clear and warm, with a nice breeze to keep the boat cool. Hills silhouetted in the distance provided a spectacular backdrop for some of the most colorful sunsets we'd ever seen. And the Philippines grew the smoothest, most flavorful mangoes we'd ever tasted.

Still, our patience had worn thin. What finally convinced us to give the Philippines another chance besides our friends' touching plea, was thinking of the people who'd planned to visit us there and knowing that once we sailed west, we'd probably never sail to Japan. We didn't anticipate the impact our decision might have on us.

Garth and I stayed in Puerta Galera just long enough to concur with the disparaging description of our Lonely Planet guide. Then we struggled for days in light winds and calm seas to reach one of several famous marine sanctuaries, all strangely named Apo Reef, where we dreamed of spectacular snorkeling. To avoid sailing at night, we made several overnight stops in rolly anchorages, where morning couldn't come soon enough. On a moonless night, unlit oil drums used to attract fish would be invisible, and striking one could prove fatal.

As we neared the reef in sparkling sunshine, we saw the iridescent hue of what looked like a swimming pool on the horizon, reflected in clouds that hovered above. But that inviting teal-colored water was too shallow to offer safe anchoring, so we carried on to the island, where moorings made staying overnight possible in what might otherwise be a nearly untenable anchorage. Near the island, depths rose abruptly from over 100 feet to 25, where coral heads jutted up from the ocean bottom. A curved sand spit stretched from the island, creating minor protection from the choppy seas that fresh south winds had churned up. Its pure white sand glistened invitingly in the late afternoon sunlight and palm trees swayed in the breeze. In the crook of the sand spit was a line of steel drum moorings, painted bright orange. We tied to one of them, relieved that we could finally relax.

We had just enough light for a brief snorkel. Garth rushed into the cool water in full gear while I lingered in the cockpit. Exhausted from several previous nights of poor sleeping conditions in miserable anchorages and reluctant to get wet at this late hour, I savored a quiet moment, assuming I'd snorkel the following day. I felt the low sun on my shoulders, and fought the pull of sleep in my eyes.

"Wendy, this water is so clear, I can see everything!" Garth said, popping his head up briefly. "You should come in." Over the side, tiny yellow shapes darted about alongside the boat.

"I know; I can see the fish from here." As he disappeared beneath the surface again, I laid stomach-down along the deck edge and propped my chin on my hands to appreciate how the incredible water clarity would let me watch schools of silvery fish shifting in unison to a silent symphony. I felt the tension of our frustrating sail beginning to dissipate.

I coveted the first solid night's sleep in days, but that proved impossible for us that night. We spent a harrowing, worried night of emergency management, as the boat wallowed in swell and wind waves that collided against a strong current. We'd seen little in the way of tides since we'd left New Zealand and didn't give tide or current a moment's thought before we settled in for the night. Perhaps if we'd been rested, we'd have noticed those telling details that might have prevented later heartache. But I've noticed that sleep deprivation has a curious effect on the powers of reason.

Just as we were settling into a slumber, I heard the steel mooring drum grating along the new paint we'd painstakingly applied in under an unforgiving Kwajalein sun. *God, I hate mooring balls*, I thought as I dragged myself from our bunk. I trusted my own anchor far more than a buoy anchored by God-knows-what and placed there by God-knows-who, God-only-knows-when. But anchoring wasn't possible here, and in our delirium, we'd forgotten to employ the techniques we'd learned to minimize the chance of the mooring slamming against the hull in the night.

By the time I clambered to the cockpit, the mooring ball had reached the transom and become entangled between the dinghy and the wind vane on the back of the transom. Garth quickly joined me. The snarled line held both the dinghy and the mooring ball firmly against the boat hull so that, with each successive wave, both smacked against the hull until we could wrestle them free. Choppy uneven waves tossed us about, leaving us unsteady on our feet and apprehensive about moving around the boat in the eerie, moonless darkness. We finally separated the mooring from the dinghy with the help of a boot hook. Then we rigged the spinnaker pole on the mast and ran the mooring line over it to hold the mooring buoy away from the boat so the wave action wouldn't cause us to collide with it.

At one in the morning, the wind and waves churned so fiercely that the spinnaker pole began snapping abruptly against the head stay. The rapid, rhythmic clanking of metal against metal was deafening. Even if we could bear the noise, we knew we couldn't ignore the stress on the pole and the forestay, so again we dragged ourselves from our bunk. As we unrigged the spinnaker pole, the boat bounced more violently than before, making work on the small dark foredeck difficult. I worried I'd whack Garth in the face or fall overboard as I unhooked the pole from the mast ring. The pole began swinging wildly in my grasp, throwing me about until Garth could lower it to the deck. We returned to bed, less optimistic about the prospects of getting rest, but our eyes drooped in exhaustion and we fell asleep anyway.

At 4:00 a.m., I awoke to the sound of water crashing on rocks. The tide must have dropped dramatically, and I was hearing waves pounding on a surface reef. With the new wind direction, the boat had swung around so that our stern was backed up against a line of jagged coral, now only twenty feet behind us. With every roll of the swell, I was acutely aware of the threatening fangs of coral that lurked nearby, ready to tear a hole in *Velella* if we drifted backward too far. For us, Apo Reef was no marine sanctuary.

"Let's get the hell out of here," Garth said.

"No. I don't think it'd be such a good idea when we can't see a blasted thing."

So we watched and waited until the first hint of dawn.

We sailed on to Coron, where we planned to get our visas renewed and resupply with groceries. We'd also heard that the area offered good diving. We worked our way down the coast of Busuonga to Coron Town in two *long* days. First we encountered a dead flat calm, and then suddenly wind rose from our destination, quickly building menacing waves that threw us about. *How does a sailor know in which direction his destination lies? The direction from which the wind is blowing, of course,* I thought grumpily. My patience was wearing thin.

We threaded our way between coral patches against a low sun. Ashore the next morning, we found ourselves baking under an unforgiving sun in another dusty, dilapidated town only to discover that the immigration office had relocated to another island. From the moment we stepped out of our dinghy, for the rest of the afternoon, we were hassled every ten minutes or so by a zealously friendly, self-appointed, "guide," who wanted to show us his cousin's store.

I braced my nerves for crossing the street, always an exciting proposition in the Philippines. At only nine in the morning, I was already overwhelmed by the oppressive heat, bright colors, and noise. In the road, drivers were busy honking and weaving, waving and hollering from cars, motorcycles, and jeepneys.

Jeepneys—pimped up jeeps, extended and painted bold primary colors, then armed with extra chrome, lights, and horns—functioned like buses. Each proudly displayed the owner's family name in swirly, gaudy letters; a crucifix typically swung from the rearview mirror, with a portrait of Jesus displayed above the driver's head. Music blared through the open windows with an excess of bass that shook the ground and shifted my heartbeat until the next jeepney pulsated a different frequency. No matter how overloaded, there was always room for a couple more passengers in a jeepney—on the roof, if necessary. The same was true for what they called "tricycles," a three-wheeled motorcycle with an enclosed side car to hold passengers that served as taxis.

A lack of pedestrians on the road was my first clue that walking was a dangerous sport. Filipinos rented tricycles for even the shortest distances, probably out of fear of being run over.

We wouldn't have had to wait to rent a tricycle, but we didn't have far to walk. Besides, we'd hired one before and discovered that Garth didn't fit. He had to scrunch down in the seat to keep from slamming his head into the frame as the tricycle bumped over each pothole.

Every few steps, someone asked, "Tricycle, Sir?" or "Tricycle, Ma'am?" With a ratio of about fifty tricycles to every customer, the soliciting was constant, and I felt like a mobile ATM machine. Since we didn't look like locals, with our pasty-white skin and my blond hair, we always seemed to get a "special" price, which we'd have to renegotiate after the service was rendered. Our budget was tighter than everyone assumed.

During a break in the flow of traffic, I dared to step off the curb. An errant tricycle swerved straight towards me as he dipped around a pothole. I flung my body against a post. Finally we scurried across the street to the relative safety of the opposite sidewalk.

Every time we turned around, there was our obnoxious "friend," pointing us in the direction of his cousin's store, as though it were our highest priority. To him, I think we were just walking wallets. When we finally relented and let him lead us into the store, the shelves were sparse and a mixture of hardware and canned goods were sequestered behind a counter filled with waiting customers. For each item, we would have to request assistance and a price. Garth sighed and nodded towards the door. No discussion necessary. We walked out. We were dripping with a grimy sweat, starting to feel depressed; all that hard sailing …for this?

Later, as we sipped a cool mango shake at a shady restaurant and dive shop, the thought of a dive on a World War II wreck finally lured us out of our funk. We were anxious to escape the noisy, dusty town and we decided a day on the water would be perfect. So we booked two dives for the following day.

We arrived at the dive shop the next morning, exhausted after a night kept awake by competing karaoke bars. No matter how hard I'd tried, I'd been unable to ignore the excruciatingly out-of-tune voices singing with gusto as though each envisioned being the next winning contestant on *American Idol*.

In the shop, others were suiting up for the day. An elderly American man with a huge paunch watched lustily as his nubile Filipina wife wriggled into a wet suit. Two young German men intently studied their dive computers. A couple of Brits, a Dane, and another American rounded out our group, a virtual diving United Nations. In the distance, several Filipino workmen shifted dive tanks across a narrow gangplank onto a bangka, an outrigger that was tied to the concrete pier.

Bangkas have high pointed bows and sterns with bamboo outriggers strapped to each side of the hull that lightly touch the water and gently balance the boat as its weight shifts. Their gangly shape reminded me of water bugs. An emergency bamboo raft perched on top of the flat roof. It looked like in the event of an emergency and need to abandon ship, only four people would be able to fit on the raft. The rest would be out of luck.

After selecting our gear and suiting up, we boarded the bangka for the day's outing. One of the Filipino crew pulled on the anchor line while another untied us from the dock. A third shifted the bangka engine into gear. We pulled away from the concrete and rebar buildings that lined the waterfront, passing a series of shacks perched out over the water on piers made of sticks. As our bangka picked up speed, I watched with concern the front tip of one outrigger dragging in the water. A cartwheel on this baby wouldn't be pretty.

The afternoon before, after studying a map of local wrecks, we'd selected dives that allowed us to venture inside a World War II Japanese freighter and an oil tanker in 80-100 feet. We stopped first at the *Kogyo Maru,* an unlucky freighter sunk in Coron Bay at the tail end of World War II. As we descended with the two inexperienced Germans and our Filipino dive master, I noticed that my air smelled a little like exhaust, and debated what to do. Then I spotted a fast-moving turtle, and forgot about my smelly air. I did my best to keep up with him, but my flippers were no match. Just as I lost sight of him, a lionfish caught my eye. And then a barracuda, a black-tipped shark, a triggerfish, and a couple of cobalt blue wrasses as we reached the wreck itself. Soft coral in a riot of pinks, reds, and purples billowed in the current from where it clung to the ship. When I emerged from the dive, I was flush with excitement. The indigo water sparkled in the bright sunshine, and a gentle breeze danced across the deck.

I wandered to the back deck where several aluminum pots, bowls, and utensils were laid out with lunch. A cooler of bottled drinks sat nearby. I was pleasantly surprised at how delicious the rice and chicken stew turned out to be, perhaps because I'd worked up a voracious appetite. Out at sea, I'd noticed, almost anything tastes delicious.

After lunch, I headed to the upper deck, hoping for a snooze. Shortly after I got there, one of the Brits appeared and lit a cigarette, so I gave up on the nap idea.

As I descended the stairs, a rapid-fire staccato of Tagalog caught my attention. The crew was hovering over the engine box. I peered around the corner, and saw that one man was epoxying a broken pipe on the engine, while the other two were smoking. Garth caught my eye and a slow grin crept across his face.

After we lounged a little longer in the sunshine, the bangka rumbled to life. Evidently the epoxy engine repair had worked. We motored on to the *Taiei Maru,* an oil tanker of the Japanese Imperial Navy that went down in October 1944. This time my air was fine. Our dive master warned us that the current would be strong, but as I hit the water I was still surprised at how fast my body zipped past the boat. I descended quickly so I wouldn't have to fight the current at the surface. At deck level in 100 feet, a more gentle current swept us along the edge of the sunken ship. This ship had caught fire before it sank, leaving large openings that let us duck inside.

I got a thrill from being able to do penetration dives, which had been forbidden in Kwajalein, even for advanced divers. Penetration dives pose the risk of getting trapped inside a cargo hold from catching the edge of a tank or an air hose. I appreciated the extra technical challenge it required and the opportunity to see intact historical artifacts that are best preserved inside a wreck. I followed closely behind our dive master so I wouldn't miss anything he might point out. As we floated through the pilot house windows past the steering station, our dive master called our attention to instruments and gear levers. Brightly colored fish darted between rungs of a ladder that led to the lower deck. Our dive master gestured toward a collection of sake bottles that floated just under the ceiling. Coils of line coated with a fine layer of soft coral formed a guarded fortress where sea anemones moved rhythmically to silent music.

With my digital camera tucked into a waterproof case, I snapped a photo each time we entered or exited a hatch or window, or ventured through a narrow passageway, and every time I spotted a new species. Our dive master swam through a shaft of light and disappeared. I lingered to snap another photo, and then dove through the gap where the propeller used to be. I emerged into open water.

Out of the corner of my eye, I noticed Garth gripping the rudder with white knuckles. He looked comical with his hair and t-shirt billowing as though he were facing a giant fan. Then the current took hold of me, and I realized why. As I swept past, Garth reached out and yanked me abruptly back to the rudder. I clutched the rudder blade tightly to counter the force of water flowing against me, scanning the blue for our dive master and fellow divers. When I spotted the anchor line about twenty yards away, I pointed it out to Garth. He nodded as though he'd known it was there all the time, as though he'd been waiting for me, anticipating how surprised I'd be by the ripping current. I thought of how far I might have been swept if he hadn't grabbed me. I might have resurfaced as a tiny dark dot on a billowing blanket of choppy waves, a half mile from the boat. Garth tempered my blind faith that everything would work out by making sure that it did.

Once I reached the surface and shed my dive gear, I headed for the empty hammock, filled with a mix of contentment and adrenaline. I could hardly think of a more peaceful place to be. My concerns about cart wheeling over a pontoon, the inadequate life raft, the epoxied engine, and a ripping current melted from my mind. And the mayhem of town seemed a million miles away.

Desperate for another escape from the town's depressing chaos, we scoured our guidebook for another, hopefully free, oasis. A freshwater lake on a nearby limestone island sounded ideal. The next day, we motored our dinghy a couple of miles across Coron Bay, and pulled into an enclosed bay, surrounded by sheer rock walls, with water that had the iridescent hue of a swimming pool. In the crowded Philippines, the rare unspoiled beauty of this island, preserved by its tribal caretakers, took my breath away.

A tribal guide led us up to cozy land caves, past scenic overlooks and downward to a sizeable freshwater lake nestled in the island's interior. Jagged vertical ivory cliffs hovered over pale blue-green water. We lingered most of the afternoon at this secluded lake, listening to birds sing and floating in water-filled caves. Tiny needlefish darted between us. Shrimp nibbled our shriveled toes and ankles until we extracted ourselves from the water before we lost the rest of our skin.

We could have easily spent days in this magical spot, but we still needed to renew our Philippine visas at the nearest immigration office, which was a several day sail away.

🌴

While we worried about encountering more corrupt officials, renewing our visas was only one of the challenges we faced. We had no wind, as usual. If we wanted to get to Iloilo before our visas expired, we had to step up our pace. I could only imagine how our hassles would compound if our Philippine visas expired before we had the chance to renew them.

Tired of bobbing and making little to no headway, I turned on the engine. I punched the RPM up to 2,300 and felt the reverberations of Garth flumping his body as he rolled over in the bunk below the cockpit, as though he was restlessly expressing his disgust. I settled into as comfortable a position as I could manage where I could still reach the tiller. Soon I was in a zombie-like state.

Over the dull roar of our engine I heard the telltale putt-putting of a muffler-less motor. Unpainted wood bangkas were nearly invisible from any distance. I made a careful scan of the horizon, tipping my head subtly, trying to identify the exact direction of the noise-source so that I'd know where to focus my eyes in the expanse of blue that stretched before me. To my left, I detected a flash of movement. A large wooden fishing bangka cut towards us, its course and speed bringing it across our path.

As the bangka drew closer, I could see five sturdy young men aboard. Three stood in the back of the main hull, one steering while two others stood behind him, their muscular arms folded grimly across their chests. Farther forward, a man braced a foot aggressively against a support for an outrigger, his hands resting on his hips. Another man sat hunched on the opposite outrigger, his arms wrapped around his bent knees, a crimson bandana encircling his head. The helmsman waved wildly, and I realized that he intended to intercept us. I tightened my grip on the tiller and stood taller. The men's stance didn't strike me as friendly, and I grew apprehensive. Their dirty t-shirts and shorts gave them the look of a group of outlaws. I pictured myself from their perspective: a small foreign woman on a "yacht," appearing to be alone. I felt instantly vulnerable. My heart began beating double-time in my chest.

We'd been lucky in all our years of sailing, though we'd left our boat unlocked and unattended almost everywhere we'd visited. A pair of Garth's Tevas, carelessly left overnight in the dinghy floating behind *Velella,* vanished while we slept on what we'd thought was an unpopulated Vanuatu island. Cash and a few music CDs mysteriously disappeared from unlocked boats in Fiji's Musket Cove during a spate of petty thefts until a local chief helped identify the culprit. Village justice had been swift and brutal, with most items promptly returned to their rightful owners undamaged. Overall, the number of incidents we'd heard about in years of sailing were far fewer than in big cities back home.

Piracy is far rarer than the petty crime and grand larceny we see every day in bigger cities, but its oddity captures our imaginations. Our anxiety about it is heightened by our fear of the unknown. Most pirates targeted lucrative large cargo-carrying commercial vessels that paid ransom or carried coveted goods that could be spirited away undetected merely by stealthily breaking the seals on a container. Still, threats against pleasure craft do happen, so we made a practice of avoiding places that sounded risky.

In the Solomon Islands, we'd heard a man on a fancy catamaran plead over shortwave radio for another boat to visit the island in Papua New Guinea to help rescue him from his dismal situation. Thieves had smashed his companionway door and stolen all his electronic charting equipment. Since he'd carried no paper back ups, he was unable to move safely in an area known for submerged reefs. Later, other frightening stories confirmed our decision to steer clear of Papua New Guinea. These were not just tall tales or rumors, but incidents that happened to people with whom we'd shared potluck meals only a few weeks earlier. One Australian couple we'd met in New Zealand had squirmed at gunpoint on a tourist bus while thieves stole their money and boat parts they'd spent an entire day collecting. Another Australian cruising couple awakened in the middle of the night to a man brandishing a knife, which he held against the woman's throat while another man gathered wallets and jewelry.

Though we'd avoided the notoriously risky piracy areas of Papua New Guinea and Mindanao in the southern Philippines, we were still sailing through an area where pirate activity had been reported infrequently in the past. As the littlest boat in the cruising fleet, we counted on being one of the least attractive potential targets. But all things are relative. Even a thirty-one-foot boat, which few in the U.S. would consider entrusting their lives to, would be considered luxurious in many areas, and certainly here. Given that there were no other "yachts" within a hundred miles, we probably looked conspicuously wealthy.

With five of them and two of us—one weighing only 104 pounds and the other currently snoring in the bunk and not likely to be at his fighting best—my prospects did not look favorable if their intentions were hostile. I considered waking Garth, but worried that I was overreacting. Perhaps with a little discouragement, they'd lose interest. I jacked the RPM up to 3,000. I didn't know if I could outrun this bangka with its five testosterone-infused crewmembers, but I thought it was worth a try.

The change in our speed must have awoken Garth, because just then he appeared in the companionway with a questioning look. He knew my stubborn desire to handle things myself and natural inclination to wait until the last possible moment to ask for help. I nodded my head in the direction of the bangka. Garth joined me in the cockpit. At that moment, the two men in the back with the helmsman held up fish.

"Slow down. They just want to sell us some fish," Garth said in a relaxed tone, as he rubbed his eyes.

"I'm not slowing down. We don't need any fish," I said through clenched teeth. "Besides, how exactly would we exchange fish for money with that gangly boat without wrecking our paint job?"

Garth shrugged. I made an exaggerated shake of my head and waved my hands to indicate to the men that we didn't want any fish. At that moment, the man who'd been glowering on his haunches held up a net, then sliced his fingers across his throat.

"He's saying we snagged his fishing net!" I said. Garth looked over our transom and shook his head vigorously. Outraged, I continued, "There's no way we could have cut his fishing net." If we *had* sliced his fishing net, we'd have a tangled mess in our propeller and would have certainly noticed. I shook my head vigorously again.

My faster rate of speed gradually created distance between us. I breathed a little easier as they slipped behind us.

Maybe I had overreacted. At only three in the afternoon, we had bright sunshine and hours before it grew dark. Still, I remained spooked until long after Garth took over his watch at 4:00 p.m., and I cooked dinner.

Though we tried to avoid sailing at night in this area, especially given the unlit buoys, we didn't always have a choice given the geography and the distances. This would be one of those overnight sails. As darkness descended, a slight breeze brewed from the east and we turned off the engine to try to sail.

I worried the men would return. Without a moon, sailing alone in the darkness was eerie. During my 8:00 p.m. to midnight watch, I fidgeted restlessly.

As hours passed uneventfully, my tension gradually evaporated. Out there, so far from any residual light, stars were so thick I could barely discern individual constellations. Waves lapped lightly against the bow as *Velella* eased through the water. I felt completely alone in my own little world, just me and my thoughts about our thrilling wreck dives and our tranquil escape to the fresh water of Cayangan Lake. I had to admit the Philippines hadn't been all bad, though I still dreaded the potentially sticky process of renewing our visas.

A noise jarred me back to the present. In front of our bow I heard voices in the darkness. In an instant, all my senses were on high alert. I strained my eyes in the blackness, but I could see nothing. I felt as though I were trying to peer through a thick woolen blanket. *They're back. Where had they come from? How had they crept up on me?*

My mind clicked into high gear and thoughts gushed into my brain like a torrent of confused waves. *This is it.* This time it would be us that people would read about in the papers. That is, if anyone ever heard about our demise at all. Perhaps we'd be judged harshly, considered poor misfortunate fools who had flirted with danger. Maybe they'd use it to justify their greatest fears, confirm their decision to stay home which they considered safe. I could hear the clucking teeth as our portraits, supplied mournfully by our grieving mothers, caught readers' eyes before they casually flipped to the movie listings. Our story might turn into an overwrought made-for-TV movie: *Piracy on the High Seas.* Still I didn't regret my decision to go sailing. Even though it hadn't always been easy, I would make the same choice again. Perhaps I'd skip the Philippines, but probably not. Despite everything, it had certainly been interesting. And at least I would have died having felt like I'd really *lived*.

An engine roared to life in front of me. I needed to waken Garth, so he could prepare for whatever we might be facing. *Dear God, if you're up there listening, I could really use a hand right about now.* The muffler-less engine at close range was alarmingly loud. Louder than even my heart, which beat wildly in my chest. At that instant, I expected lights to shine brightly in my eyes as they hopped aboard and tossed me over, or worse: grabbed my wrists and pushed me down. I braced myself for whatever might come next.

Yet what came next surprised me. That pulsating engine quickly grew faint. And then I was alone.

By the time I calmed down, a sliver of moon appeared on the horizon, and Garth was rousing himself to take over his watch. He was surprised by my enthusiastic embrace and kisses. As I described my experience to him, in the moon's reflection on the water, I saw a shadow slip past, sending a jolt through me yet again. In a moment it was gone.

"Did you see that?" I said, pointing into what must have looked like thin air.

"No." Garth replied, looking at me with a ruffled brow. "Maybe you should get some sleep."

When I returned to relieve him four hours later, Garth blurted, "You know, I thought you were losing it before you went to bed, but I had that happen to me twice while you were asleep. I nearly had a heart attack." I stopped before clipping on my harness to look at him. "The second time, I saw a cigarette ember just before I heard the engine start up. Maybe we snuck up on a sleeping fisherman and scared him as much as he scared us." He shuddered. "It's creepy."

"I can hardly wait until morning." I said, thinking of the two hours I had yet to endure before the sun made its way over the horizon. "Let's figure out how many more miles we have to go. Maybe we should do a little motoring. I'd rather not spend another night out here with all these unlit fish attracting devices and mysterious fishermen, or pirates …or whatever they are."

When we anchored outside the city of Iloilo, where there was an immigration office, we discovered just how exposed the anchorage was. The curve of the land offered little protection from the winds that gusted down the narrow strait between the island of Panay and Guimaras, where we were nestled. Added to our agitation about renewing our visas was the worry that *Velella* would drag anchor. Or be run down by an errant ferry. Or that our dinghy would be gone when we returned to collect it from the only wide spot along the beach, next to the city's sewage outflow.

"Ah, yes…Isn't yachting glamorous?" Garth said in a mock-satisfied tone with a wry smile as we picked our way around sewage that trickled from a large cement pipe that dead-ended at the water only fifty yards from where *Velella* was anchored. The stench was powerful enough to turn my stomach.

"Quite," I replied imitating a clipped British accent, pausing to step over the plastic bags that littered the grey sand. I stopped to shake off the sand—and God knows what else—that had crept under my Tevas. I shuddered to think about it.

"I think this needs to be a quick stop."

"Yup," I concurred, nodding emphatically.

"I sure hope our dinghy is here when we get back," Garth said, giving me a lingering look.

"No kidding."

We hoofed our way towards the immigration office full of dread, dodging the mayhem of cars, tricycles, and Jeepneys that scurried haphazardly around the paved streets. Yet our worries about renewing our visas were unfounded.

The moment the ink dried on our visa stamps, we found a large Western-style grocery store that seemed straight out of the 1950s, where we overloaded a grocery cart with pasta, rice, flour, sugar, and cans of tomatoes and roasted peppers. Then we stuffed our purchases into our backpacks and expandable tote bags until they strained at the seams. We trudged back towards the dinghy, as overloaded as a couple of pack mules, sweat dripping down our backs and our faces covered with grime. The dinghy and oars were still there, fortunately, though it was filled with grimy sand, evidence that children had found our wooden dinghy an appealing play platform.

At dawn's first light, we escaped Iloilo's exposed anchorage to seek a more protected one. Once again we endured a windless sail, followed by sudden squally conditions that tried our patience. Almost instantly, we were awash in flying spray and laid over. When we reached the southernmost bay on the island of Negros, due to the stellar combination of sketchy charts and the difficulty of identifying coral patches below tumultuous waves, we faced another reef entrance that threatened to turn our home into kindling. What drew us there was rumor of a well-protected bay near where a Hong Kong friend would be passing through. We anticipated a happy reunion with her, but began to have our doubts. We were on the verge of giving up when a fishing bangka waved us over and led us safely through the pass. The placid green water inside seemed like an oasis.

But the surface tranquility of this well-protected bay was deceiving. Port Bonbonon was rife with tumultuous expatriate politics. Expatriates, proud of their rugged individuality, bristled at the interdependence that living in a small community demanded. In a matter of hours, we learned that Nigel, an Australian resort owner, was at war with the Swiss-German resort owner, Bruno, due to some past transgression I never completely understood. Both resented Bruce, the American who had a spring on his property that supplied the water to the area. Like most of the balding, shriveled expatriate men we'd met in the Philippines, all were married to Filipina women a generation or two younger, and were raising a second family young enough to be their grandchildren. Any conversation with inhabitants that lasted more than a few minutes quickly descended into sniper fire about someone we'd just met. As I looked around at these people, it occurred to me that people we'd encountered who'd settled for "the easy life" showed signs of boredom: heavy drinking, bickering, and self-created dramas. Perhaps the path of least resistance, while it offered a temporary respite from the struggles of life, ultimately held no great opportunity for growth, which was what made life most interesting.

A weatherproof bay such as this offered an irresistible oasis to more sailboats than we'd realized traveled the entire country. While most boats were merely moored there—many on the verge of sinking from neglect—we found ourselves immersed in a small community of voyaging sailors. And where cruising sailors congregate, potlucks and cocktail parties are sure to follow. Our social calendar wasn't quite as jam-packed as it had been in the South Pacific, but I was again purring with delight. I realized just how acutely isolated I'd felt without a community and how that isolation had drained the sparkle from my cruising experience.

Our time together was short. Our lifestyle was one of constant change, hellos and goodbyes. Yet even a brief encounter with others living the vagabond-sailor lifestyle we had chosen gave us a chance to vent our inevitable frustrations while reminding us why we'd chosen to live this way. After two weeks we needed to be on the move again. We had more visitors coming.

Garth had pointed out how naïve I had been to plan three meetings with friends in places hundreds of miles from each other. After meeting Elly from Hong Kong near Port Bonbonon at the southernmost point of Negros, less than a week later, we had a reunion with Randy from Guam and Annie from Kwaj at the north end of Mindoro, followed by a charge north to Luzon to meet the Hong Kong racing fleet as they arrived in San Fernando. The country was much bigger than I'd realized and our mode of transportation wasn't always the most efficient, traveling at the pace of a fast walk, *if* we had wind.

But I had stubbornly refused to listen to his reasoning. I wanted to see everyone, and that was that.

The wind funneled between long narrow islands, creating some areas where the wind blew powerfully strong and others with geographic wind shadows, where not a breath of air could pass, ever. We went from shivering and getting thrown about in raucous, wild conditions to frustrated and baking under an unforgiving sun on water as still as a bird bath. Our normal approach of patiently accepting whatever wind we had and resigning ourselves to *getting there whenever we got there* didn't work here. A mysterious but frightful engine noise kept us from motoring as we anxiously watched hours tick by on the countdown to Randy's arrival.

We squeaked back into Puerta Galera the second day of Randy's visit, bleary-eyed but excited to see him. An hour after Randy vacated his hotel room, Annie arrived for a whirlwind visit. And then we were underway again. On the marathon sail north to San Fernando, fleets of parked fishing bangkas perched off the coast of Luzon had us weaving an erratic pattern that added tension and miles to our trip. The slow rhythm of sailboats collided with the time-sensitive hustle of the outside world. Though we'd done it to ourselves, by the time we reached San Fernando and the Hong Kong racing fleet, we felt burned out.

A few days later, we set sail for Japan .After a grand reunion with sailing friends from Hong Kong who'd raced to San Fernando, the anchorage quickly emptied of the sleek race boats returning to Hong Kong. Not wanting to be the last boat left to raise the interest of customs officials after we'd checked out of the country, we rushed our departure.

Our sail along the western Luzon coast began pleasantly enough, with light winds behind us and calm seas in warm sunshine. Late in the day, we reached an uninhabited anchorage where we could have stopped, but since conditions seemed ideal, Garth suggested we sail on.

Within an hour of making our decision not to stop, the wind suddenly rose and shifted forward and the boat healed dramatically as waves built to steep peaks. Avalanches of water crashed over the side, breaking over us, soaking us every few seconds. Nothing in the forecast had hinted of the wind and waves we were seeing.

As the bow plowed into each wave, the violent motion of the boat threw us off balance, and we both struggled to remain where we perched in the cockpit. Garth's braced legs stretched across most of the cockpit. I laced my legs across his, bracing my feet against the opposite seat edge, but my position felt precarious, and I lurched with every wave. I wrapped my arm around the winch next to me in a death grip, the edge of metal digging into my upper arm through my foul weather jacket. We both wore harnesses clipped to the boat on six-foot tethers, but that offered little comfort or support in the jarring motion. The slippery, wet decks seemed treacherous, and I imagined that if I relaxed for a moment, I'd slide down the cockpit into the water below where I'd bump alongside the hull until Garth could pull me back aboard.

"This is horrible," I whined. The boat creaked and groaned in protest along with me. The watery horizon looked like the Himalaya for as far as I could see.

Garth's jaw was set. His eyes gazed into the distance, though focused on nothing in particular. He said nothing for a few seconds. Then he sighed heavily and said, "I can't take this anymore. The boat just can't take this kind of abuse. Something is going to break, and I've just had it with fixing things over and over again."

I stayed quiet.

A wave crashed over us. I managed to duck under the dodger in time, but Garth, too tall to fit under our dodger, didn't have that luxury and the wave soaked his head and shoulders. Water dripped down his nose and cheeks. He blew the water away from his mouth.

"You know, if someone offered me a dollar for this boat right now, I'd take it," he said, void of any energy. After all the crap that we'd dealt with in the Philippines—corrupt officials, perpetual rip-off attempts, windless sails, and spooky night sails through a fleet of unlit fishing buoys and bangkas—I could relate to the exasperation I heard in his voice.

He yelled into the wind. "You can have it for free if you can get us onto an airplane right now."

For a moment, I let myself consider abandoning *Velella* and getting on an airplane to fly home, but I just couldn't picture it. I felt a sudden flood of compassion for *Velella*, our friend who had brought us so many miles.

Besides, go home, to do what? As bad as it seemed right then, I didn't want to do anything else. If there was one thing I'd learned about our crazy lifestyle, it's that the emotional highs were higher and the lows lower than I'd ever felt at home, where I'd spent days on end on autopilot, checking off tasks on my to-do list. Just as we'd been through bumpy patches together as a couple, we'd worked through them; and the process of overcoming the adversity had made us appreciate what we had that much more. If I could just find the patience to get through this, the payoff would be there. It had before, and it would again. I shook my head resolutely.

"We could face this crap all the way to Japan," Garth continued, "These kinds of conditions in the Bashi Channel would be impossible." A guidebook had warned that winds along this coast were notoriously strong, but these conditions were even more intense than we'd expected. "We could crack off and head west for Kota Kinabalu." Now that sounded appealing. As though reading my thoughts, he said, "You wanted to keep heading west around the world anyway." Then in a defeated tone he continued, "Let's just forget sailing to Japan."

I heard the catch in his voice, and it tugged at me.

He stood up and unhooked the wind vane, which had been attempting to steer straight despite our bucking motion. "I'm heading for Kota Kinabalu."

"Wait!" I shouted. In this moment, I had the opportunity to steer our course westwards, where I could postpone the inevitable march homeward that seemed to propel Garth forward. But a nagging voice inside warned me not to take advantage of the situation. I didn't want Garth to make such a momentous decision in a moment of intense frustration. I knew how much he wanted to sail to Japan and that once we sailed west, going back would be difficult, and likely something we wouldn't do.

Garth was restless with the cruising life because he needed a new goal. Each new country had offered challenges, but was that enough to sustain me for years more? Throughout my life I'd faced change. Yet change for the sake of change wasn't what had made life satisfying. It was the personal challenges it posed and the opportunity to grow from them.

"You've got a better idea?" He crooked the tiller in his elbow as he shook water off his fingertips, blew on them, and rubbed them together. The temperature had dropped alarmingly fast when the wind began to howl. I shivered.

"Why don't we just turn around and sail back to the last anchorage? We could regroup and then figure out what to do," I said. I looked at him pleadingly.

I knew it pained him even more than it pained me to sail back. On any outing, Garth always favored making a loop at any cost, rather than backtracking. But I knew it would give us the chance to see what was happening with the weather and discuss our options with a calmer perspective. Our future hung in the balance for a few moments. I held his gaze.

Garth sighed and turned the tiller pointing towards the coast rather than Kota Kinabalu. I gradually eased out the jib. He reached past me to ease the mainsheet. Once the wind was behind us, our motion settled.

I went below to plot a course, and then yelled the heading back through the companionway. Garth reset the wind vane and adjusted the sails for our new direction.

Afterward, we both sat quietly, lost in our thoughts. Given a little perspective, our previous exasperation seemed completely out of proportion. I wondered if we'd lost our edge, our adventuresome spirit.

When I heard stories later of testosterone-filled Volvo Ocean Race boats—known for their brave forays into the brutal Southern Ocean—that passed through this area and experienced similar rough conditions and significant gear breakage, I felt like less of a weenie. Several of them had holed up in this same bay, their crews whining to weather routers and the media about what they'd faced in the South China Sea while they waited for conditions to improve.

Sometimes we can only take so much and need to cut ourselves a little slack. Typically, when Garth and I don't like our options, we avoid making a decision in the hopes that our choices will improve if we wait long enough. Sometimes that strategy works, and sometimes it doesn't. This time it did. We spent the following day in a tranquil anchorage, checking the weather and reading peacefully as though we hadn't been battling for our sanity less than twenty-four hours earlier. When the wind didn't roar like it had the previous day, we recovered our courage to carry on for Japan.

AN UNEXPECTED PIT STOP
IN LAN YU, TAIWAN

Several days later, in the notorious Bashi channel we crossed our inbound track to Hong Kong. We hoped to avoid the tide rips and gales that had made for boisterous sailing exactly one year earlier. Conditions were mellow, though we knew they wouldn't last. To the north, a gale hovered over Ishigaki, our Japanese destination. With winds blowing fiercely in our direction, it was only a matter of time before we faced the worst of it.

Friends who'd sailed this route spoke fondly of a tiny island, Lan Yu, thirty-three miles east of Taiwan. Taiwanese customs officially required we visit Taipei or Kao-Hsiung and hire a costly ship's clearance agent before we ventured to this off-lying Taiwanese island. But the building wind and seas provided incentive for an "emergency" stop before conditions grew worse.

Along the southern tip of the island, enormous tide rips tossed us about, confirming the chart's stern warnings. Armed with nothing more than a sketchy description of a hidden harbor on its western shore, we poked our way along the rugged coastline as close as we dared in the surge, looking for this mysterious entrance. Waves crested as they reached the shallows of this high rocky island, and then sprayed spectacularly to the height of the mast as they struck shore. It was a landfall we didn't want to get wrong. First we entered a narrow channel between a rocky islet and an impressive breakwater, but we backed our way out as the depths decreased and the area narrowed abruptly. My heart fluttered an extra beat. This couldn't be the entrance. People sitting along the breakwater didn't return our wave and we'd raised no reply on the radio. Fishing boats in the vicinity paid us no attention. We were on our own.

We poked *Velella*'s nose around the other side of the islet, where we found a wider entry into what was evidently a port. But what had looked like an empty wharf from afar was in fact a cramped concrete dead-end open to the surge. As if to make the danger evident, a wave picked us up and hurled us towards the hard concrete wall opposite.

"This is a death trap!" Garth exclaimed as he slammed into reverse and backed out at high speed. My blood pressure spiked, and I could feel my heart beating wildly in my chest.

Our cruising friends wouldn't have spoken so favorably of what we could see; this couldn't be what we were looking for. We ventured back around the islet but crept closer to the rocky shore than we had dared earlier. Keeping his hand on the gear shifter, Garth drove *Velella* ever closer, while I called out the depths and scoured the horizon for an opening.

"I don't like this. I'm going to bail in about twenty seconds," Garth warned.

Just as the depth dropped below twenty feet, and we'd closed two thirds of the distance to the shore, I spotted a gap at the end of the fortress-like concrete breakwater.

"There it is!" I shouted. I heard Garth exhale.

Through the narrow opening I could see a modest enclosure that housed a mixture of open skiffs, a couple of larger western-style fishing boats and some of the most unusual vessels we'd ever seen: rafts made of large plastic PVC pipes with boxy wooden structures lashed to the top that reminded me of home-made flatbed trucks. Each featured a crude "cab" where one could escape the weather.

We motored in slowly, hoping someone would suggest where we should tie up. Sure enough, a man gestured encouragement to raft up on the outside of these unusual flat-bottomed fishing boats stacked four-deep. Soon, three men in orange jumpsuits stood alongside the man who first waved us over. Despite their close resemblance to penitentiary inmates, we learned that these men were actually young officers of the Taiwanese Coast Guard.

Stationed in one of its most distant outposts, perhaps these men hadn't seen a lot of action. They seemed unsure how to proceed with our unsanctioned arrival. In broken English, they asked the purpose of our stop. We explained that we needed water. We didn't know whether stopping to avoid a gale would be considered legitimate and needing life-sustaining water seemed like a plausible excuse for an emergency.

Of course, we *always* needed water, since we carried only forty-five gallons. Through the liberal use of salt water—which was notably abundant—and careful rationing of fresh water, we usually managed to get our supplies to last three weeks. We probably could last another two weeks, but only we knew that.

Two officers promptly passed us three boxes, each containing 36 2-liter bottles of water. Their efficiency made me wonder if we would have to leave as soon as we'd topped our tanks.

As Garth and I laboriously decanted ten 2-liter bottles one by one, two officers disappeared with our passports and boat documentation, leaving one observing us from shore.

After a few minutes, the senior man returned. I expected him to ask us to leave. Instead, he said, "Come for lunch."

We quickly changed out of our filthy passage-making clothes which were salty from regular wave dousing, but were acutely conscious of how sweaty and stinky we must have been. We forgot that to reach shore we had to clamber over four grimy fishing boats and up a series of truck tires on a ten-foot seawall.

The officers escorted us past a herd of black, white and brown ruminating goats to a white painted cinderblock building. There behind a plain metal desk, a young lieutenant apologized profusely for his limited English and for inconveniencing us as he posed the standard questions that we answered every time we checked into a country: boat description (type, length, tonnage, hailing port, and documentation number); departure port, date and time; and the names and passport details of the crew. Perhaps they would let us stay after all.

After a few minutes, Lieutenant Huang showed us to a Formica banquet table in a back room that was empty except for a couch and an entertainment system. I concluded we were in the barracks when I saw two sleepy young men in t-shirts, shorts, and socks rise from the couch to join us. None spoke English, though their smiles eased the awkwardness as we dipped into platters of rice, stewed meats, fish, vegetables, and scrambled eggs, and washed it all down with cold sweet tea.

Afterward, our hosts invited us to use showers in the barracks, going so far as to offer traveler's toiletry kits complete with tiny plastic packets of shampoo, soap, and even paper-like towels. When we emerged from luxuriously long, hot showers, Lieutenant Huang explained apologetically that they had more questions.

First he requested a detailed list of every port where we'd stopped since our departure from Seattle. After six and half years, that numbered quite a few. With the assistance of a schoolteacher translating over the phone, Garth patiently explained, and they finally agreed that details for our three most recent ports would be adequate.

Next they wanted the GPS track of our route. I guessed that, worried about his superiors in Taiwan looking over his shoulder, the young officer was covering his bases. I worried what our odd detour during our emotional meltdown a few days earlier might look to an officer's trained eye: suspiciously like an illegal rendezvous.

Through our translator, Garth explained that our chart would provide far more useful information than our squiggly GPS track out of context, and the officers finally agreed. So we returned to the boat to fetch our chart, which meant navigating the truck tires on the seawall and four fishing boats littered with fish scales with chart in hand. After our return, Garth and the officers wrestled our gigantic chart onto a microscopic copy machine, and, with the help of a minor geography lesson from Garth, pasted a series of snapshots together to encompass our entire route. Finally the officers seemed satisfied. Except that they needed just one more thing.

"Excuse me, so sorry to ask," the young lieutenant began tentatively. It seemed to be his favorite phrase. I looked around the sparse office, wondering, *what now?* With his mouth scrunched into a pucker, the man said, "Our headquarters office has asked if you would leave and return so we can take picture of your arrival." Garth looked amused, and then his smile spread into a wide grin. We all shared a hearty laugh.

The odd request forged us into a single team, working to satisfy the Taiwanese bureaucracy as we handed back the boxes of water and untied *Velella's* lines for a brief harbor tour. I felt like a celebrity as we staged our "arrival" and "emergency water transfer" with multiple cameras recording our every action.

Officially clearing into the country took two more days, but cost nothing. In the interim, our escape from the gale raging to the north would prove an unexpectedly fascinating respite.

We expected little more in Lan Yu than a brief pit stop, but we found an intriguing culture we'd never heard about. It was these unexpected discoveries that were the most precious part of our life afloat.

While we waited on shore for clearance, then for the gale to abate, a handsome young man named Adder took responsibility for us, apologizing for his poor English. Invoking his favorite phrase, "so sorry," several times within minutes, he invited us for dinner at his mother's house with his sister, Theresa, who spoke better English.

That evening, Adder and Theresa picked us up in an old white Toyota sedan and drove the short distance to their mother's white cinderblock, two-bedroom home in the quiet village of Yeh-yu.

Adder led us into the simply furnished living room and showed us a children's picture book about the Lan Yu culture while Theresa and her mother bustled in the kitchen. "The Lan Yu people are famous for their traditional carved and painted canoes in black (soot), white (lyme), and red (ochre) pigments. They venture out in the canoes to catch flying fish during the season between April and July," it read. Drawings depicted narrow canoes that rose to a high point on both ends, painted white and elaborately accented with common geometric designs in red and black. The text continued, "The men hold a special ceremony with dances and costumes to honor the opening of flying fish season." Drawings showed men dressed traditionally, with only a modest covering over their genitals, their butt cheeks open to the breeze. I shivered. In another drawing depicting the ceremony, the men wore grey-striped open vests and what looked like deep bowls of silver inverted over their heads with cutouts for their eyes. "They consider it bad luck for women to be out in or near the canoes."

As we flipped through the picture book, Theresa's toddler zoomed around the room, defiantly tossing every item that Adder placed on the table onto the floor: napkins, chopsticks, and soup spoons.

After Adder set down the soup and bowls and returned to the kitchen to carry the remaining dishes of food, the boy leaned over the bowl and spit into the soup.

Did I really just see that? I thought. I looked over at Garth.

He flinched then shook his head slowly. Theresa had told us he'd been home with a cold that day. I shifted uneasily, wondering whether to warn the others, and, if I didn't, how I might gracefully extricate myself from partaking in the contaminated soup. Not wanting to appear an ungrateful guest, I said nothing. We ate the soup anyway, which I regretted several days later when I awoke achy and congested.

After the soup, Theresa served rice and stewed vegetables. As we finished, Theresa explained, "The Aboriginal people of Lan Yu are more closely related to Filipino than Taiwanese Chinese. Most of our words are the same."

I'd noticed that Theresa, Adder, and their mother were dark with chiseled cheekbones and slender noses. Their narrower faces were quite different from the flatter, pale faces and widely-spaced eyes of the Taiwanese Coast Guard officers. With the Philippines just across the Bashi Channel, it made sense that the original inhabitants closely resembled the Philippine people. I vaguely remembered reading in Jared Diamond's *Guns, Germs, and Steel* that all Pacific cultures could be traced back to the original inhabitants of Taiwan who preceded the Chinese, a Diaspora that also included Indonesians, Malays, and Filipinos. How interesting to think that Theresa and Adder might share ancestors with people we'd seen in the Pacific.

Theresa said, "I stayed in Taipei for a while, where I trained as a nurse, but it was difficult to live there. They did not accept me as Taiwanese because I look different." Her dark, elegantly-proportioned features looked beautiful to me. "I came back here because I couldn't get a job. Adder also trained there as an X-ray technician, but he still needs to take the test before he can work at the hospital with me."

Theresa's eyes lingered on Adder for a moment. He shrugged sheepishly, and I detected an undercurrent of tension between them.

After we cleared the dinner dishes, Theresa offered to take us around the village. She and Adder led us into a sparsely stocked souvenir shop, featuring dusty resin models of colorful Lan Yu canoes, packages of dried flying fish and faded postcards. Theresa explained that Lan Yu was a vacation spot for Taiwanese, who came by ferry during calm summer weather.

As we stepped outside the shop, Theresa stopped to buy something inside. When she appeared on the step, she held up a delicate double-strand beaded bracelet like an offering. Its tiny red, black, and white beads were threaded together with small white blouse button accents. Her gesture touched me, and I beamed with gratitude as she placed in on my wrist. We stopped to take a photograph together in front of a plastic mannequin modeling traditional dress, an outfit that had intrigued me in the picture book but looked far less fetching on a plastic sentry.

Along the paved street, a fishy smell assaulted my nose. To my left, a school of drying fish hung on strings from a bamboo framework. From their eye-less heads to their powerful V-shaped tails, they appeared nearly intact except for a telling slit up the belly that explained their lack of girth. Underway, I'd seen thousands of flying fish burst from the waves and travel impressive distances while airborne.

Theresa noticed my gaze. She explained how the fishermen dried their catch immediately to preserve them to eat in the off season, or sell.

I remembered packages I'd seen in the store. I thought of many flying fish that had leapt from the waves in the night to escape a predator, only to find themselves propelled by their translucent wings straight into *Velella*'s path. We might have supplemented our diet with their fresh meat, but I'd always found them too late, frozen to *Velella*'s deck in rigor mortis in the harsh light of late morning.

Our tour of this compact village was brief. As darkness fell, the echo of a dog bark ricocheted around the silent concrete village. We bid goodbye to Theresa, who would be heading to Taipei on the mainland the following afternoon, and arranged to meet Adder the following day. Adder had offered to lend us his motor scooter so we could drive around the island.

When he didn't show up like we expected, we wondered whether we'd misunderstood his sketchy English. Later someone came to the boat to tell us he was sick. Eventually Adder arrived looking apologetic, riding a different scooter. He had a chipped tooth, notable road rash on his arms and face, and smelled faintly of stale alcohol. We shared an awkward moment. The tension that had passed between Theresa and Adder the previous evening came back to me. We might never know for sure, but I suspected he'd been on a bender and had crashed his scooter. I wondered if he was caught in frustration between two worlds: the modern one he'd been exposed to in Taipei, where he'd received his advanced training, and he had come to grasp the reality of limited opportunities back in his sleepy village. Perhaps our arrival had reminded him of that.

We spent the next day circumnavigating the island with the use of Adder's borrowed scooter. With the Coast Guard's permission to move freely, we set off along the perimeter road that hugged its formidable coast, Garth driving and me glued to his backside. Straddling the narrow vinyl seat with the wind in my face, I remembered when a waiter in the Cook Islands generously lent us his motorcycle to attend a memorial service for 9/11. Garth's first time driving a motorcycle was on the wrong side of the road at night in probably the only traffic jam Rarotonga has ever had.

As we leaned into our first curve, I relished the free feeling of moving fast and effortlessly with the wind buffeting my face. Traveling at the brisk pace of twenty miles an hour held a new excitement after so many months of sailing or walking at less than five miles an hour.

"Wow, you can cover a lot of territory with one of these inventions!" Garth shouted over the wind.

"Yeah!" I agreed, thinking of how many hours it might take us to do the same on foot, our typical mode of land transportation.

The seaward side of the road fell away to rugged volcanic rocks cut by violent wave action. The inland side of the road rose abruptly to steep mountains. Low clouds skidded overhead, occasionally parting to reveal jagged peaks covered with a low green scrub. To our left, explosive blasts of water shot into sharp crevices, sending spray and foam flying, intimidating reminders of the gale we'd avoided. Each thunderous wave sent a shudder through surrounding earth.

We zipped past low shrubs that had stubbornly taken hold in rocky crevices and the occasional plots of taro that grew within narrow terraces cut into the hillside. We passed several deep caves, which, of course, I had to investigate. I imagined Japanese soldiers seeking refuge in their dark depths as they had in Saipan. Several larger cave openings were blocked by monumental wrought iron gates, and I wondered whether they had stored munitions during World War II. I later learned that the caves stored radioactive material. A tribal chief, convinced he was granting permission to open a fish-processing factory that would create jobs for his people, trustingly signed a document he couldn't read.

The road detoured around a narrow indentation along the rocky shore. In front of us stood another fortress-like retaining-wall. Inside it a few fishing skiffs tugged against their tethers. Waves pounded against the outside wall, water rising in splashes that blew inland in the wind. I imagined the islanders facing the wrath of a typhoon, thankful for these impressive barriers to keep the waves from punishing every inch of their shore. Also within the forbidding concrete enclosure lay a stony beach, dotted with those exquisite white canoes from the picture book. We stopped for a closer look.

Ever mindful of fishermen's superstitions about women standing too close, I did my best to appreciate the fine details from a respectful distance, all the while resenting Garth's maleness and ability to study them at close range.

Some were simple, painted all white with a narrow outline of red on the pointed tips and below the waterline. The keel, narrow as a blade, nestled between smooth, round stones the size of a fist. Other canoes were more intricate, with their sides divided into multiple panels. Each panel featured stripes, zigzags, or a crude human figure surrounded by five curlicues. That curlicued symbol was repeated in elaborate figureheads mounted on each canoe tip. Each one depicted a man standing atop an equally detailed canoe surrounded by ten circles sprouting rooster feathers. Each canoe had something that resembled a bull's-eye painted on both ends. Red, black and white dots demarcated the panel edges, and along the tip of the gunnels. I used my feeble telephoto lens to zoom in on details that caught my eye. As ever, many of my pictures included Garth's backside.

"Look at the stripes painted inside the canoes," I said. The longer I looked the more detail I noticed.

"These aren't just painted. Each pattern is carved into the wood," Garth said as he knelt down to take a closer look. I was frustrated I couldn't get closer.

"Here, can you take some pictures up close?" I said, turning off our cheap digital camera and holding it out to him. Shifting into reporter-on-the-ground mode, I was obsessed with documenting every angle of these fascinating canoes and capturing the artistic expression of this unusual culture. The larger canoe featured subtle touches of yellow paint in addition to the predominant red, black and white.

Garth was fully absorbed in his inspection. "Interesting," he said. "The pieces of wood that hold the canoe together are fitted using wooden pegs. You can barely see the seams." He was oblivious to my question and my growing agitation. "They row instead of paddle them! See the beefy oarlocks fitted to the gunnels?"

I hadn't noticed that yet, probably because he'd been standing in front of them. "Please?" I held out the camera and waited.

After a moment, he turned around and looked at me. Wordlessly he took the camera, made a cursory attempt to capture some details, and handed it back. I checked the images to make sure they were in focus, disappointed he hadn't taken more. Winding our way around the island, I cajoled Garth into taking more close-up photos each time we spotted these graceful canoes.

Given Garth's obsession with boats, we'd spent a lot of time in our travels studying various types. His background in designing boats made me notice and appreciate their differences more acutely than I might have. These intricately carved and painted narrow canoes were so unlike the other boats we'd seen during our voyage: from the gangly double-outrigger bangkas of the Philippines, to the boxy junks of Hong Kong, the oddball contraptions concocted from scrap and PVC piping in Saipan, the impressive sailing canoes of the Marshalls and Kiribati, or the thinly-carved wooden shells in the Solomons and Vanuatu barely big enough for a single person. These Lan Yu flying fish canoes were the most intriguing native vessels we'd seen.

Our scooter let us cover territory at a rapid clip. We sped past more goats than people. Each person we passed paused briefly in their business to wave, including a woman stooped over tidy rows of taro wearing a low peaked, wide brimmed hat of vegetable fiber like ones featured in the picture book. We paused near traditional houses tucked into the ground to withstand high winds, some covered with a roof of foliage or grass thatch and others with modern roofing material. I sputtered for a moment when one of our friendly greeters was a man dressed exactly as the book had depicted, bare butt cheeks and all.

Like many places we'd visited, a blend of modern and traditional stirred together into a slightly symbiotic, slightly tenuous brew gave Lan Yu an endearing innocence of a bygone era. The curse of the temporary visitor is that we never fully understand the richness of the places we visit. Yet, we stop to *really look* in a way we often don't in familiar surroundings. What we take away without a doubt is an awareness that many ways of living exist that may be equally valid.

And though Garth had grown weary of life as a perpetual traveler—to be *in* a place but not *of* it—I still yearned to see as much of the world as possible before homogenization reduced unique cultures such as these to a distant memory.

After four days, three of which we'd spent checking into Taiwan, the storm had abated over southern Japan, and we had ideal weather for heading on to Ishigaki. We were hardly anxious to go. The kindness of people here had astounded us. Each morning we'd awoken to discover pastries left anonymously on deck as gifts. Every day, coast guard officers had generously invited us to the barracks for lunch and had encouraged us to join them watching movies in their lounge. Once we did accept their invitation, but the only English-speaking movies that interested us didn't feature enough explosions and car chases, and we could sense their restlessness. Though we couldn't communicate well, they seemed glad for our company.

As we prepared to leave, Adder and four officers came to see us off, bringing two more boxes of water along with our passports and clearance documents. As a gesture of gratitude, I presented them a DVD containing twelve action movies with Chinese subtitles that we'd bought in the Philippines for less than $2. Their eyes grew as big as if they'd won the lottery. We'd nearly doubled their collection with a single disk. One officer sheepishly asked Garth, "Is okay we take picture with your wife? We like picture with pretty girl." Probably the only blond they'd ever seen was in the movies. When we untied the lines at last, these men, who knew nothing of our existence only four days earlier, seemed more concerned with our safety than we were and requested we email to let them know we'd reached Japan safely.

CHAPTER
19

JAPAN AT LAST

As we worked our way north from Taiwan the temperature became notably cooler, reminding me that we were emigrating from the tropics, where we'd sailed the last six years. A wall of low clouds awaited us at the Tropic of Cancer as though it were a barrier, checking my resolve. I was sad to leave the tropics but excited to reach Japan after nearly four years of anticipation.

Part of me knew that it brought me a step closer to sailing home, something I still wasn't sure I wanted to do. After so many years of being unable to stand or sit comfortably in *Velella*'s cramped cabin, Garth's patience was wearing thin. I could understand how uncomfortable he'd been trying to squeeze his large frame into such a tiny space; I was gradually starting to accept that I couldn't drag Garth around the world if he didn't want to go.

As we drew closer to land, Garth and I noticed the Kuroshio Current was sweeping us more than thirty degrees from our heading, which, combined with variable winds, made it nearly impossible to give the port of Ishigaki our exact arrival time, as we were required to do. This was our first hint of the complex regulations we had to navigate.

After our radio call went unanswered, we passed through a formidable series of confusing breakwaters, until we spotted several sailboat masts. We pulled alongside a floating steel pontoon. Surrounding us were fifty-foot wooden fishing vessels laden with nets, buoys and outriggers, a couple of day-sailors and a few idling dive boats, awaiting customers. Japanese flags fluttered in the breeze.

A sizeable entourage of uniformed officials promptly arrived at our boat and efficiently checked us into the country, but then perplexed us by requesting our exact itinerary for the next three months. *How could we possibly guess each and every bay where we might stop when we didn't know how long it might take to travel between them, especially once we factored in that ever present variable: weather?*

Garth shrugged and said tentatively, "Everywhere!" Unlike our encounter in the Philippines, where each officer acted like a greedy free agent, these bureaucrats didn't much care what our answers were, just that they be precise enough to satisfy the blanks in their forms. So with the help of two patient officials, we laboriously concocted a list of bays to satisfy them. Whether we could actually follow such a route was anyone's guess.

Ishigaki is the southern-most of the Nansei-Shoto (southwestern islands), which are sprinkled like stepping stones between Taiwan and the main islands of Japan. We planned to work our way north towards the main islands of Japan—weather permitting—until our three-month visas expired. I'd been to Japan a number of times already, but sailing through its myriad islands on our own boat was a completely different experience than visiting its larger cities for business. And much more challenging, we were soon to find.

Our stay in Ishigaki was brief—only as long as the week during which we had a free slip. The abundance of empty tourist shops so early in the season gave the town a ghostly feel. We found the town compact and easy to get around on foot, yet architecturally modern and culturally unremarkable, except for signs in kanji and strings of carp streamers in honor of Golden Week. Flower boxes overflowing with marigolds, bougainvillea, impatiens, hibiscus, and orchids infused a flash of color to low-rise concrete apartment blocks. What impressed us was the warm welcomes from locals. An older man with a small sailboat down the dock stopped by several times, always with a merry smile, and occasionally a bottle of Shoju, a powerful fermented beverage similar to brandy, and a generous platter of sushi, which we polished off together. Koji's English was non-existent. Initially, we showed him the article about us from Kazi magazine to bridge the language barrier, but mostly he seemed content just to share our company.

Occasionally, Mike Quinn, a Texan who'd settled in Ishigaki after a tour at the military base in Okinawa, acted as interpreter. One afternoon when we were all sitting around the boat sipping on a beer, I heard Koji-san say "Clinton-san" and point towards Garth. He said a few more words in Japanese, and Koji-san and Mike shared a laugh.

"What?" I asked, my curiosity piqued.

"He said that he thinks Garth looks like President Clinton." When Garth and I had first seen a photograph of Bill Clinton, we'd noticed how much he resembled an older version of Garth. They shared a sturdy frame, rosy cheeks, bright blue eyes, and a slightly rounded nose. While Koji-san was the first to state this comparison, he was not the last. Though my Japanese never improved markedly during our visit, on several other occasions I recognized "President Clinton" buried in an otherwise unintelligible string of Japanese words followed by titters. Each time, I think I startled the speaker by seeming to understand Japanese when he thought he could speak candidly.

One afternoon on a walk to a nearby grocery store, we stopped to dispose of our garbage. We both stared silently at an intimidating row of recycle bins. The Kanji written on them meant nothing to us; no universal symbols gave any hint of what was supposed to go where; and the bins, empty of contents, featured no clues to help us. Just then, Koji-san drove up in his little white pickup and noticed our perplexed expressions. He gave a hearty laugh and motioned for us to hand him our garbage bag, which he tossed in his truck.

At the grocery store, we faced endless rows of plastic boxes containing God-knew-what. Once again, the Kanji labels offered no helpful information to us suddenly illiterate folks. Was it sweet or sour? Did it need to be cooked or could it be eaten raw? Even in the produce section, we saw neatly packaged vegetables—the epitome of perfection in their plastic coffins—which we didn't recognize. A young couple wearing kimonos brushed past us on their way to the refrigerator case, where I recognized milk cartons, puddings, and yogurts, definite signs of western influence. At these prices, I decided to stick with foods I recognized or that featured pictures to help identify them, though I was intrigued to experiment. Ironically, avocadoes, which nearly cost a mortgage payment in the U.S., here cost only a dollar, so we stocked up. I hoped that when we reached larger cities that weren't recognized tourist destinations we'd find cheaper prices and more English-speakers.

Sailing between spring storms, we traveled north to Okinawa, the best known of these islands. Since its role in the last great amphibious operation of World War II, the U.S. occupied and administered the area until it returned to Japanese ownership in 1972. The U.S. still leases land for active military bases.

With such convenient proximity to an air base, I arrived in Okinawa with hopes that my dad would hop a space-available military flight to meet us. But when I checked email, once again there were no messages from my father to indicate whether he might be coming.

Of course, Garth had predicted this development. "If he's not on his way, he's not coming."

Garth had indulged my naive delusion and splurged for a pricey marina slip in Okinawa, not because he thought we'd see my dad, but because he was as curious to see this historical place as I was. Yet what we found our first afternoon when we'd stepped ashore to find an Internet café was a sprawling island nearly bereft of any sign of history. What little remained from before the war seemed overrun by freeway overpasses. Traveling on foot, as we typically did, clearly would not work here. Without a visit from my dad, I knew a rental car was out of the question. *Double-damn.*

Getting into town had been fairly easy once an American servicewoman, who drove past, pointed out a bus stop. On the Kokusai-dori, amidst the steak restaurants and kitsch, which included Godzilla, Ronald McDonald, and Hot Dog Man, we escaped the rain for a few hours inside a shopping arcade where we saw big jars of Habu snakes pickled in alcohol.

Getting back to the boat again was more complicated. We studied the confusing route map at a modest bus station. The bus we'd taken into town did not appear to work in reverse. We asked the only person in the vicinity, and though he had seemed unsure— either because of his unfamiliarity with the bus routes or with English—we unwisely followed his advice anyway.

When we boarded the bus, the driver impatiently waved us in, and we were left wondering whether we'd chosen the right bus. From a machine next to the driver, we grabbed a ticket imprinted with a zone number and took a seat. On an electronic reader board above the driver's head, we monitored the current price for each zone as we traveled. The longer we sat on the bus, the higher the number of Yen rose for the zone number on our tickets. When the price topped five dollars each, the price we'd paid coming, we were still nowhere near our destination. Then the bus driver turned east, away from the marina where we'd parked the boat. We passed several more highway overpasses and strip malls. We grew more agitated. The bus turned north, and soon the price rose to nearly $10 each.

Oh boy. We no longer knew where we were. Garth and I exchanged nervous glances.

Just as I was thinking about getting off the bus, the driver turned west.

Garth said, "Wait. The price is going back down!" He pointed at the prices for our zone number. "We must be on some sort of loop route. If nothing else, we could at least wait until the price gets reasonable again or return to Naha. Maybe the price will be back to zero by the time we get there."

When we reached the western edge of the island and turned south, I grew hopeful. Then I began to recognize scenery from our walk earlier. I said, "There are the stores we walked by when we were looking for the bus stop." I pushed the button for the bell when I saw that familiar bench near the marina gate; we pulled out five-dollars-worth of Yen, and got off.

"Hey, a full island tour for only five dollars." Garth quipped, as we walked back to the marina.

By the time we reached the boat in the steady drizzle, I was disappointed and irritable. Garth gritted his teeth, but after spending the next several hours in the dark, cramped interior of *Velella* listening to me complain over the rain drumming against the cabin top, he couldn't help but express a long overdue, "I told you so."

I steamed for the rest of the evening.

Determined to see something before we left Okinawa so it wouldn't feel like a total bust, I studied the Japan Lonely Planet guide someone had given us for sites I could reach by bus. While I knew about Okinawa's war history, what I hadn't realized before we'd reached Japan was that these southern islands of Japan had once been a mighty kingdom, the *Ryukyu*, which had strong links to China until the Satsuma of Japan invaded in 1609.

Since Garth no longer shared my enthusiasm for tromping around Okinawa and a day apart might do us some good, I wandered around the old Ryukyu royal capital by myself on the first truly sunny day we'd seen since we'd reach Japan. Though the brutal eighty-two-day battle that flattened Okinawa also destroyed most of the 450-year-old Shuri castle, the original castle walls and gates survived. Many of the internal structures were reconstructed. Inside its imposing stone walls were courtyards, formed by a series of high wooden gates, and buildings topped with heavy terra-cotta-tiled roofs. Shiisa, ceramic figures in the shape of fierce lion dogs, guarded the rooftops. According to Ryuku legend, a predatory sea dragon tormented villages and dined on villagers until shiisa chased the serpent away. Shiisa still protected many dwellings from evil spirits. We'd seen the figures for sale in the tourist shops of Ishigaki and atop the heavy tiled roofs of traditional wooden structures in the Ryukyus. Some were fierce and intimidating, others comical.

After being in Asia for more than a year, it felt odd to be in the presence of so many Americans, many from the nearby military bases. They weren't the occasional, intrepid travelers we'd encountered along the way, but hordes of military families who were probably experiencing a foreign culture for the first time. As I marveled at the gleaming, garnet-red paint of the recently restored royal family residence, I'd hear a whiny voice nearby say a little too loudly, "Isn't there a soda machine anywhere?" or "Man, you could play a good game of football in here!" Though they spoke my language, they seemed more alien to me than the respectful Japanese who didn't.

Spending the day alone and picnicking in the peaceful regal castle grounds overlooking Okinawa gave me a new perspective. I had to admit that Garth had showed remarkable patience and understanding. After all, he had been right and in retrospect our argument seemed rather trivial. Once I'd wasted another $15 figuring out the bus system, I returned to the boat feeling refreshed and excited to share what I'd seen and done during our hours apart.

From Okinawa we sailed to Amami-Oshima, where we found an oasis of protected bays tucked within a cluster of islands. The scenery, with its gleaming white sandy beaches and Caribbean-colored waters, blew all our preconceived notions about Japan. Except for the temperature, which was much colder than the oppressive heat we'd grown used to, it looked invitingly tropical. Even with overcast, gloomy skies, the water was as bright as a resort pool. Where we beached the dinghy, we broke off pieces of the red clay cliffs that shrouded the beachfront and crumbled them in our fingers. From the boat, we'd heard announcements broadcasting the same music as the ice cream trucks of my childhood summers. There was also a pier with occasional passenger ferry service, so we assumed we'd anchored off some sort of resort, but as we walked along the shore road we found ourselves passing sugar cane, rice, and taro plantations.

Along the roadside, a jeep stopped and the driver waved us over. He definitely wasn't Asian, with curly grey hair, blue eyes, and a beak nose. He introduced himself as Pat and as I was trying to place his accent, he told us he was from Switzerland. He invited us to his house for coffee.

As we chatted in the car, I gradually realized that *Kuroshio*, the boat we'd parked next to in Subic Bay four months ago had once been *his* boat. "So Sarah and Clement bought *Kuroshio* from you?" I asked. I took a moment to reconcile the uptight man they'd described with the relaxed one before us. "That means that the Japanese charts we're using were once yours."

I could see a hint of remorse cross his face. The huge roll of Japanese charts, they'd given us had been hard to come by and were worth a fortune. Since we'd left the South Pacific, we'd encountered few world cruisers like us and it felt good once again to be in the company of a sailor who understood our scrimping, vagabond lifestyle.

When we asked him about the announcements, Pat rolled his eyes and said dryly, "Oh that's Big Brother talking. The announcements encourage people to stop for lunch at noon, urge children to return home to help their mother prepare for the evening meal at 6:00 p.m., and suggest that it is time to put the little ones to sleep at 8:00 p.m."

We turned and drove down a long gravel driveway to a house hidden in a jungle of lush tropical foliage. A young Japanese woman appeared with a baby on her hip and a broad smile of unusually perfect teeth. As the daughter of a dentist who suffered through two episodes of a mouth filled with braces, I tend to notice teeth. Unlike the Philippines, where dentist offices populated every town and nearly every smile was picture-perfect, the Japanese we'd seen so far had remarkably crooked, yellowed teeth.

Pat introduced us to his wife, Monica, who spoke fluent English. We slipped off our shoes and went inside. Like a typical Japanese home, its interior was subdivided by internal walls with sliding paper screen doors. Tatami mats covered the floor. Pat and Monica and their three children welcomed us as though we were old friends. We spent the rest of the afternoon and evening with them sharing a dinner of soba noodles and chatting.

At the end of the evening, Pat insisted he drive us the short distance back to the boat. When Garth protested, Pat told us that deadly Habu snakes were active at night. He explained that these venomous creatures from the pit viper family came out onto the roadway after dark. "Don't ever go out without a torch, in case you're stuck out at night," he urged. Timely local knowledge saved our skins from ignorance.

We spent the next several days with the family, inviting them out to our boat and appreciating the amenities of their home. We relaxed in their *ofuro*, a traditional wood heated soaking tub, after scrubbing away the grime in a cool shower. We used their computer to catch up on email and their washer/dryer to do laundry. They gave us cucumbers and lettuce from their garden. We shared our smoked salmon from the Pacific Northwest which we carried for special occasions.

As we prepared to leave Amami-Oshima, Pat asked us where we were headed next. When we told him we didn't know exactly, he seemed surprised. "Didn't you check in and tell them your plans when you arrived here?" he asked.

We hadn't.

"You're supposed to check in each place you stop. Didn't you know that Amami-Oshima was a closed port? You need special permission to come here." He explained that all foreign vessels were prohibited from all but the major shipping ports without advance permission, which is sometimes only available at the prefecture office inland. "You might want to keep a low profile. You could get into a lot of trouble."

After the freedom we'd experienced so far in our journey, I suddenly felt like a teenager accountable to my mother.

Without cruising guides and unable to speak the language, we were woefully ill-equipped to navigate the rules of an unusually complex and obtuse system. When Pat saw my worried expression he shrugged and said, "I've lived here on and off for twenty years, and though I am fluent, I still can't read Japanese. In fact, it's probably better if you don't speak Japanese at all, because then officials won't expect you to know the rules."

🌴

From the Ryukyu Islands, we steered for Nagasaki on the northwest coast of Kyushu. This area close to Korea is sprinkled with islands that our Hong Kong pal, Tets, told us offered some of the best cruising in Japan. Nagasaki, nestled into a narrow channel with lush high hills on either side, offered a protected harbor where we didn't have to worry about the safety of the boat. Or the cost of a marina slip. We discovered when we pulled in that Dejima Marina granted foreigners free moorage for a week.

While Nagasaki is best known as the second atomic bomb site, we discovered its prewar history intrigued us as much. A wayward

Portuguese ship initiated Japan's contact with the west in 1542. Europeans introduced guns, which, of course, revolutionized warfare in Japan. But, more importantly, the arrival of other Portuguese trading ships turned Nagasaki into a profitable trading port. Missionaries followed close on the heels of traders, bringing their teachings as they tend to do. Christianity spread rapidly. Within a few years, several hundred thousand people had converted to Christianity. In 1587, the shogun considered the strong influence of Christianity a threat, so he expelled most foreigners and instituted a period of national seclusion except for tightly controlled trade in Nagasaki. Only Dutch, Chinese, and Koreans, who the shogun perceived to be more interested in trade than religion, were allowed to remain under strict rules within the boundaries of a tiny fan-shaped island off the shores of Nagasaki.

Until Garth and I reached Japan, we hadn't realized that from the mid-1600s to 1855, Nagasaki was the only port open to the outside world. Until Pat explained in detail, we hadn't fully grasped that without special permission the only ports open to foreigners today were the busy ports where ships traded. This explained the convoluted rules we'd encountered trying to sail through this country.

For over 250 years, all trade, Western technology, and culture passed through Dejima Island. Its unique status as the only point of entry for Western influences turned Nagasaki into an important scientific and cultural center where people flocked to study art, technology, and medicine. The original Dutch-trading enclave, Dejima Island, had since been absorbed by land reclamation. It was nearly indistinguishable from the modern high-rises that surrounded it, save for a sign and a diorama we stumbled upon. We peeked through the fence of the reconstructed trading post, but ultimately decided to save our money instead of paying the exorbitant entrance fee. Instead, we fleshed out historical details through exhibits in the *free* Dejima history museum and in the company of an English-speaking historian who patiently answered our many questions about Japanese culture and history.

After leaving the museum, we hiked "the Dutch Slopes," an incline where hints of Dutch architecture remained in the form of wooden clapboard houses that overlooked the harbor. We strolled across a picturesque collection of centuries-old stone bridges, which elegantly stretched across the river that gurgled through the city, and peered down on some of the meatiest koi I'd ever laid eyes on. We cut through street arcades filled with Japanese antiques, fine paper goods, and kimonos. I was enchanted, and we hadn't even seen what originally drew us here.

We poked along a street lined with as many as twenty temples, the result of a decree by the shogun. A string of imposing archways covered with heavy tiled roofs marked the entrances to the temples, each surrounded by peaceful gardens populated with Buddhist deities and heavy weathered bronze bells dating from the 1600s. The most notable was the Fukasai-ji Zen temple, because not only was it one of the oldest temples in Japan—having once hosted dignitaries, including U.S. President Grant—but because it was possibly the most garish thing I'd ever seen. The original temple burned completely following the atomic bomb explosion. Rebuilt in its place was a spectacularly gaudy structure in the shape of a turtle. As though erupting from the turtle's pale green back, an eighteen-meter-high metal sculpture of the Goddess Kannon stands surrounded by three smaller metal sculptures of worshipful children. The effect was positively outlandish. Garth and I entered the building through the throat of the turtle beneath its ugly metal head. Inside, alongside memorials to victims of the atomic bomb blast and fallen World War II soldiers stood the largest Foucault pendulum in the world outside of Paris and Leningrad. Its slowly swinging pendulum was the last thing I expected to find in this already incongruous temple. As Garth and I studied photos of Nagasaki before and after the blast, a female caretaker told us that each day, a bell chimed at 11:02 a.m. to mark the exact time of the atomic bomb explosion.

Unlike Hiroshima, much of Nagasaki remained intact after the bomb was detonated. Its high hills, along with a lucky shift in the wind direction, protected the town from total devastation. While luck improved its chances for survival, it was bad luck that turned Nagasaki into a target in the first place. Americans selected Hiroshima as the number one target for bombing, yet Nagasaki was not on the original shortlist. Only after months of debate did the target list shift to include Nagasaki, because of the presence of the Mitsubishi Shipyard. On that fateful morning, the primary target for the second bomb was the industrial city of Kokura. Smoke obscured Kokura so the B-29, *Bock's Car,* headed for its secondary target, Nagasaki. Aboard was its deadly cargo, "Fat Man," the plutonium bomb named for Churchill. Ironically, the bomb missed its intended target, the Mitsubishi shipyards in the south of the city, and instead scored an almost direct hit on the largest Catholic Church in Japan. At the epicenter of the bomb blast stood a lone black marble pillar and slab resembling a coffin laden with brightly colored strings of origami peace cranes.

Our visit to the nearby atomic bomb museum was sobering. I stared somberly at the exhibits, soaking in as much information as I could before museum stupor set in. The horror astonished me. I took notes so I wouldn't forget. Everything within 6.5 miles of ground zero was reduced to ashes, including some pretty substantial buildings. A third of the city was wiped out instantly or in the firestorm that followed. A wall of hot air more fierce than a typhoon travelled at the speed of sound covering 11 kilometers in thirty seconds. Everyone within 1,000 meters died immediately from the intense heat, dramatic pressure differences, being crushed, or impaled by flying glass and debris, inhaling or ingesting particles, and fires. Many without any visible injuries died later from radiation exposure. The death toll was 75,000 within hours of detonation. Another 75,000 were injured.

I listened to accounts from survivors. Lost in the sound of voices, recounting their firsthand experiences, I lost track of Garth for a time. One woman told how she struggled to free her crushed limbs. Another recounted how she located her family. A doctor described the challenges of treating the injured and sick, with a severe shortage of medical supplies, while not knowing whether his family had survived. He said rescue operations were hampered because few medically-skilled people survived, and medical supplies were scarce. More than 120,000 people were left homeless in the aftermath.

Across the room, I saw that Garth was as entranced as I was. Like me, he was probably remembering the details we'd read about the war before visiting Tinian and Okinawa. Several books about Japan portrayed a Japan entrenched in pursuing this hopeless conflict like a freight train out of control. *Enola Gay* detailed the development of the bombs and the mechanism to deliver them. *Embracing Defeat* examined the aftermath of the war and rebuilding Japan politically, socially, and economically.

I had come full circle: from Tinian where the B-29 began its journey; to Okinawa, where Bock's Car touched down after its deadly mission; to Nagasaki, the victim of its deadly cargo. I thought of how, as *Bock's Car* struggled to reach Okinawa with barely enough fuel to land, the people of Nagasaki struggled for their lives and dealt with the horrible consequences of this man-made destruction. There are always two sides to every story, and it is only learning more that helps us grasp its complexity.

Travel gives us the chance to see the other side. It forces us to stop and open our eyes to the ugly truth. It lets us see that humans across the planet may look different and speak a different language, yet we come face-to-face with the realization that we humans have the same basic needs. We yearn for the same things, like love, compassion, health and peace, though we may not know how to achieve it.

At the site of the bomb blast and museum Garth and I encountered no animosity toward us as Americans for the devastation our country had inflicted. Instead, we met young people in school uniforms eager to practice English with tourists and a resolve that this destruction must never happen again. Perhaps peace begins with forgiveness.

🌴

From Nagasaki, we wove our way through the mountainous islands west of Kyushu that Tets had described. Light winds made for long days sailing at a slow pace. Several times, we'd identify a promising bay on the chart only to find it filled with rows of buoys marking nets, traps, or pearl farms.

Late one afternoon, we anchored in the bight of a larger bay filled with pearl farms. It was a tight squeeze, and I worried that we shouldn't have anchored there, but that late in the day we had few options, and we would only stay the night.

While I was cooking a pasta dinner, a fishing boat pulled up unnervingly close to *Velella*. Through a porthole, I watched with fascination as fishermen dropped a net hung from floats and then steered in a tight circle back to the first float. They worked together to pull the net closed, then hauled a heavy net aboard.

A moment later, the fishermen pulled alongside. With a glowing smile, one silently handed us a fresh squid. But before we could even thank him, he was gone. The incident reminded me of a similar incident in the Marquesas, when an outrigger canoe appeared, a sparsely clothed native handed us a freshly caught tuna, and then disappeared into the night. No translation was necessary.

The following day, we pulled up to a fishing pier on the tiny island of Takashima for the night. As we tied the boat to the pier, we positioned the large typhoon fenders we'd found on the beach in Ishigaki to protect our boat from the sharp edges of corrugated steel. A heavyset gentleman with a wide face stopped a faded, green sedan and got out. He pointed at the boat, then at us. We nodded. "America?" he said, noticing the American flag waving on board. We nodded again. Then he furrowed his brow and scrunched his face in concentration, then shook his head and sighed. We laughed. He poked around his trunk, pushing aside a few old newspapers and plastic bags. Then he grunted and pulled out a warm beer that had been tucked into a crevice. He wiped it on his pants, shrugged, and handed it to us with a smile. Then he bowed awkwardly, got back into his car, and drove away.

Garth shook his head. "Well, that was interesting," he said, laughing.

Later, two men pulled up in a pickup truck and walked over to the edge of the pier where we were tied. The tide had dropped our boat lower than the pier, making it difficult to get on and off the boat.

"Hello," the younger, shorter man said, looking down at us. "Where from?"

"America…Seattle" I said.

"Ahh." He smiled. "I once lived in San Francisco."

"I was born in San Francisco. I lived there when I was a boy," Garth said.

"Ahh." Our English-speaking friend nodded sagely. He sat down, letting his legs hang over the edge of the pier. The other followed. He asked our names, then told us that his was Jiro and introduced the older man as Kohei. His English still came easily.

I thought of the map in the back of the dictionary we'd bought in New Zealand and went to retrieve it. On the diagram, I pointed at Seattle. They nodded.

Kohei reached into a paper grocery bag and wordlessly handed around a couple of beers. Then he handed us a small plastic container of some unidentifiable substance. The Kanji writing on the lid provided no clues about its contents. We tentatively placed a few morsels into our mouths and began to chew. Permeating my mouth was the flavor of rotted seaweed but with an extra bitterness and a slimy texture. When horror flashed across my face, they laughed. Jiro explained that it was eggplant. Normally I like eggplant, but this was undercooked and pickled with seaweed. I shuddered. Garth nudged me. They smiled. I went below and pulled out a package of Wasabi peas to contribute to our informal picnic.

Jiro absently grabbed a handful of wasabi peas and popped them into his mouth. As he chewed, his eyes widened suddenly. He coughed and sputtered, then took a quick swig of beer and swallowed quickly.

"Hot!" he said. We laughed.

"You've never had them before?" I asked, surprised that someone from Japan would be unfamiliar with wasabi peas. He shook his head and coughed again. Jiro examined the package we'd purchased in Hong Kong that I now realized had been made in Thailand.

I ducked below to grab locally-bought peanuts and seaweed crackers, and when I returned, they beamed with pride.

I picked up the dictionary again and traced our route around the Pacific. They nodded with amazement. I explained that we'd been sailing for nearly seven years and talked about the many countries we'd visited. Jiro then translated the details for his silent friend. The two men spoke briefly in Japanese. Kohei nodded with raised eyebrows.

Then Jiro asked "Where you go next?"

"Fukuoka," Garth said.

"After Japan?"

"We'll sail to America," I said.

"Japan to America?" He said slowly, shaking his head. Before Jiro could translate, Kohei looked instantly surprised.

Kohei then stood up, squared his body, gave a full bow from the waist, then kneeled, and bowed low—nearly prostrate to the ground. His gesture touched me deeply, though I was well aware we hadn't done it yet.

"You are very brave," Jiro said, then after a pause added, "crazy, maybe." We laughed.

"Yes, maybe a little crazy," Garth said. We nursed our beers to the last drop. Kohei shook his head again, then looked at his watch and said something to Jiro.

"We must go," Jiro said with a hint of reluctance in his voice. We smiled and waved as they returned to their truck, sad to see them go.

Our cruising life gave us the time to let situations unfold and see where they might lead. Time was our most precious gift. Before we went sailing, a busy schedule and too many possessions left me little time to reflect. I'd slowed down a lot since then. Would I be able to retain this sense of peace when I returned to the frenzied atmosphere back in the U.S.?

The shortest route from Western Kyushu into the Inland Sea we knew would involve some challenging sailing. Indeed it did.

Our route took us through Kanmon Kaikyo, a narrow nine-mile-long cut between the islands of Kyushu and Honshu with heavy shipping traffic and currents as strong as thirteen knots. Adverse winds kept us anchored outside the channel for days in the shadow of gigantic oil tanks and acre-sized warehouses, as well as smaller ships—100 times our size—who were also waiting to pass through. This grim industrial area had been the original target for the bomb that had ultimately devastated Nagasaki. The time on our three-month visas remained ever-present in our minds as we entertained ourselves with books and card games during two days of rain, gusty winds, and then thick fog. Gradually the wind clocked around to the west with an ideal wind speed of seven to ten knots.

While we waited, we checked and rechecked the currents and tides, acutely aware how critical timing would be. Our engine wasn't strong enough to counter an adverse current of even three knots—and certainly not the thirteen that we could encounter if we got it wrong. We aimed to arrive at the narrowest point under the bridge during slack water just before the flood so that we'd be gently flushed in the direction of our destination. Starting early against the last of the ebb gave us extra time to pass through while the current was mild enough to maintain control.

We were nervous about navigating this busy shipping channel with so little confidence in our engine. But if we didn't cut between Kyushu and Honshu, we'd have to sail hundreds of miles around the bottom of Kyushu. I might be exaggerating a bit to say that'd be like sailing around Cape Horn because you're afraid your engine might quit while going through the Panama Canal, but to me, the analogy seemed appropriate especially given such a short sailing season. Our decision to visit Nagasaki and the western islands put us in this position with little time left. In hindsight, it might have been faster to sail around. But it is an experience we'll never forget. Perhaps, neither will the Japanese coast guard.

At what we calculated would be the tail end of the ebb, we up-anchored and motored eastwards into the narrow channel. With a light breeze on my face, I strained to read an oversized reader board which indicated the current under the bridge seven miles away. I could make out a 3W.

"Looks like it says three knots from the west," I announced.

"That seems about right," Garth said from where he stood, tiller in hand. That meant the current was flowing in a westerly direction at a speed of three knots against us. The next current reader board showed, 2W, which meant the current was dropping. We expected the adverse current to keep declining until slack water, when it would shift in our favor and give us a gentle boost.

We had ideal conditions for sailing in a narrow band just outside the shipping lanes and made steady progress the first few miles. Ship after ship passed, heading the opposite direction. As we rounded a curve in the channel, wind funneled down the narrow slot directly from our destination. With little room between the shipping lane and the shore to sail against the wind, we fired up the engine. For several minutes we motor-sailed up the slim channel, marveling at the steady stream of car carriers, oil tankers, and containerships flagged from around the world.

Then the engine made a ghastly grinding sound of metal-against-metal. I rushed below to shut it off before we wrecked it. I looked at Garth. He shook his head and a look of disgust crossed his face. "I spend so much time fiddling with that damn engine, and when we really need it, we can't count on it." He blew out a stream of air. "So honey, you ready to short tack along the shore?" We'd have to tack back and forth against the wind in the twenty-five-yard slot between the channel markers and shore.

"You think we can pull this off?" I asked nervously, noting how incredibly narrow it was outside the shipping channel. We'd be tacking every two minutes until we got to the bridge, which could take us an hour. Every tack had to be perfect. If not, we risked losing ground, hitting a rock near shore or wandering into the path of a hard metal ship.

"Do we have a choice?" he said. The current changed directions. Turning around would have us sailing into an adverse current. Continuing would let the current help push us through the passage. If we took took long, the current could rise to levels that might be impossible to steer. We could get caught in a whirlpool, spin out of control and career into a ship. A steady stream of ships passed nearly nose to stern. None would be able to maneuver around a sailboat. At this point we were racing for our lives and our home. No, we didn't have a choice.

"Let's tack," Garth said. I wrapped the jib line around the winch, put the winch handle into position, and braced my legs. "Tacking." Garth pushed the tiller over hard. I pulled in the line as fast as I could. I handed him the line and winched in the last bit. It was a good tack. He pulled up the traveler so he could point the boat as high into the wind as possible. We'd done this before when we were racing and dueling with another boat for position. I thought of all the times we'd challenged ourselves to sail in the fluky winds in the narrow channel under the Agate Pass Bridge back in Puget Sound or the time we ran out of gas under the Montlake Bridge and had to tack our way through "the Cut," a channel no wider than a hundred feet. At that moment, I was grateful for our practiced teamwork. This time the consequences of screwing up were far more dire. I felt the adrenaline kick into high gear. I readied the winch for the next tack, which came only a minute later.

"Ready? Tacking," Garth said. We repeated our maneuver again and again. Over the years we'd worked out a system that was paying dividends now when we needed to be on top of our game. Garth steered as high as he could, feathering as much as possible to reduce the number of tacks we'd ultimately have to make and get us through this narrow death trap before the current became unmanageable.

With only a third of the channel left to navigate, a Japanese Coast Guard vessel motored into our path and stopped directly in front of us. Perhaps the officers expected us to stop, but there was no way we could. Garth kept steering straight towards them. I hoped they'd get out of the way before we got there.

"Perhaps they don't realize that we're going to get swept up this channel no matter what we do," Garth said. "I'd prefer to do it under control." There was nowhere safe to anchor. Turning around with the tide against us would have been impossible. Perhaps no one expected a sailboat would attempt to sail through here nowadays. But what choice did we have at this point?

It felt like a game of chicken. Finally the vessel shifted to our side as we kept sailing. Several uniformed officers appeared on deck. Over a megaphone, one officer announced, "You must take down your sail."

Garth yelled over the wind, "We have to sail. We have no engine."

The man repeated, "You must take down your sail."

Garth again yelled, "We must sail. We have no engine."

Then the man asked, "What is your destination?"

I was dumbfounded. What made him think he'd hear our replies when he was using a megaphone? Garth pointed at the bridge. I held up the radio microphone to suggest they call us by radio. A minute passed and we tacked while they looked on. After we settled onto the new tack, I called them on the VHF and explained that our engine had quit and we'd soon be through the channel anyway.

"Please be very careful," a voice replied tentatively.

"We'll stay outside the shipping lanes," I said. I hoped. The channel was getting narrower. We continued to make steady progress towards the bridge at the top end of the channel.

Velella neared the narrowest section under the bridge where there was no room outside the hundred yard wide shipping channel. Three ships approached in a steady line. They loomed over us, casting a long shadow. Bridge supports took some of our sea room, so under the bridge we would have to venture into the channel. We tacked towards the line of ships into a wall of standing waves. Just then we got another call on the VHF. Could they have picked a worse time?

After we tacked back and they'd called a third time, I finally answered. A baritone voice asked me to spell our vessel name, state our port of entry into Japan and nationality. It was as though we were starting all over again. How could they be so oblivious?

The voice asked, "Please state your last port."

"Fukuoka," I said breathlessly as I prepared the winch for the next tack.

The voice asked, "Please state your destination." I felt my blood pressure rising.

"Shikoku. Stand by," I said, putting down the microphone to tack. I pulled in the sheet as the jib came across the bow. I winched in the last bit, and then wound line around the opposite winch to prepare for the next tack.

Garth pulled up the traveler. I resumed microphone-duty.

"This is *Velella*, go ahead," I said into the microphone.

"What is your estimated time of arrival?" the voice asked.

"It depends on the wind. Our engine is not working," I replied.

"How long will it take to repair your engine?" the voice asked.

"I don't know," I said. "We don't yet know what the problem is."

"What will you do if you cannot get your engine working?" he asked.

"We are a sail boat. Sail to America, I guess."

"Sail to America! Sail to America?" the voice said, rising several octaves. The microphone clicked off, and I imagined stunned looks and chatter among the officers listening.

Garth chuckled.

"Yes, sail to America," I said. "Stand by." I set down the microphone again as we maneuvered the boat through another tack.

When I came back on the radio, he asked, "How many people do you have onboard?"

"Two."

"Two?" the surprised voice repeated. "Two. Ah so, desuka." Finally they understood. There were two people on board doing all the sail maneuvering through a narrow channel filled with large ships, and one of them was the woman they were interrogating. I wondered whether they could see the situation we were in. After a silence, he came back on the radio. "Please contact customs when you arrive in Shikoku." He signed off just before we darted across the channel between two fast moving ships a thousand times our tonnage.

My heart thudded a staccato beat as we slipped between them.

When we passed under the bridge, the reader board indicated the current was flowing east at four knots. Garth steered past the channel marker and resumed a position on the shoulder of this busy thoroughfare.

"That enough excitement for ya?" Garth said, face flushed. "You can't say we live a dull life." I nodded vigorously.

Within a half hour, we heard an announcement on the VHF in English that the current under the bridge was eight knots and rising and that passage would be closed to all vessels unable to power more than fifteen knots.

🌴

We had just started to relax, when a guy on a nearby fishing boat started frantically waving flags. As *Velella* drew closer, I spotted a line of nearly submerged small white buoys. We tacked away, and he calmed down. Then another fisherman started waving frantically and honking.

"Watch out, I think he's also connected to that same net," I said to Garth. They might have been easier to spot had they been in a straight line. "Those floats are nearly-invisible!" Garth turned below them. Once the danger had passed, I added, "I can't believe fishing boats are stringing lines and nets across a vast area so close to a major shipping lane."

Garth said through clenched teeth, "Yeah, I've noticed Japanese fishermen seemed to push the right-of-way rules as far as they can."

By the time we cleared this fishing group and then another, the adrenaline had worn off and my nerves were shot. Yet hundreds of fishing boats still dotted the horizon, along with countless ships, some of which were cutting the corner outside the shipping lanes.

On the forms we'd filled out in Fukuoka, we'd indicated that we would sail out of the Inland Sea straight to the south of Shikoku Island and estimated our time of arrival to be 5:00 p.m. the following day. As the day wore on, the wind died to nothing, and I mean nothing, zilch, zip, nada. Not even a ripple on the water. With no wind or engine and dusk descending upon us, we were feeling the pressure. Being near a busy shipping lane in the fog, surrounded by fishing boats doing the unexpected while we had no steerage made for a long tense night. We didn't know it would be only the first of several.

To the south, another slot between two promontories funneled the current. On watch alone while Garth slept, I struggled to make headway. We'd never make it through before the current turned against us. I battled for every inch in short wisps of wind, heavy mist and fog, and then lost all my progress as the tide changed. Several times I sailed past, then drifted back towards a group of dimly lit fishing buoys. I couldn't remember office stress that had surpassed this.

The closest anchorages were too far to reach. Once we anchored Garth could take a look at the engine, though he was doubtful that he'd be able to fix it. He assumed that a fix would require parts we'd never be able to get before the weather turned for the season and we needed to sail for North America. Finally we made enough progress to sail into a nearby bay and anchor. Garth inspected the engine, but found no obvious source for the problem. Discouraged and exhausted we went to bed.

The following morning, still without an engine, we sailed off again in a mildly promising wind only to have it die once we were too far to return. Finally after our fourth agonizing day of drifting in a foggy drizzle without any sign of real wind, out of sheer desperation I broke down and tried the motor again, hoping I wouldn't hear that bone-chilling squeal.

Ten minutes later, when we did hear it, Garth was below. As I reached down to turn it off, he yelled, "Wait! The noise isn't coming from where I thought it was. It's coming from the shaft seal." I endured that wretched sound a moment longer while he fiddled with something below. And then it stopped. Later he explained that air had gotten into the shaft seal, which was normally lubricated with water. The horrible grinding noise was merely the sound of it running dry. To fix the problem, all Garth had to do was burp it. After four interminable days of frustration and nearly getting ourselves pulverized by a ship and causing an international incident, we'd made a whopping seventy miles of progress. And all because the shaft seal needed to be burped.

The following day, the wind picked up enough to make decent progress under sail. But by then, we'd wasted so much time bobbing around, we had lost days of sightseeing time and had to skip several planned stops. Typhoon season wouldn't wait.

As we pulled into Wakayama, we were sure that we'd violated every rule the Japanese Coast Guard had ever imagined. We'd never stopped where we'd declared that we would and had been mostly MIA for over nine days. Yet when we arrived, customs officials greeted us with a smile, handed us refrigerator magnets, cell phone straps, and engraved pencils, and nodded sagely when we explained that our timing was totally dependent upon the weather.

Later, when we told our friends Yuki and Tomi, who we'd first met in New Zealand while they were circumnavigating the Pacific, that we'd sailed through Kanmon Kaikyo, they told us we were crazy.

🌴

"What was it like to come home after your cruise?" I asked Yuki as we climbed the steps to the imposing Wakayama Castle. Its whitewashed walls and heavy grey-tiled roof towered over us behind a fortress of stone. We paused to take photos, each of us squinting in the bright sunshine. A gentle breeze rustled the leaves on the graceful burgundy-leaved maples in the gardens.

Yuki had arrived at our boat that morning with cucumbers and green beans from her garden, explaining that Tomi was working and would join us later for dinner at their house. It had been four years since we first met them in New Zealand. We'd gotten to know them better in Fiji as we commiserated about the rough passage we'd both survived and shared directions to the customs and immigration offices. She and Tomi had picked their way north from our last rendezvous in Fiji through the islands towards Japan, arriving there shortly after we'd reached Kwajalein following our Solomons meltdown.

That morning she'd looked around *Velella*'s cramped interior and with a hint of melancholy in her voice, and said, "I miss the sailing life." They'd been back just over three years. Yet her English was still perfect. I'd asked how she'd maintained her fluency back in Japan where few spoke English. "Reading English novels," she answered. Embarrassed by our overflowing bookshelves, I handed her a stack of books we'd just finished. She eyed them with the sort of eagerness I reserved for fresh vegetables after weeks of sea rations.

Her comment had intrigued me. I wanted to know more. I was still trying to reconcile myself with the idea of returning home. I wasn't finished with the sailing life. This I knew.

Garth was looking forward to the next phase, to challenging his engineering skills among colleagues again and finally building the boat he'd been designing since we'd sailed to Mexico nearly six years earlier—and in his mind far longer. I knew how important that was to him, though wondered where the money would come from. Unlike Garth, I didn't have a plan. I was returning only reluctantly, though I longed to see friends and family.

Yet I had an unsettled feeling about even that. I worried that we'd no longer fit seamlessly into the community we left behind. We'd changed and undoubtedly so had our friends. We didn't even know what we'd missed. Though I'd hungered for news of our hometown and the lives of our friends—anything that extended my connection to the life and people I'd left behind— I'd noticed that replies to my emails came less frequently the longer we were away. Several who did write replied with vaguely dismissive statements along the lines of, "Nothing exciting going on here," or "Compared to what you're doing, I've got nothing to report."

I'd begun to wonder how many friends were still reading my updates and whether we had gradually become irrelevant to their lives after being away so long. There's a saying "Absence makes the heart grow fonder," and another "Out of sight, out of mind," and I wondered if we'd passed that critical moment when one turns into the other.

When I looked over, Yuki's thoughtful gaze indicated that she was still considering my question. I realized that I'd asked a rather bold question of someone from a society that avoided such directness and worried she'd feel awkward speaking so candidly. We silently made our way up the steps into the interior.

My thoughts drifted to an Australian couple we'd met in Kyushu who'd told us they were on their third voyage. Though our time together had been brief, we'd felt an immediate affinity with Mauro and Pauline. When I had told them we were planning to set sail across the North Pacific to return home, Pauline blurted, "You don't want to go home and just be an American in America, do you?" I hadn't thought of it that way before. We'd been considered "exotic" for years. Then, with a tinge of horror in her voice, "Rejoin the rat race?" It was as though her piercing blue eyes had seen though my reservations.

"How long have you been out?" Mauro asked.

"Seven years." I said.

"Ooch." Mauro shook his bald head. "That's a long time away." I nodded from what felt like a distance of a million miles.

Pauline said, "Our boat practically fell apart on us by the time we reached Hong Kong. We had no money to fix it, so we sold it and flew home to Australia. But we quickly realized when we got there that, even after two years away, it no longer felt like home." Like many long-married couples, they completed one another's sentences, like teammates on a relay.

Mauro grabbed the baton from Pauline. "We'd changed. We were no longer the same people we were when we left. We'd done all these things that had stretched us, and our friends were still doing the same things, unaware that time had passed." His comment struck me as harsh. Maybe they just had grown apart.

Yet the conversation gave voice to a general unease I'd been feeling. Something I never considered before we left was that our voyage would change us and that we might reach a point where we'd be unable to return to the life we'd left.

Pauline added, "We quickly decided we had to get back out there again. We set a goal and saved our money." This too struck a nerve. Wasn't this exactly what we were proposing to do? The only reason I'd agreed to sail back was the hope that we'd return to the cruising life again soon. Next time on a boat that fit Garth.

She went on. "We did nothing but work for four years. Then we bought a boat and left again." Their brief time back in Australia sounded so devoid of the ties that bind us to place and make life worth living. I wasn't sure I could survive that kind of life.

I had truly loved Seattle when we left. Yet that connection faded the longer we were away. Could I love living there again, I wondered. Or had I unknowingly sentenced myself to a life of feeling like I didn't belong anywhere? We'd met many sailors who, once exposed to this alternative lifestyle, were permanently afflicted—as though infected with malaria which returns with a periodic feverishness.

Shore side life has a way of conspiring to make extracting oneself difficult. I remembered all the things I had to do to disengage before we left—closing accounts, changing addresses and training people not to expect us to be readily available by phone or email—and dreaded repeating the process. Every moment ashore compounded the risk. I'd tasted freedom. To me now, shore life felt like entrapment, full of expectations, obligations, and complications. *Could I learn to love it again? Or would I forever be aching to go? Forever caught between two worlds?*

I came alongside a display case featuring traditional warrior dress, which reminded me of the TV miniseries *Shogun*. As I stood there, I pictured the forbidden lovers Anjin-san and Mariko stealing intimate moments together under the beady gaze of warriors dressed just as the figures in the case before me. Thrown together from two widely divergent cultures in a time of adversity, they forged a bond deeper than ones each had known before. They'd been caught between two worlds.

Yuki swept across the polished wooden floor to stand beside me. When Garth appeared next to us, she finally spoke.

"Coming back to Japan was difficult," she said hesitantly. I hoped I hadn't made her uncomfortable with my probing question. She looked over at me and her steady gaze deflected my worry. "After we reached Japan we didn't sail directly home, though our families were impatient to see us." She grew more animated. "We sailed through Japan as though we were tourists. We didn't want our trip to end." She turned to me and pressed her lips together.

Garth caught my eye from the other side of the display case. Yuki reached up to tuck a strand of her short dark hair behind her ear. I nodded, and she went on.

"Tomi has a small dinghy which we sail sometimes, but it isn't the same. We miss the freedom of life . . ." She made a sweeping gesture towards the view out the castle windows of Wakayama and the water beyond, "out there."

After we left the castle, we headed for a grocery store where Yuki helped us buy supplies for our upcoming passage. Yuki's help was invaluable, telling us what was in those mysteriously labeled packages and suggesting ingredients like miso soup paste and noodles that could last for months without refrigeration and make easy-to-cook meals underway. Provisioning with someone who'd tackled that stretch of ocean with far less experience than we had somehow made it feel less daunting.

We got so absorbed in provision shopping, we nearly forgot to buy octopus for the evening's meal. We quickly dropped our stores on *Velella* then drove on to Yuki's house. There we met up with Tomi, whose English had improved markedly since our last meeting. During dinner preparations that evening, we flipped through Tomi's sketchbook featuring fine watercolors of places we'd both cruised. A circumnavigator who'd single-handedly sailed around the world via all the great capes also joined us for dinner. As we sat down to eat, he and Tomi echoed what Yuki had said earlier about the difficulty of returning home after their grand adventures.

Over a delicious feast of the local specialty, Takoyaki—tiny round balls of a soft, lightly toasted mixture of octopus, flour, and mild cheese—we reminisced about boats, people, and places we knew in common. At the low wooden table, sitting cross-legged with a glass of Kirin in hand in the company of fellow cruisers, I felt understood.

I savored the moment. I'd worry about the future tomorrow.

Since they'd featured us in *Kazi Magazine,* we'd remained in contact with Tomoko and Yuichiro. After New Zealand lost the America's Cup, our friends had moved back to Tokyo and followed our halting progress around the Pacific by email. They must have doubted whether we'd ever reach Japan. (I certainly did.) First we'd wrecked our electronics in the Solomons. Then we'd spent two years in Kwajalein repairing our boat and earning money to afford those repairs and pay for a new roof for our house back in Seattle. Then another year had passed since we'd left Kwajalein while we detoured through Hong Kong and the Philippines and debated our future.

When I emailed to let Tomoko and Yuichiro know we'd finally arrived in Japan, Tomoko's reply seemed almost surprised that we'd finally made it. After we pulled into Yokohama, outside Tokyo, not far from where they lived, Tomoko wrote, "We'd love to see you and do another interview with you for the magazine, but right now we are in Beijing doing an article about the Olympics and won't be back until next week. Can you wait until next Tuesday?"

We were already behind schedule. Garth and I had planned to leave Japan in early July before typhoons started pounding the area. The massive breakwaters protecting harbors and the oversized Styrofoam typhoon fenders that boats carried hinted that typhoon season was no joke. We hoped to avoid needing that type of protection. Plus, we still had to sail 5,000 miles to North America. At the pace we travel, that would take ages and we hoped to arrive *before* fall storms began buffeting the Pacific Northwest coast. We needed as much margin as we could get. Garth expressed reservations about waiting, but I convinced him to delay our departure so we could see Tomoko and Yuichiro.

Because we were foreigners, Yokohama Bayside Marina discounted our slip fees from $60 to $15, but we were used to anchoring for free. We flirted with the idea of finding a free anchorage, but in such a heavily populated area we knew our chances of finding an open bay were low. Experience had taught us that what initially appeared to be clear bays on our older charts were often overrun with fish nets, marinas, or new islands.

A new development on the weather chart convinced us to stay put: Another deepening low east of the Philippines where north Pacific typhoons usually form.

"Let's see what happens with this low. I'd rather be in a protected marina than any of the coastal anchorages around here if we're going to see typhoons this early in the season," Garth said. I wasn't about to argue. Besides, I had a number of Tokyo-based friends I wanted to see and being in the marina simplified logistics significantly.

During the week and a half that we awaited Tomoko and Yuichiro's return from Beijing, between social engagements we squeezed in time to prepare for our last passage across the North Pacific. And, of course, we closely watched the weather chart. As the days passed, the low on the weather map turned into a full-fledged typhoon. Normally typhoons veer west towards Vietnam and Hong Kong at this time of year. But this typhoon was curving north, unusually early for the season. Each update of the forecast showed it curving ever closer to Tokyo. Uh, oh. Typhoon season had come early to Japan and we sat directly in its path. Just what Garth had tried to avoid. The tension between us rose.

Everyone around us carried on as though impending doom wasn't awaiting us. And so Garth and I went sightseeing, trying to ignore the bull's-eye that hovered over Tokyo and our floating home. With Tokyo-based friends we poked around popular Tokyo sights as well as Enoshima Island's beachfront, shrine and gardens. We paused for a traditional tea ceremony where a kimono-clad older woman brought us thick, bitter green tea and sweets on a delicate bamboo tray. We sampled a chalky pink one that tasted remarkably like sweetened chalk, a white cake-like one filled with bean paste, and a translucent gelatinous pale blue-green one with a subtle flavor I couldn't place. After the tea ceremony, we walked past carefully cultivated bonsai trees that were only a few feet tall despite being hundreds of years old. I wondered how they'd survived the fire-bombing of Tokyo during the war.

Despite the distractions, Garth seemed preoccupied. I imagined the imminent typhoon weighed heavily on his mind. The 5,000 mile sail across the North Pacific weighed heavily on mine. The typhoon only made it seem more ominous. Yet if we had left as originally planned, would we have missed the typhoon altogether? Or would we have been caught in its fury at sea? At a Buddhist temple, brightly colored tags spun in the wind from the slender branches of a weeping willow. At a nearby table, I penciled my wishes for a safe passage across the North Pacific on a neon green tag.

🌴

Despite the ominous forecast, the day we met Tomoko and Yuichiro dawned sunny with blue skies and gentle winds. But I'd noticed a pattern. The days before a typhoon arrives seem deceptively calm and clear. While the camera captured photos of *Velella* with a firm click, Tomoko recorded details of our travels since our New Zealand interview. Afterward, the four of us drove to Kamakura for an afternoon of sightseeing in the former Japanese capital, a peaceful town of notable Buddhist temples, Shinto shrines and picturesque gardens. As the afternoon unfolded, Tomoko and Yuichiro's English gradually grew less stilted as they remembered the language they hadn't used for more than a year.

They took us to Daibatsu, a bronze Buddha built in 1252 that sits over thirty-six feet tall. The size of his sandals alone was an impressive sight. When I ventured inside the bronze Buddha, though it was a cool day I immediately understood the need for the ventilation provided by amusingly large doors cut into his back. At a signpost Garth silently pointed to the English words that read, "The statue sits in the open since the hall that once housed it was washed away in a tsunami in 1495." Wow. . I'd almost forgotten about the weather. My stomach tightened. As we climbed the stone steps of an ancient temple surrounded by blue and pink hydrangea blossoms, I tried to ignore my growing agitation, knowing that we'd be facing another typhoon within the next couple of days.

We stopped for a timeless tradition, afternoon tea. At the entrance to the slope-roofed tea house, we paused at what looked like a vending machine. Yet the graceful tea house didn't look like a vending machine kind of place. Tomoko and Yuichi exchanged a few words in Japanese and Yuichi began punching buttons and plugging yen coins into the machine. The machine spit out two receipts, which he handed to a man standing expectantly nearby. The man disappeared into a back room and we grabbed a table overlooking the gardens. Outside I saw no sign of the typhoon that loomed in the distance. A few moments later the waiter delivered skewers of small white rice balls coated with a mildly sweet and sticky brown sauce with a subtle hint of soy. Tomoko and Yuichi watched closely for our reaction. Chewy but delicious, I decided. I nodded my approval and they relaxed. The waiter returned with two bowls of watery gelatin with wide translucent noodles. As I attempted to fish the noodles out of the bowl with my chopsticks and dip them into a bowl of molasses, the noodles slithered back into the bowl with a monumental splash, sending brown gooey liquid splattering over me, Garth, and the table. Tomoko and Yuichi sprang back from the table, giggling at my ineptitude.

In the late afternoon, we drove to the home of Yuichi's parents. My eyes took in the finely manicured garden and the exquisite antiques in their tatami room, and I asked if this was the house where Yuichi had grown up. It was. For the last four years, we'd carried a quilted silk ornament Yuichi's mother had made, which he'd given us for luck during our New Zealand interview. After Garth thanked Yuichi's mother for the ornament she pulled out stacks of hand-made silk figurines, insisting we take some home. They remain among the most treasured souvenirs I have of our seven year voyage. After they treated us to heaping plates of sushi, Tomoko and Yuichi dropped us back at the marina. We said our goodbyes, unsure when we'd see each other again.

As the typhoon moved closer, we stayed glued to the weather forecasts, monitoring minute by minute the danger posed to our home and health, as we began our precautionary steps. We moved *Velella* into a smaller, more protected slip in the lee of a beefy breakwater behind several rows of boats and strung a spider's web of lines to hold us securely. Suspending the boat midway between the pontoons made getting on and off the boat difficult. To protect the boat hull in the event we smacked against the dock or another boat, we rigged the oversized typhoon fenders we'd carried for months, just in case. Finally they would earn their keep. After shrinking in horror at the $80 hardware store price tag, we'd salvaged two fenders from a deserted beach only to slowly realize they were infested with ants. It had taken me months to chase down the last of the wayward critters.

We'd been through this before, but would we be so lucky this time? One by one our friends emailed status reports of their experiences further south and west as the typhoon rolled over them. Sailors in the Ryukyu Islands where Pat and Monica lived reported damage to their toe-rail and stanchions when a fishing boat dragged anchor into them. Yuki and Tomi reported severe winds and heavy rains, minimal roof damage and a few minor boat casualties in the Inland sea. Given their relatively protected position behind Shikoku, I feared what that must mean for us.

We waited nervously for the worst. The wind and rains lashed their fury and the boat surged back and forth in the slip. Garth worried the lines would pop from the strain as the wind blowing against *Velella*'s hull yanked them taut. The boats around us tugged fitfully at their mooring lines. If one of them broke free, we could suffer the consequences even if our boat remained secure. A ninety-foot steel motor yacht that had moved into the slip we'd vacated wrenched a cleat right out of the dock and started swinging wildly downwind of us. Its crew and marina personnel scurried to secure it before it could wreak any more havoc.

Dressed in full foulies, I leaned into the wet wind to make my way to the boater's lounge where I could track up-to-the-minute weather information on the Internet while Garth remained aboard. Rain pelted loudly against the cathedral high picture windows and streaked down their fronts, turning the scene into a blurry impressionistic painting. Compared to the slamming, wrenching of the boat and symphony of groaning nylon lines, ashore the typhoon seemed little more than a blustery rainy day.

Finally the wind dissipated. We'd survived another typhoon, this one, by twenty five miles. Once again, the tense watching and waiting had been the worst part.

Still looming before us were 5,000 miles of open ocean that boiled in the wake of this departing typhoon.

CHAPTER
20

RETROGRADE MANEUVER: NONSTOP ACROSS THE COLD NORTH PACIFIC

Two days later, on July 18, 2007, we left Japan for Seattle. At roughly five miles per hour, we could expect to sail east for at *least* forty-two days nonstop before we'd see land on the opposite side of the Pacific. That is, *if* we made progress in the right direction every day.

Before we'd left Japan, we stocked our little boat as much as we could to sustain us during what we expected would be a long, arduous journey. The problem was that our capacity was so limited. *With* jerry cans, we carried a whopping eighteen gallons of diesel. Out of 5,000 miles, we could only expect to motor for 100 of them, which meant we needed wind to get there. As for fresh water, we carried forty-five gallons normally, but with all our water jugs filled to capacity, we had seventy gallons, thirty-five each for drinking, bathing, or whatever. (I'd probably taken a single shower using that much water back home.) We'd have enough water, if we conserved carefully, relied mostly on saltwater for non-drinking, and caught water along the way. Hopefully.

As always, I'd stocked up on groceries, buying several months worth of food. Uncooked food. In the frenzy of preparing to go, Garth forgot to top off the propane tanks, which we didn't realize at first, so we had less than six weeks of fuel for the stove and oven at our normal usage rate. We were heading into colder waters, and with my penchant for hot chocolate and inclination to bake in cooler (calm) weather, we worried we wouldn't have enough. Again, if I was careful to conserve, we'd make it. Hopefully.

To reach Seattle, we needed to sail slightly north of due east, but waves and winds left over from the typhoon drove us south. Once the wind and seas finally diminished, they quickly died to nothing. The typhoon had sucked all the wind from its path as it moved eastward across the Pacific ahead of us.

On the ninth day out of Japan, we found ourselves sitting on a glassy ocean without wind in any direction. Weather charts Garth downloaded from the short wave radio showed that the void stretched for hundreds of miles around our position. Motoring made little sense, as it wouldn't have gotten us far and we might need the fuel later for an emergency. So there we sat. Waiting.

After two weeks of nonstop sailing we still had 4,673 miles to go. I made the best of the light winds by getting creative in the galley, making focaccia, and grilled sandwiches, until Garth remembered about the propane.

🌴

On July 27, we lost our ability to transmit over short wave radio. That meant that we had no way of speaking to anyone outside of our little world beyond the range of our VHF radio—twenty-five miles. When we left Mexico for the Marquesas, we didn't have this capability, but after we'd added it in New Zealand, we'd grown used to having it. Something we had once considered a luxury, we now considered a necessity. Leaving Japan with possibly a couple of months stretching before me, I had counted on being able to communicate with the outside world to help keep me going for so long. But I'd have to learn to live without it once again.

We sailed on.

🌴

In the vast north Pacific thousands of miles from land, there's not a heck of a lot to look at—even less if it's foggy. We had been sailing nonstop for nearly four weeks, a week longer than our longest passage to date from Mexico to the Marquesas. Neither of us had seen a ship in more than two weeks. Once fog settled upon us, even dolphins, whales, and birds were no longer visible. Forget passing time by marking the movement of the sun, moon and stars across the sky. Even the thin line separating water from sky was fuzzy.

At 4:40 in the morning, I'd been awake for maybe forty-five minutes. I yawned, rubbed my eyes, and shivered. Fortunately summer dawns came early at this latitude. Moisture hung thick in the air, collecting and glistening on my cheeks as our momentum propelled me through it. Lines creaked as they moved in their blocks in time with the gentle shifting of the boat. Water, cast aside by the cut of our bow, gurgled alongside the hull.

Finally wind had returned to aid our progress. Garth and I alternated keeping watch in four hour stretches. We'd had contact with no other human beings for weeks now. Even our contact with one another was compromised by a need to get enough sleep while keeping a constant vigil.

With nothing on the horizon to focus on, my thoughts drifted to what awaited us at the end of this journey. We'd been gone for a long time—seven years sailing the Pacific and Asia, at our own pace, by our own choice. It had been a priceless experience, full of incredible encounters with people and wildlife. We'd overcome seemingly insurmountable obstacles and thrived. We'd changed in that time. So had the country and friends we'd left behind. We'd missed 9/11, one of the most monumental events in our nation's history, and had missed nearly the entire two Bush administrations. I wondered how it would feel to be back and how I would adjust to the frantic pace of American life after the tranquil life of sailing.

A flash of color in my peripheral vision instantly jarred me out of my reverie. A bright orange ship emerged out of the murk on a collision course, closing the distance between us unnervingly fast.

Normally when I spotted a ship, I could take evasive maneuvers with a minor course correction to put us on widely divergent paths. At least if I'm paying attention. But this one was too close.

I could see him, but could he see me? A white boat with white sails against a white sky. I doubted it. I had minutes to get his attention before impact. The fog thickened, and he disappeared from view.

Oh-my-god, Oh-my-god, Oh-my-god …

I was scared to take my eyes away from where I'd last seen him. Our radio wasn't within reach. Neither was our horn. Our pitiful horn sounded more like a party favor, anyway. There's no way anyone would hear it. Usually I had all these plus a floodlight at my fingertips. But this wasn't a typical shipping route, and after weeks of seeing nothing, it seemed ridiculous to expose them to perpetually salty air. And to waste all that battery power running the radio— to talk to *who* exactly?

The ship re-emerged. God was he close. At least I knew where he was. But I still had a BIG problem, getting bigger by the second.

I felt like a bug on the freeway faced with a rapidly advancing windshield. Within minutes, this ship could turn our home of eight years into debris, plunging us into the cold North Pacific. My heart pounded in my chest and my body started shaking uncontrollably.

I frantically banged on the hull with my knuckles.

"Turn on the radio, quick!"

He popped his head up and squinted at me with bleary, unfocused eyes.

"Huh, what's going on?"

Wordlessly, I pointed to the dramatic color interrupting our featureless horizon. His eyes popped open, and he gasped, instantly wide awake. Before I could get any words out, he reached for the radio.

"Orange ship, this is the sailing vessel *Velella*. We are directly off your bow on a collision course. Do you see us?" Garth said, carefully enunciating each syllable.

Garth's eyes locked on mine, then settled on the ship. We strained to detect a reply, cocking our ears towards the speaker as though that would help. Tick, tick, tick, I heard our clock softly marking time. After what seemed like an eternity, a whistle and two clicks crackled through the speaker. The ship's bow abruptly swung away. I exhaled.

Fog billowed around us, masking the surprisingly brilliant color, enveloping it briefly. When the orange reappeared, I watched it slip behind us back into the murk, like a phantom. Only my irregular heartbeat hinted of our recent danger. My heart took some time to resume a slower beat. The horizon resumed its uniformity.

Garth returned to the world of slumber as best he could. I continued my watch, trying to shake the memory of our nearly fatal encounter, which now felt like a hallucination.

Four hours on, four hours off. *Only 2,959 miles to go.*

Storm petrels chirped at dusk, and albatross gracefully glided over the boat throughout the day. Huge tunas leaped out of the water, a number keeping pace with us for a time. We trailed a fishing line, hoping to catch one to vary our diet, but none fell for our lure. All day our lure skipped along as lonely as the moment I'd eased it into the water. On the rare occasion we did snag a fish, we couldn't reel it in fast enough before another predator feasted on our catch.

One evening as I was serving stove-top burritos, I noticed an albatross swooping near the end of our line. "We should take in the fishing line. That albatross looks a bit too intrigued with our lure," I said.

"Let's eat first," Garth said, taking a bite.

I was chewing absently when I heard a twang. The bungee attached to our fishing line went taut. Dragging from the lure was a cascade of water over a flap of white wings. No! The albatross had dived for the line and gotten snagged in our lure. We set our dishes aside.

"There's no way he'll survive," Garth said. He slowly reeled him in. We were sailing at five knots. I was hopeful, but as Garth drew the bird closer, I could see that his neck was broken. I grasped his impressive size for the first time. The albatross was far larger than he'd appeared while soaring in an endless sky.

"This is heartbreaking." I said.

Garth gently unhooked the webbed feet of the lifeless bird from the lure and eased him into the water. He shook his head as he let go of it, muttering something unintelligible about the "Rime of the Ancient Mariner."

The white, feathered carcass in our wake attracted the attention of several other birds, and I imagined them gathering for a bird funeral, as we sailed on, wondering what lay in store.

I try not to be superstitious, but we'd taken steps to appease Neptune along the way—pouring him a spot of blackberry wine at the equator. Though it wasn't the rum he's reputed to prefer, we had months of ideal sailing afterward.

Already uneasy about the Sisyphean task ahead of us, I wasn't sure we hadn't pressed our luck just one time too many.

What else could we do but sail on?

🌴

Each day, Garth downloaded a weather map and each day it indicated a gale brewing in our vicinity. At first, we shortened sail in preparation, but when a gale didn't arrive and we saw it vanish from the weather map, we stopped taking precautionary measures, figuring we'd face conditions once they arrived.

When we reached the International Date Line, we had a glorious day with vivid blue skies and perfect winds behind us. After bathing in the sunshine, we celebrated with Kahlua-and-Milk and chocolates I'd saved for the occasion. We'd sailed 2,700 miles since we'd left Japan twenty-four days earlier. I tried not to think about the fact that; after all this sailing, we were just over halfway there.

Garth noted our position in the log book and then reprinted the date. Because we were sailing eastwards across the dateline we regained the day that we'd lost six years earlier when we crossed from Tonga to Fiji. The second time we saw August 9 wasn't quite as pleasant. The clouds rolled in, and our world became enveloped in thick fog once again. Our world became suffocatingly small. There were ships we heard or smelled but never saw.

Still, we sailed on.

Low, dark clouds pressed in on us day after day, sometimes the fog was so thick, we could barely see past the bow. Since our SSB had stopped transmitting, our floating world became even more isolated, with only music and books as company. We had one another, but standing watch in shifts meant we saw little of one another when we were both coherent.

Just before I fell asleep one night, I read a scene from the book *The Secret Life of Bees* in which someone dies and is laid out in a coffin. My subconscious must have associated the coffin in the novel with my cramped, dark bunk that reeked of fetid air, because I awoke in a panic, my hands sweaty, and my heart pounding in my chest. I climbed out of the bunk, pulled on clothes, and clipped on my harness. I pushed past Garth in the cockpit.

"What are you doing? You have another hour and a half before you're on watch!"

"I don't care. I can't stand another moment down there. I need air."

"Are you okay?"

I gulped deep breaths of air until my heart slowed. Garth watched me intently.

After weeks of sensory deprivation, could I be losing my grip on reality? I was weary of scanning a gray, featureless horizon hardly distinguishable from the sea. At times, I couldn't even see that, as though I were looking through an out-of-focus camera. Every day, the same view in every direction: gray sky and clouds and nothing else. Little distinguished one day from another. This voyage was stretching on interminably.

"I don't know," I said after a minute, peering into the fog. I felt like I was suffocating. I needed to do something, anything, to shake free.

Garth laid his hand on my upper arm. His touch soothed me.

"We should be over the fold on the chart by the afternoon," he said, smiling in feigned excitement. We'd been sailing for over a month, but we were still far from land in either direction.

"Humph." I grunted.

He spent a few minutes gently rubbing my back. I watched the waves dance in their haphazard way.

"Are you sure you want to begin your watch now?" Garth said.

I nodded numbly. After several more minutes, he gave me a gentle squeeze and went down to bed.

Gradually the dark sky grew pale; then the sun gleamed beneath an umbrella of clouds as it emerged over the horizon. The low cloud cover hinted that the sun's appearance might be fleeting, but for now, it beamed gloriously, and I drank it in. I lay on the foredeck and looked straight into its rays, gathering as much of its soothing brilliance as I could.

Before that moment, I'd wondered how much longer I could endure. But that blessed morning sun gave me a glimmer of hope.

And I sailed on.

Beyond the bow, a dark pinnacle appeared that I gradually realized was the nose of a sperm whale. Each time I saw a whale, I experienced a rush of delight and a flutter of apprehension. This impressive creature exceeded the size of my universe, so I had a healthy respect for the consequences of getting too close. I had read enough about whale-sailboat encounters to know that sailboats often don't fare well.

Instead of slipping beneath the waves, the whale held his position. I had to alter course to avoid sailing into him. With a quick pull against the tiller I chose a side to pass, hoping he would remain where he was. I felt the change in wind angle on the back of my neck on my new course. I took in a sharp breath and held it. *Velella* slowly slid past the whale within a hundred yards. I exhaled.

Once the danger seemed less imminent, I debated grabbing my camera or waking Garth, but assumed the whale would disappear in moments. His proximity was mesmerizing, and I didn't want to break the spell, so I just sat and watched. He remained with his nose jutted proudly above the waves.

Then another whale cracked the surface. I'd broken into a pod of whales. These two whales were a safe distance away, but how many of them were there? I tried to imagine what *Velella* looked like from their perspective—a black rounded bottom, with a large fin rocking in the waves—like a whale.

The first whale began slapping his tail. Then the other whale joined in. Had my presence upset them? I was glad I was too far to feel their splashes—a single splash could swamp the boat. I sat paralyzed as *Velella* plodded through the waves away from them.

My fear dissipated as the distance between us grew. And then I was saddened when they disappeared from view. I wondered what they had been trying to communicate. Perhaps they were just waving hello.

The whales set me to thinking about all the amazing wildlife we'd seen during our seven-year voyage. In Mexico, pelicans creating a huge splash as they dive-bombed the water in hopes of catching a fish during their descent and then another when they popped to the surface, and turtles so abundant that we wove erratic courses around them. There were the narrow black-and-white sea snakes that had wriggled on the surface in Mexico, the same kind that undulated lazily at a depth of twenty feet in Niue or were as thick as my arm and six-feet long in Vanuatu; the booby and mahi mahi that rode with us as we crossed the equator; and the brilliantly colored tropical fish the current carried me past under snorkel in Fakarava. Mother Nature was capricious and arbitrary and could humble us at any moment, but her rewards were unexpected surprises like this.

With no air pollution, noise pollution, or light pollution to mask nature's wonders, we could see, smell, and hear much more than we ever knew existed. Stars normally eclipsed by the glare of artificial lights crowded the sky, so dense that I could barely distinguish familiar constellations from my childhood. The beauty was that we had the time to notice.

Dolphins and whales had visited us many times, but I never tired of them. Dolphins burst out of waves with a suddenness that set my heart racing and frolicked alongside us for miles with a joy that was contagious. In the moonless darkness, dolphins cut torpedoes of phosphorescence through the water, making for a thrilling light show. From our dinghy in Honeymoon Cove, we had sat transfixed as dolphins methodically herded fish around us. Whales had breached when we'd left Tonga and New Zealand and again when we'd left Japan, as though to say goodbye. And here were several more whales, providing a mid-ocean milestone.

They encouraged me to sail on.

🌴

At 1,000 miles from land, we had no wind and were drifting along at less than two knots. We decided to motor to charge our batteries and heat up the frigid cabin; at the same time, we made some progress towards our destination.

Garth turned the key and the engine roared to life.

I leaned down to shift the engine into gear, but something didn't sound quite right. And then I realized what it was—I was missing the sound of the engine-cooling water spitting out behind the boat. Without it, the engine would burn up within a matter of minutes.

"Turn it off!" I shouted. "The cooling water isn't flowing."

Garth immediately shut it off. "It's probably clogged with growth."

We'd noticed that emptying the sink and flushing the head—both of which required an open pipe for liquid to flow—had become a challenge.

Garth went below and pulled open the engine compartment. He unhooked all the hoses to clear the blockage, then said, "Stand by for a geyser when I open this pipe."

"Wait!" I grabbed a plastic cutting board to protect the nearby bed, "Okay, go ahead."

But when Garth opened the seacock, there was no geyser—not even a trickle.

"Wow," he said. He grabbed a sail batten and rammed it into the pipe to scrape away the growth while I stood by with my plastic shield. When he finally broke through, water slowly began to puddle at the bottom of the engine-water intake pipe. After a little more scraping on the engine intake, water finally flowed freely.

Garth reattached the hoses and closed the engine compartment. "Let's hope we get in before the sink and the head don't work anymore," he said as he washed his hands. Neither pipe was accessible, as the engine-intake pipe had been. I imagined being reduced to using the bucket for dishes and everything else, and this was not something I cared to experience. Would that be worse than running out of propane? I wasn't sure which option I'd choose first, but none of them struck me as appealing.

We moved out to the cockpit. I settled in next to the tiller, but Garth walked to the transom and looked over the side.

"No wonder we're hardly moving," he said. "Come take a look at the growth on the rudder."

I moved over next to him and looked down. Attached to the back of the boat were hundreds of barnacles, three inches long, spaced less than a half an inch apart. Garth had scrubbed the boat bottom the day before we'd left Yokohama; all this growth had occurred in just over a month's time on a boat that had been constantly moving—albeit slowly—and because of it, we were getting slower every day.

I wondered whether it made sense to have one of us go over the side in the frigid water to clear the pipes. Given that I was the only one with a wet suit, I figured it would be me. None-too excited about the prospect of hypothermia, I kept the idea to myself.

We sailed on.

"Land Ho!" I shouted. Finally.

I had no doubt. What I was regarding now looked completely unlike the clouds on the horizon that had posed as distant mountains for thousands of miles, though I'd known they couldn't be. Garth came up and took a look for himself.

"Yup. There it is. We weren't hallucinating." He watched for a few moments before retreating below.

Over the course of the day, I watched the shapes grow bigger as we drew closer. I shook my head in amazement that the seemingly insurmountable feat we'd undertaken was coming to a close. We'd just sailed 5,000 miles out of sight of land with a sort of blind faith that it would be there on the other side. And there it was.

We had plenty of wind, and I thought we might just make it in the next day, after forty-six days of nonstop sailing. I began to fantasize about a full night's sleep. *Together.* I couldn't keep myself from checking our position periodically and recalculating speed and distance to guesstimate when we might arrive.

"Don't count your chickens," Garth reminded.

I'd been disappointed in the past, but I found containing my excitement nearly impossible. Land looked so close, as though I could touch it. The mountains loomed large, their evergreen peaks ever more lush as the sun brightened the sky, and we closed the distance.

Tears flooded my eyes when I spotted a clump of Pacific Northwest kelp, its copper ribbons undulating in the waves. My sentimentality surprised me. I'd loved to pop the tubular floats under my sandaled feet at Golden Gardens along the high-tide line. Years had passed since I'd seen this once familiar sight, which I'd often considered no more than a floating threat to the prop or a beached pile of decaying sea life, a smelly host to flies.

The navy-blue ocean turned to a dark green as we closed in on land. The wind built through that day and night. The gentle waves grew steeper and closer together. Garth had noted a southerly gale forming on the last weather chart, but we hoped to make it in before it arrived. When we got close enough for radio reception, Garth turned on the weather station. As I listened to current wind speed and direction for familiar place names on the Canadian coast, memories of beach walks and rock hopping along the shore during our shakedown cruise around Vancouver Island came rushing back.

Then a weather notice interrupted: "Gale warning in effect for west coast Vancouver Island north and south part, with the exception of Estevan Point. For Estevan Point, *storm* warning."

I looked at Garth and sighed. It was just our luck that the point just in front of the bow was Estevan Point. The red-roofed lighthouse tower on the point taunted us. The rocks and trees looked so close. I checked the chart repeatedly, anxious about where we were in relation to charted underwater rocks. The water was so churned up, we might not be able to spot them.

We were trying to make landfall in Ucluelet, the nearest port for Canadian customs clearance, but adverse winds had pushed us north. With storm and gale warnings all along the coast and building winds, we reasoned that we should just try to make it into the nearest protected anchorage and radio customs to explain our predicament.

I was delighted that the closest spot was Hot Springs Cove, a place infused with happy memories of hiking along a mossy boardwalk under a tree-covered canopy, followed by a soak in natural hot springs. We fantasized about soaking in steaming hot water, all the more alluring because we hadn't had a proper bath in a month and a half.

If we could just make it in. At 6:00 p.m., with three more hours of daylight, we were within five miles of Estevan Point, but the rising wind had shifted so that it was coming directly from Hot Springs Cove. We tacked back and forth, yet with each tack, we made little to no headway. All that growth on the bottom of the boat was keeping us from making much forward progress, and we were mostly just slipping sideways. Motoring made no sense because we could still sail faster than we could motor. I felt like I was experiencing one of those slow-motion danger dreams, when I needed to move but couldn't.

Finally, Garth stated the obvious, though I didn't want to hear it: "I don't see how we can make it. We're not making any headway."

Our dreams of soaking in fresh hot water evaporated; we couldn't get in before the storm, and we knew we wouldn't be able to make landfall until the storm subsided. I turned the boat away to find a safer distance off the coast. Garth went forward and dropped the main to the third reef point to prepare for higher winds.

Garth picked up the radio microphone and called Vessel Traffic Control: "This is the sailing vessel *Velella*. We are hove-to off Estevan Point. Our location is forty-nine degrees, 11.2 minutes north; 126 degrees, 46.7 minutes west. Just wanted to let you know we were here." He set down the microphone. In the log book, he wrote "VERY DISCOURAGED" in bold letters so large I could read them from the cockpit, and then he crawled into the bunk.

We couldn't do anything but drift until the storm abated. The storm itself was not the worst of it, for we'd faced high winds and challenging seas many times. Instead, it was the torment of having our prize dangled before us before it was ripped from our grasp. We'd been so close.

Land disappeared behind rain-sodden clouds. The sound of the wind howling in the rigging became intense. The rain blew sideways, and the seas became mountainous. Watching for shipping traffic was hopeless in those furious, heaving seas.

I stewed at the hand that fate had dealt us. I was on watch, but it was blustery and cold, and I didn't care anymore. I was getting jostled about and was tired of trying to brace myself against the motion.

After a while, I crawled into the bunk after Garth. We lay there, cuddling for a while, not saying anything. What was there to say? I'd cheered Garth up the week before, but I felt spent and couldn't muster anything positive to say to brighten the mood. I gazed at the Marquesan paddle hung next to the bunk that had offered me solace in the past during rough weather, its intricate patterns of waves, dolphins, mantas, and turtles offering a cheery counterpoint. That and the feel of Garth's warm, solid body next to mine soothed me.

After a few minutes, remembering that I was on watch, I said, "Well, I should at least go take a look."

Garth grunted.

I climbed out of the bunk, put on my foul weather jacket and harness, and climbed the ladder to the cockpit. Outside I grasped the top of the dodger, scanning the horizon, but not expecting to see anything but waves and the nearby shore.

To my horror, I saw a freighter moving away from our position. It had evidently passed while we'd both been down below, oblivious. My heart fluttered momentarily—a bit late.

For the next two days, Garth and I went impassively through the motions of living and keeping watch, while the storm blew its fury. The motion was unpleasant, but not untenable. The hardest part was the waiting. Instead of feasting at anchor, we shared a single spoon, eating reheated canned chili out of the pot.

Once the winds dropped, Garth raised the mainsail. But just after the sail reached full hoist, Garth gave an anguished cry, and I looked up to discover that the stitching on the mainsail had given way. The fabric remained attached at the front and back end, with a gaping hole in between, hardly useful for turning wind into forward motion. Garth grumbled as he dropped the sail back to the third reef point.

With a triple-reefed main in light winds and our large light-air genoa, our progress was slow. We spent the entire day sailing the thirty-five miles we'd lost. And since we'd lost our excuse to sail into magical Hot Springs Cove, we headed for Ucluelet.

In the late afternoon, we began to worry whether we could make it in by dark, or face yet another night offshore, during which we'd forfeit our hard-won miles to keep a safe distance in the darkness. We drew close in the fading light, then turned on the engine to pick through the rocks that dotted the shoreline outside of Barkley Sound. Spotting them in the surge left by the storm kept us on edge through Carolina Channel until we turned around Francis Island and worked our way up the narrow channel into Ucluelet.

With our engine at full throttle, we could barely reach three knots of speed. We struggled to reach the customs dock before we were enveloped in complete darkness. Every yard seemed to take forever. Finally, the last hint of light vanished from the sky. Unable to safely go any farther, we steered for the end of the deserted fuel dock. As *Velella* neared the dock and slowed, I leapt off the boat with a mooring line. My legs buckled, and I fell flat on my face. My little-used legs weren't prepared for such momentum after forty-nine days.

We'd done it. We were finally stopped.

To celebrate our long-anticipated arrival, we grabbed the last bottle of bon voyage gift booze that our friends Mary and Joel had given us seven years earlier, a bottle of port wine, to be drunk after our first storm. Though we'd held onto it through a number of situations that had certainly qualified, there was something special about saving that last bottle until the end. We'd earned it. The final storm removed all doubt. After seven years, Mary and Joel were right; we were happy for any port in a storm.

RE-ENTRY

I'd thought that the exhausting forty-nine-day non-stop sail from Japan to North America would be the hardest part of our 34,000-mile odyssey. But the toughest part was yet to come.

After a miserably wet sail to Seattle against thirty-five-knot winds and a steep chop, we found that a severe slip shortage meant we had nowhere to moor *Velella*. Shilshole, the largest marina in the area, was under reconstruction, and hundreds of displaced boats were fighting for a few slips. Garth called over thirty marinas and found nothing but waiting lists of three, four, and five years. Our only option was to anchor for free among derelict and abandoned boats in Eagle Harbor, across Puget Sound from Seattle. Instead of snorkeling in sparkling turquoise water or reveling in the wonders of a fascinating new culture, I was bailing icy water out of our dinghy to row ashore in the pouring rain.

Eventually we found a slip for the boat and could begin to rebuild our land-based lives. Garth began a new job with some former colleagues. He awoke before dawn each morning to catch the ferry and returned home exhausted long after dark. Without Garth's steadying presence, I felt adrift.

While I knew readjusting to land life would be difficult, I wasn't prepared for the intensity of the emotions I would feel. I'd moved regularly as a child and from country to country throughout our voyage. But this transition was different; I was a reluctant participant. Instead of immersing in my new environment, for a time I fought against it. Meanwhile, Garth, with a set of clear goals, set about pursuing them and faced a far less tumultuous transition.

Fortunately an opportunity to do freelance reporting for a local sailing magazine, *48 North*, fell into my lap. I spent far more time on the articles than their meager financial return merited, but it gave me some small feeling of purpose and pulled me back into the local scene. That and the words from a novel: *Be where you are.*

One afternoon, I was working on an article about a recent regatta. A weak spring sun had lured me from the table out to the cockpit where I found an unsecured Wi-Fi signal that let me avoid the library on such a nice afternoon. It was a day when the monochromatic scene brightened into the neon-green of moss-covered branches against china-blue skies and snow-capped peaks that sat like bookends on either side of evergreen-dotted hills. The sun buoyed my spirits, and I tapped away on my keyboard.

I noticed a guy in his early forties staring at me from the boardwalk that ran near the docks. Several minutes later the guy was still staring. *What is he looking at?* I wondered. Finally he strolled towards the marina gate, and I resumed studying my computer screen. Then a shadow passed alongside the boat and stopped. It was him.

"Are you Wendy?" he asked.

I nodded and shifted uneasily. How did he know my name?

"I've loved your articles in *Latitude 38* magazine for years—about your voyage. I recognized the boat and thought I'd come say hi."

What an unexpected surprise. I felt terrible that I'd been suspicious of him.

"I'd love to go cruising like you did."

I remembered how powerful stories I'd read during our voyage had cast light on life's shadows. This brief conversation inspired me, and I began to think about how I could share our story even more.

Writing steered me towards a new goal. I joined a writing group, which offered companionship, steady encouragement, and a regular date on my calendar. It was a start.

My transition to land life hasn't always gone smoothly. My first few trips through U.S. airports in a post-9/11 world left me shell shocked; I felt overwhelmed by the pace of shore life, grim news reports, perpetual marketing, mind-boggling choices in the grocery aisles, and a profound sense of insignificance in a world of databases and automation.

Even months after our return, I found myself periodically saying "over" at the end of leaving a voicemail message as though I were speaking on the VHF or SSB radio. And even now, I feel like an alien in disguise, brought up short whenever conversations turn to TV shows and movies that appeared while we were away.

But over time, I've rebuilt a place on land where I feel like I belong and have discovered that the rewards are directly proportional to how much I invest of myself, just like when we traveled.

The curse of the curious mind is that it always hungers for more. There are worse afflictions, and I am fortunate that Garth possesses a similar curiosity about the world, though it manifests itself in different ways.

🌴

"What about box number seventeen?" Garth shouted up from the basement.

"Box seventeen? Uh, yeah. That would be good. It's got the mugs and the bowls."

"How about fourteen and twenty-one?" Garth shouted back, "They're in front." I checked my list, congratulating myself on my foresight. I'd moved enough times in my life to have earned a doctorate in moving. Mom had trained me well.

"Yeah, bring up box number fourteen, but wait on twenty-one. It's got our old sailing trophies."

I heard Garth grunt at the bottom of the stairs and resumed working. A few minutes later I heard a muffled, "What *is* all this shit?" I chuckled, remembering that when we first met, he'd moved all that he owned in the passenger seat of his Fiat Spyder.

For nearly nine years aboard, we'd made do with five plastic cups, four plastic plates and bowls, six mugs, two pots, and a single cast-iron skillet. And it had seemed like enough.

I paused a number of times to think back about our lives before we'd gone cruising and how we'd spent months whittling down to the sparse furniture and twenty-nine boxes that we'd been unpacking for hours. I felt so different from the person who had carefully packed away these items all those years ago. I'd had so many incredible experiences since then and, even though they'd been challenging, I wouldn't trade them for all the material goods in the world.

Next to me, leaning against the dining room wall, was my beloved Marquesan paddle that carried with it so many memories of our seven-year voyage. Every time my eyes rested upon its geometric swirls rife with meaning far beyond its dolphins, manta ray and turtle, I felt as though I were seeing an old friend. I reached over and ran my fingers over the waves carved above its blade.

Moving back into the house filled me with conflicting feelings. My blood had grown too thin to withstand another Seattle winter aboard *Velella* with an anemic space heater. I'd managed to stay sane through one winter, but there was no guarantee what would happen if I risked a second. I had to let go of the past to embrace the future. So, with a firm commitment from Garth that—whether or not we built a boat—we'd go voyaging again, I agreed to move back into our house.

A part of me was excited to uncover family keepsakes that had been packed away for years and to host a patchwork gathering of friends and family for a holiday celebration.

Still I yearned to travel and remained wary of taking steps away from it. Moving back into our house truly marked the end of our journey.

A little later, I heard metal clanking from the basement, followed by a groan and heavy footsteps on the stairs. Garth appeared in the basement doorway with a grimace on his face.

"What?" I asked tentatively.

His hand came out from behind his back, accompanied by a sonic ring and a circular grouping of aluminum tubes in varying lengths held together precariously by a shredded string. A smile spread slowly across his face. As he extended his hand, I saw that dangling from his fingers were the wind chimes I'd managed to rescue surreptitiously in the "great cleanout" before we'd left.

"You think you're so slick," he said.

I laughed, "All they need is a little restringing."

EPILOGUE

For the next three years, Garth and I steadily worked toward our goals. Garth polished his design skills and took on ever larger projects at work. I wrote and polished stories. We lived simply and saved our earnings.

Garth interviewed boat builders and scoured the classifieds and local streets for a warehouse suitable to build the boat he'd been designing all these years. But he had little luck finding something affordable. Garth's *ideal* warehouse—Dave and Candy had finally gone sailing—had long since turned into an auto repair shop. Garth grew frustrated and began to consider purchasing a used boat. But after months of searching he'd produced few candidates that excited him.

Just as I was completing the final edits to this story and nearing my goal of publishing, Garth found an affordable 1920's farmhouse with a workshop big enough to build his dream boat. How did I feel about this? Like the universe was presenting the next challenge.

GLOSSARY

Abeam: The widest part of the boat. For example, when seas the hit the side of the boat from the side on, and completely soak everything. (Also known as beam seas).

Aft: The back of the boat.

Anchor chain: The chain that connects the anchor to the boat. Helpful to keep from losing the anchor and to make it useful, as in anchoring the boat where there are no marinas.

Awning: A big tarp that offers shade—essential in the scorching heat of the tropics.

Backstay: Wire at the back of the boat that helps hold up the mast. Handy for tying things to, like awnings, or for hanging onto while doing various things, especially if you're a guy.

Bilge: The lowest inner part inside a boat's hull under the floor boards, where hair and lint collect; the goal is to keep it as dry as possible. Water above the bilge usually means you have a problem, one of which could be sinking.

Block: A contraption that lines run through that give you extra leverage. They also allow you to exert pressure or to lead a line in a new direction without wearing a hole in whatever they touch.

Block and Tackle: A pulley system that allows a weakling like me to exert great force that would otherwise be impossible.

Boom: Bottom of the main sail that'll whack you in the head or the chest when changing course and the sound that it makes when it does that.

Bow: The pointy end of the boat.

Bow Pulpit: A handy stainless steel frame that usually helps keep us on the boat when it's bouncing wildly and we're trying to anchor or work with the jib (the sail in the front).

Celestial Navigation: Navigating by the stars. Requires serious math skills, an almanac (a book that you need to buy each year which is now more expensive than a device which tells you exactly where you are, also known as a GPS).

Channel 16: Emergency and hailing channel on the VHF radio: Not to be used for long conversations with friends about recent book reads and dinner plans in crowded anchorages, but somehow always is.

Charter: Renting a boat either with or without crew. A bareboat charter means the boat comes without crew—not that everyone aboard is naked, though during our Greek honeymoon we often were.

Cockpit: Where you sit to steer the boat and watch for ships or host cocktail parties when stopped and the weather is nice.

Companionway: Opening into living area below decks. Usually has a ladder or steps that are a great place to perch and puts you totally in the way of anyone who might want to enter or exit the interior.

Dodger: A large pram-like hood stretched over the companionway to hopefully keep it dry inside the boat.

Dragging anchor: When the anchor slides along the bottom; Traveling while not actively steering, which you do not want to do while you are sleeping or in the vicinity of rocks, reefs or other boats, or . . . ever.

EPIRB: Emergency Position Indicating Beacon; a safety device you hope you'll never need that, when activated, is designed to indicate where your boat sank and where to start looking.

Fend off: Something you do to keep the boat from hitting something. Often an air inflated fender helps soften the blow.

Forepeak: The cramped triangular shaped bunk under the pointy end of the boat. Also known as the V-berth because of its shape. Our garage where we stacked all our junk.

Forestay: The stainless steel wire that runs from the front of the bow to the top of the mast and helps to hold the mast up.

Foulies: As known as foul weather gear, because when the weather is foul, that's what we're wearing. We wore them a lot more often in the Pacific Northwest than anywhere else along our route.

Galley: Kitchen in plain English. Though on tiny *Velella*, it also happens to be the living room, dining room, and bedroom.

GPS: (Global Positioning System) A device which tells you where you are in numbers through latitude and longitude and needs to be translated onto a chart/map to figure out where that is. Now many people have them in their cars or even cell phones, but when we left few people besides boaters had ever heard of them.

Genoa: A large front sail used in lighter winds. When we weren't too lazy, we pulled it out so we could make progress.

Gimbal(s): A device on which things hang that helps to keep them level when all hell is breaking loose. A gimbaled stove was key to cooking underway without burning myself.

Gybe: Changing course when the wind is behind you by bringing the sails across to the other side of the boat quickly. Can be dangerous if you're standing in front of the boom and you aren't looking.

Gunnel/gunwhale: The edge of the deck. Rolling from gunnel to gunnel isn't good under any circumstances, not to mention unpleasant.

Halyard: The line that takes the sails up.

Hatch: An opening into the boat that lets water in when it's open, and often when it's closed, too.

Head: Toilet and toilet area. So when a sailor refers to the head, he's often not talking about thinking.

Head stay: The wire at the front of the boat that helps hold the mast up and that one of the front sails (jib or genoa) attaches to.

Jib: The smaller front sail. Not the main sail or the *colorful* sail, as one friend calls the spinnaker.

Leeward: The downhill side of the boat; If you are going to get seasick, this is the best place to do it.

Lifelines: The lines that run around the boat to help keep you in or that you trip over.

Mainsheet: The line that adjusts the main sail.

On the Beam: Winds from the side and makes the boat heel over at an awkward angle. In this state of affairs, nothing that you set down actually stays where you put it and you have to walk a little like Igor in *Young Frankenstein* to move around the boat.

Plotter: A square plastic ruler-like tool for measuring angles to determine a course to sail; Also helpful for knowing where you are and to avoid running into rocks. There are several different types. Garth wanted to carry one of each kind. Not quite the same as a chart plotter which is an electronic gizmo we couldn't afford that automates the process.

Portholes/Port lights: Boat windows that often open and leak saltwater onto your seat cushions, your head, or important electronic equipment.

Preventer: Line holding the boom to one side of the boat so that it won't swing across the boat suddenly if the wind catches the other side of the sail and kill someone.

Reefing: Reducing sail area when the wind increases, hopefully before capsizing or breaking something.

Rudder: The blade part of the tiller that sits in the water. Its position determines the direction of the boat as water flows around it. Helpful for climbing aboard, if you're a snake.

Running: In boating this doesn't usually mean leaving town before paying your bar tab, but rather sailing with the wind behind you.

Sailmail: Very limited—emphasis on *very*—means of sending a few lines of text through radio waves, to one or two very important people. Transmits at a rate that makes dial up speeds seem blazingly fast. It is persnickety, because it relies on radio signal strength which varies widely, but a miracle when it works for feeling a little less isolated in the middle of nowhere. Most boats now have this capability to communicate. This technology eluded *Velella* and her crew throughout most of this voyage.

Sextant: A device that is incredibly hard to use on land and nearly impossible to use when moving around like a cork running through rapids.

Sheet: Besides bed linen, it's a line used to bring in the bottom corner of a sail.

Slack water: The brief time period when tide pauses between flood and ebb tides before reversing direction and there is no current. Slack water presents a good time to pass through a narrow channel that usually has a strong current flow so that water isn't flowing against you or spinning you out of control.

Single Sideband Radio: See SSB.

Slatting: When you are trying to sail in little to no wind and waves and the sails crash from side to side with a jarring force that'll rattle your nerves and your dental work. To be avoided whenever possible to preserve your sanity, your sails and, of course, your dental work.

Spinnaker: One of those colorful sails that people use when the wind is behind them. Sailing with them is a little more complicated than the other sails but much faster when the wind is light and coming from behind the boat so worth it.

Spinnaker Pole: An aluminum pole clipped to the mast on a mast ring fitting which is used to hold the spinnaker out so it can catch the wind and is especially helpful when there isn't much wind.

Spreaders: The cross bars up high that catch the edge of the sail where birds like to sit. They help keep the big stick (called a mast) up.

SSB: Radio that can communicate thousands of miles, albeit with lots of static; With a special modem and a computer, it can be used to communicate cryptically short emails through Sailmail.

Stanchion: The stainless steel short vertical poles that run along the edge of the deck through which a life line runs. If they are bedded properly they *might* keep you from going overboard.

Tack: Verb meaning to change course, by bringing the wind to the other side of sails when sailing against the wind. Zigzagging across the water so that you can sail in the direction from which the wind is coming. Tacking is often essential but usually doubles the distance you have to cover to get somewhere.

Tide Rips: Uneven waves that result from an area where forces on the water work in opposing directions, for example where water meets against wind waves. Churned up water that could, well, soak you.

Tiller: Stick for used for steering smaller, simpler boats; attached to a rudder which is in the water.

Transom: The back panel of the boat. There's no more boat after the transom. Where names and hailing ports are often written, though not on *Velella*. *Velella's* transom is varnished and usually needs another coat.

Traveler: In addition to a person that goes from place to place searching for adventure like me, it's also a sliding track used to change the angle of the main sail. A handy tool when trying to point high into the wind.

V-berth: The cramped triangular shaped bunk under the pointy end of the boat. On Velella, the V-berth served as our garage where we stacked all our junk.

Velella: We pronounce our boat name Vel-ay-la, though others may say it differently. The Latin name of a sea creature, VelellaVelella, that resembles a blue raft with a sail. Nicknamed *by-the-wind sailors*, because they go where the wind takes them, a policy that our *Velella* might have found easier to follow.

VHF: Radio used for calling within twenty-five miles. Their purpose is to prevent collisions, though I've found nearby ships rarely answer. Mostly used by cruisers to schedule cocktail parties.

Waypoint: A point on the chart near where you want to go that gets you close before you really have to pay attention and sweat the details.

Wind Vane: The silent crew member that does all the driving, never complains, and needs to be heralded as the best piece of mechanical equipment ever invented to keep us from having to steer constantly; We do have to keep looking for other boats, rocks, reefs and the like and sometimes even micromanage the wind vane when wind conditions are fluky. We nicknamed our wind vane "Jacques" because he sometimes developed a bit of an attitude when he was not adjusted properly when conditions changed.

Windward: The direction from which the wind is coming and often our destination. The high side of the boat.

Zephyr: A nearly imaginary puff of wind, in which *Velella* typically tried to sail. A blue T-bird we used to race against before we bought *Velella*.

Velella underway

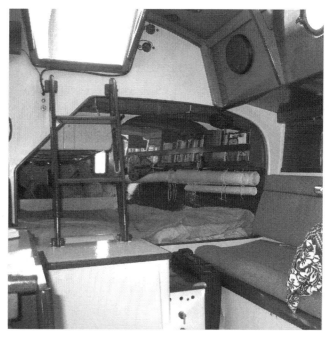

Inside our floating world

Honeymoon Cove, Sea of Cortes, Mexico

Tiki. Marquesas   The Beauty Shot, Fatu Hiva

Fakarava

Exploring Caves, Nuie

The Dream

Ocean Planet Race Prep, New Zealand

Pre-start Haka, New Zealand

Great Barrier Island, New Zealand

Fijian Market Vendor

A Wee Paddler, Vanuatu

Shy Girl in Vanuatu

Pandanu Forest

Kastum Dancers, Vanuatu

Would you buy a carving from this man? Solomon Islands

River Guide, Solomon Islands

The Big Ass Red Trailer, Kwajalein

War Ruins

Hong Kong Lantern Festival

Luk Wu Gorge, Hong Kong

Yet Another Lovely Waterfall, Pohnpei

Snoozing in the Philippines

Tricycle Riding, Philippines

Cave Swimming, Coron, Philippines

Canoes in Lan Yu

Japanese Mystery Foods

Japanese Tea Ceremony

Shredded Japanese Courtesy Flag

Home again

ACKNOWLEDGEMENTS

I couldn't possibly have written this book without my cheer-leading team led by Garth—if you can imagine it. Besides being my sugar-daddy, his encouragement, wisdom, humor, and balanced perspective kept me out of trouble and out of an insane asylum. My family and dear friends formed the foundation for the squad, all acrobatics aside.

So too the gentle taskmasters of my Wednesday Writers Group, a group of accomplished authors whom I greatly admire and for whose red pens I have a deep respect. They are Debra Daniels-Zeller, Sandra Earle, Kathy Gerht, Elsie Hulsizer, Sheila Kelly, Sharon Morris and Jan Schwert.

So many contributed to the evolution of this writer that go back to ancient history, beginning with the storytellers that have brought me comfort and escape throughout my life to the teachers from my formative school years who cultivated my love of literature and respect for proper English (including the one who called me "Miss Grammarian" in college.)

My thanks to mentors who helped me develop the craft of writing: Theo Pauline Nestor and my fellow students and pilgrims at the University of Washington; Corbin Lewars and my fellow students at Hugo House; Nick O'Connell and fellow students of the Writer's Workshop; as well as contributors to Traveler's Tales, Wanderlust and Lipstick, Fields End, PNWA and the Whidbey Island Writers Conference.

My deepest admiration goes out to Seattle7 writers led by Garth Stein and Jennie Shortridge who've given so generously of their time and talents to other wanna-be authors of all stripes and engage their creativity to raise funds for literacy and make our world a better place. And also to fellow writers Janna Cawrse Esarey, Lin Pardey, Beth Leonard, Frances and Jo Robinson, Robert Birkby, Carol Cassella, Kit Bakke, Maria Ross, Ingrid Ricks, Elizabeth Corcoran

Murray, Christy Karras, Jim Thomsen, and Amanda Castleman for their friendship, inspiring examples and encouragement. Thanks to my editors Jessica Trupin, and Mick West, and the production team who worked their magic to produce this book.

And finally to the many non-writing "civilians" who regularly offered friendship and who kept me going me by telling me they enjoyed my stories and anxiously awaited this book. This is for you.

Wendy Hinman

READERS GUIDE FOR
BOOK CLUB DISCUSSIONS:

1. A theme of the book is living simply and living in the moment. How does Tightwads on the Loose develop this theme? Wendy and Garth traded luxury for freedom. Do you think they were happier from paring down their lives to a simpler existence?

2. How did coming from a prosperous country like the United States pose dilemmas for Wendy and Garth as they tried to survive on a small budget? How were they perceived by locals? Other cruisers? Discuss how economic disparity influenced Wendy and Garth's perspective of the countries they visited. Do you think their privileged status in foreign countries made their adjustment back to U.S. life more difficult?

3. How has Wendy and Garth's seven year odyssey affected the way they viewed home, family, community, and country?

4. How are travelers changed by the cultures they encounter? How do travelers change the cultures they interact with? Is this good or bad? What examples do you find in Tightwads on the Loose?

5. Where were you during the events of 9/11? How do you think it affected our society? Imagine you had missed this event altogether as Wendy and Garth did. Would you be surprised by the changes it introduced to modern society? How do you think news and our media culture affect the way we live? Did Wendy and Garth see life differently after being away from it?

6. Wendy and Garth's route traces the path of WWII destruction, which provides a sobering backdrop to their carefree lifestyle. How does that backdrop affect how you, the reader, view Wendy and Garth's lifestyle? How does it influence your perspective on current events?

7. Wendy is tempted to take the easy route. What do you think changed her mind?

8. At the close of this adventure, Wendy struggles with what to do next. What ultimately helps Wendy's transition? Were you surprised by Wendy's change in attitude about building a boat?

9. What do you think Wendy and Garth were searching for? Do you think they found it?

AN INTERVIEW WITH WENDY HINMAN, AUTHOR OF TIGHTWADS ON THE LOOSE:

What surprised you most about your voyage?
Away from societal pressures, friends and family, I had to figure out what I wanted. That sounds easier than it is. I realized that the most satisfying things in life aren't necessarily the easiest choice. Our biggest challenges became the most memorable aspects of our voyage. Our efforts were focused on survival at a primal level yet also on enjoying the world around us. Now that we're back on land it's important to preserve that sense wonder and openness and to keep things in perspective by asking honestly, *does my survival depend on this?*

Garth and I really struggled with a decision about when to come home. We saw examples of people who didn't have goals and suffered from boredom. We clearly needed goals, yet we gained so much when we just lived in the moment and saw where it would take us. I really noticed how in our society, we don't allow ourselves much unstructured time. We become human doings instead of human beings, and our relationships and community suffer when we don't have enough time to think about what we are doing and why. Yet humans grow restless when we are not in pursuit of a longer range goal, something beyond meeting our immediate needs. It's a delicate balance.

What did you find most challenging in writing the story of your voyage?
Probably the toughest part was deciding which stories to tell in the book. After seven years, as you can imagine, I had an overabundance of material. I had to leave out entire countries and friends who had a strong influence on our experience. When we had multiple situations that were similar, such as close encounters with ships, stormy weather,

or touching interactions with local people and cultures, I had to choose some over others. Sometimes I chose to tell about one because it seemed representative, other times because of when and where it occurred and what else was going on in the story. Also I tended to choose events that dovetailed into a single idea that framed the story. The upside is that it leaves me with a lot of material to play with for other stories. Mostly, I was surprised to realize that with the same facts I could have told a very different story.

One story I wanted to tell was about how hard it was to return after such an experience, something no one talks about but is quite common among people who return from a long time away in a foreign culture. I found it challenging to convey how difficult a transition it was without losing perspective on what a lucky opportunity we'd had.

What did you find most overwhelming upon your return after living remotely for so long?
- Going from hot humid weather to freezing rain.
- Moving from living a predominantly physical outdoor life to a sedentary indoor one.
- Transitioning from a lifestyle in which not a soul in the world knew where we were to one where we were expected to be always plugged in by cell phone and Internet.
- Shifting from a spontaneous, leisurely existence to a hectic one.
- Finding a balance between joining the frantic pace and feeling alienated by it.

What message would you like to leave with readers?
We can be happy with nothing or miserable with all the comforts one can imagine. What makes the difference is taking the time to stop and appreciate the moments along the way. What makes life satisfying is not in reaching a goal, but in facing the challenges on the journey.

54082665R00211

Made in the USA
Columbia, SC
25 March 2019